Questions

about

life and morality

Christian Ethics in South Africa today

Louise Kretzschmar

Len Hulley

(eds)

JL van Schaik
RELIGIOUS BOOKS

Published by Van Schaik Publishers
1064 Arcadia Street, Hatfield, Pretoria

First edition 1998
Second impression 2005
Third impression 2008
Fourth impression 2008
Fifth impression 2008
Sixth impression 2008

ISBN 978 0 627 02358 3

Cover design by Brightmark
Typesetting in 10½ on 13 pt Palatino by Sonja Reinecke, Studio S
Printed and bound by Digital Print Solutions, Cape Town

CONTENTS

LIST OF CONTRIBUTORS

David N. Field: Lecturer in Systematic Theology in the Department of Religious Studies, University of the Transkei

Len Hulley: Professor in Theological Ethics, University of South Africa

Nico Koopman: Lecturer in Systematic Theology, Huguenot College, Wellington

Louise Kretzschmar: Senior lecturer in Theological Ethics, University of South Africa

Mokgethi Mothlabi: Associate Professor in Theological Ethics, University of South Africa

David F. Olivier: Senior Lecturer in Systematic Theology, University of South Africa, presently seconded as Project Coordinator of the Gold Fields Faith and Earthkeeping Project attached to the Research Institute for Theology and Religion, University of South Africa

Neville Richardson: Associate Professor in Theological Ethics, School of Theology, University of Natal, Pietermaritzburg

Des van der Water: Coordinator for Systematic Theology and Ethics, Theological Education by Extension College, Johannesburg

André van Niekerk: Part-time lecturer in Theological Ethics, University of South Africa

Charles Villa-Vicencio: Professor of Religion and Society, University of Cape Town, presently seconded as Director of Research in the Truth and Reconciliation Commission

Ethics in
South Africa today

Louise Kretzschmar and Len Hulley

When one engages in conversation in an academic or a social group one is almost inevitably faced with questions about society that have moral implications. People in high profile positions are also aware of the problem. During a courtesy call by the Presiding Bishop of the Methodist Church, the Rev M Dandala, on the Acting Prime Minister of Swaziland, Dr S Nxumalo, the church in Africa was challenged "to strive for peace, stability and unity in the troubled continent of Africa". Dr Nxumalo went on to amplify what he meant by "troubled continent" when he said that he saw as the great challenges facing African nations problems brought about by, amongst others, "disrespect and disobedience, low morals, crime, corruption, family disintegration, fallen and shaky governments" (*Dimension* August 1997:1). He believed that the churches were in a position to do something about this state of affairs. When one examines the matters raised by Dr Nxumalo, it soon becomes clear that he regarded the majority of the problems facing African nations as being ethical in nature.

A similar point has been made by the outgoing bishop of Kimberley and Bloemfontein, Bishop W Z Gill, who challenged churches in the country to speak out about "all the ills which were impacting negatively on the social and economic conditions of the country" (*Diamond Fields Advertiser* 22 May 1997:4). In particular, he highlighted the following:

> The high crime rate, child and women abuse, poor health and medical services, the high rate of bank robberies, violence and murder, the poor economy and poverty, corruption within the government, unstable education conditions, abortion, AIDS, and alcohol abuse (*Diamond Fields Advertiser* 22 May 1997:4).

Corruption and crime

In a recent newspaper report it was stated that research has found "that the rate of crime in South Africa has increased at double the rate of population growth over the past four years" (*Saturday Star* 11 November 1995:5). Statements such as these need to be seen against the background of the fact that all crime statistics are based on crime reported to the police and not on crime perpetrated. This means that as greater numbers of crimes are reported, statistics could soar alarmingly. But these statistics are misleading since they would seem to indicate an increase in crime whereas, in fact, they indicate an increase in reported crime. Nevertheless, it does appear that crime is on the increase.

Another important matter has to do with the increase in levels of brutality in crimes committed. Thus, for example, "it is one thing to go out to your garage in the morning and find your car missing, but it is a different matter to be hauled out of your car at gun-point. It is a crime of personal violation and is particularly threatening" (*Saturday Star* 11 November 1995:5). South Africa seems to have a "pathologically high rate of violent crime" in comparison to other countries. Here, murder and assault make up 16 % of reported crime, for 72 other countries, the average was 3 % of reported crime. Whereas the international average for assault rates was 142 to 100 000 people, the rate in South Africa was 840 per 100 000 people (*Saturday Star* 11 November 1995:5). Other important figures include:

- 1 vehicle hi-jacking every 54 minutes
- 1 murder every 30 minutes
- 1 rape every 18 minutes
- 1 robbery every 6 minutes
- 1 vehicle theft every 6 minutes
- 1 theft from a vehicle every 3 minutes
- 1 housebreaking every 2 minutes (Nedcor as quoted in the *Saturday Star* 11 November 1995:5).

It is because of startling figures such as these that commentators speak of a "culture of violence" or a "spiralling crime rate".

Statistics concerning violent crimes such as murder, rape and housebreaking may cause us to forget that the crime problem is part of a larger moral problem within our country. The spiralling crime rate must also be viewed in relation to the wider issue of immorality and corruption. Corruption takes many forms. These include so-called white collar crime (eg theft within government departments or private businesses) as well as the involvement of the police in crime and corruption. During 1996, 1 076 policemen nationally were under investigation for corruption (*Saturday Star* 17 May 1997:11). Crimes committed by policemen include: involvement in motor car theft and illegal re-registration of such vehicles, the theft or "loss" of police dockets for charged criminals, and involvement in crime syndicates. Corruption also includes all forms of fraud, the failure to do one's work properly, greed, inefficiency and indifference on the part of the public at large.

Concerning corruption, it would be a mistake to censure the present administration while forgetting the corruption committed by the previous government. Under the previous political dispensation, officials commonly abused their positions. In addition, homeland governments were particularly dishonest as were central government departments such as the Development Aid which worked alongside the homeland governments. In addition, secret budgets made it possible for security and other officials to misuse funds for their own benefit and the lack of transparency meant that ample opportunities were created for various forms of bribery and corruption (*Saturday Star* 17 May 1997:11). In the new South Africa, various cases of dishonest bureaucrats have been uncovered. These include the sale of matriculation examination papers, thefts within pension offices, fraud in the Housing and Land Affairs Department, and irregularities in the Low Cost Housing budget. A particularly well-known example relates to the *Sarafina 2* scandal which involved the misappropriation of funds. Telkom and the Post Office lost R201 million due to employee fraud in the 1995–1996 financial year (*Saturday Star* 17 May 1997:11). Other groups such as the Independent Broadcasting Authority have been severely criticised for misuse of travel and entertainment budgets and various other forms of self-enrichment.

Joe Qwelane, a controversial correspondent of the Saturday Star newspaper, made the following comments with regard to South Africa and the issue of governance and corruption:

> I am of the opinion that South Africa is this continent's last real chance to disprove the belief that once blacks come to power, everything goes down the tubes: thriving economies seize up, self-enrichment at the expense of the masses becomes the order, and wholesale corruption replaces orderly governance everywhere. I will go further and say another thing: if here in South Africa we fail to get it right and opt to go "the way of Africa north of the Limpopo", chances are that the survival of sub-Saharan Africa will be so greatly endangered that we could very well face a new spectre of colonialism (*Saturday Star* 24 May 1997:10).

Qwelane went on to point out that countries such as Botswana and Namibia have been shining exceptions to the general rule, but he still stressed the need for South Africa to take cognisance of negative examples from other African countries. He also pointed to the particular responsibility of black professionals and intellectuals:

> That is why, in my opinion, it is imperative that the crusade against the corrupt but powerful few who turned state organs into their own little fiefdoms must be led by black professionals and intellectuals: in this very instance it must be blacks who must be seen to campaign for clean and transparent conduct in public life (*Saturday Star* 24 May 1997:10).

According to a recent newspaper report, white collar crime cost South Africa almost R4 billion last year and less than 10 % of the 50 000 commercial cases reported to the police actually resulted in a conviction (*Saturday Star* 17 May 1997:1). This sum is so vast that the R113 million that South African banks lost in armed robberies during 1996 almost pales into insignificance.

This raises the issue of South Africa's future (and that of the continent as a whole). At the risk of oversimplification, at least two main perceptions can be identified: the Afro-pessimists and those speaking of an African Renaissance. In the eyes of Afro-pessimists, the African continent is doomed to an unending cycle of corruption, authoritarianism, famine and war (*Saturday Star* 24 May 1997:11). In contrast, President Mandela, although recognising that the problems in Africa are both complex and long standing and will not lend themselves to simple solutions, said:

> The time has come for Africa to take full responsibility for her woes, use the immense collective wisdom it possesses to make a reality of the ideal of the African Renaissance whose time has come (*Saturday Star* 24 May 1997:11).

Rather than looking towards Western Europe, Southern Africa is increasingly looking to other countries within Africa and the Pacific Rim. According to Deputy President Thabo Mbeki:

> It knows and is resolved that, to attain that objective, it must restrain tyranny; oppose all attempts to deny liberty by resorting to demagogy; repulse the temptation to describe African life as the ability to live on charity; engage in the fight to secure the emancipation of African women; and reassert the fundamental concept that we are our own liberators from oppression, from underdevelopment and poverty, from the perpetuation of an experience from slavery, to colonialism, to apartheid, to dependence on alms (*Saturday Star* 24 May 1997:11).

Mbeki pointed to recent improvements in the economies of sub-Saharan African countries. In 1995, the average GDP growth was 4 % in comparison to 1,4 % between 1991 and 1994 (*Saturday Star* 24 May 1997:11). Although he stressed that he would like to see much greater growth, up to 10 %, there were indications that the situation was beginning to swing around. Individuals such as Thabo Mbeki and Nelson Mandela are of the opinion that we should speak in terms of an African Renaissance and work towards the achievement of such a Renaissance. But they are often opposed and ridiculed by the "Afro-pessimists".

This raises the question of where the church stands in all of this. Is it part of the problem or is it part of the solution? To what extent are South African churches conscientised and mobilised to play a significant role in bringing into being a South Africa in which we and our children would like to live?

AIDS

AIDS (the Acquired Immune Deficiency Syndrome) is a disease which affects the systems of the body which resist sickness. This is why the words "Immune Deficiency" are used. In other words, no-one actually dies from AIDS, people die from a variety of diseases such as tuberculosis and pneumonia, because the immune system of their body is no longer functioning and therefore the body is unable to fight these diseases. A distinction is often made between what is called "full blown" AIDS, which is the actual disease itself, and HIV, a virus which affects the immune system of the body (HIV stands for Human Immuno-Deficiency Virus). This virus enters the white blood cells of the body and makes it impossible for the body to defend itself against illness or disease.

How does a person contract AIDS? AIDS is spread mainly through sexual intercourse with an infected person. However, one can also contract AIDS as a result of:

receiving a blood transfusion of infected blood (if it has not been properly screen-ed); the use of a knife which has contaminated blood on it (eg in the case of circum-cisions or tribal markings); the use of contaminated injection needles (eg by drug addicts); and an unborn child can be infected by a mother who has HIV. While poverty and migrant labour are not causes of AIDS, they have accelerated the spread of the disease since some people have been separated from their families and have not been able to resist the temptation of having sex with a number of other people outside the marriage bond.

In a recent report in a South African newspaper, it is stated that the North West Province is amongst the worst AIDS zones in the whole of Africa, comparable to Uganda during the 1980s when the AIDS epidemic in that country was at its height. According to this report:

> The latest AIDS statistics show that 25 percent of pregnant women tested in the province are HIV-positive – a 17 percent increase in one year and an esti-mate which health care workers claim is conservative (*Pretoria News* 23 May 1997:12).

In certain parts of rural KwaZulu-Natal it has been estimated that 1 out of every 4 people tested at the clinics are already infected with HIV. Recent statistics indicate that the worst affected province is KwaZulu-Natal, closely followed by Gauteng and the North West province. World wide it has been estimated that more than 10 million people are infected with the AIDS virus, of these 6,5 million live in Africa south of the Sahara.

The AIDS epidemic raises several ethical or moral issues, such as the responsible and moral use of sex. Also significant is the responsibility of both the church and the state in keeping families together and thereby limiting the temptation to engage in sex outside of marriage. Local economic growth is important to limit migrant, labour and education concerning the causes of AIDS is vital so that people can be conscious of the risks of unrestricted and unprotected sexual intercourse. Finally, what should the attitudes of Christians be towards those who have AIDS and what will the consequences be for our society if nothing is done to stop the spread of AIDS? What can the churches do to promote good health, positive family interac-tion and healthy sexual relationships?

This brings us to a discussion of what the task of ethics is in situations such as those described above. It must also be borne in mind that the task of ethics is not a purely academic task, but it has significant implications for the faith and witness of the Christian church.

The task of ethics

It seems clear that many people think that we need to develop our moral sensitivi-ty and our understanding of moral issues. We believe that the way to do this is not to hit people over the head with a whole bunch of "thou shalt nots". We cannot leg-islate people into better moral beings, although laws can keep the baser kinds of immoral behaviour in check, provided of course that people can be apprehended and made to pay a penalty for their behaviour. We believe that one has to help people to regard moral living as an expression of their faith and then enable them to judge what a moral course of behaviour would be. Here we agree with the comments of Dr Nxumalo quoted at the outset of his introduction. The church is one institution which may be able to do this if it takes its mission to call upon people to amend their lives, as an expression of the Christian faith, seriously.

What, then, is the task of ethics? Elsewhere it has been argued that the task of ethics encompasses three vital elements: analysis, the proclamation of salvation or liberation, and practical involvement (Kretzschmar in Villa-Vincencio 1994:16–22). By analysis is meant the need to identify the nature, extent and causes of the many ethical problems that exist in our world. This analysis will include a description and evaluation of our personal existence as well as an examination of our social or structural context. After analysis, the next important step is to identify what the "good news" is in relation to the bad news that the analysis has identified. This is because:

> The Christian gospel is, then, concerned with the liberation of persons and groups from the bondage of all forms of sin. It is equally concerned with the movement towards the healing and transformation of persons and societies (Kretzschmar in Villa-Vicencio 1994:20).

This emphasis on the application of the Gospel to social needs neither denies nor removes the importance of the personal appropriation of salvation. Conversion, discipleship and growth towards spiritual maturity remain vital elements of the Christian faith. Nevertheless, the good news ought not to be restricted to the personal spiritual needs of individuals. Biblical faith is always about repentance, new life and wholeness, whether for individuals or groups. It does need to be appropriated, but it must not be truncated.

Practical involvement is the third vital element of the task of ethics. It is not enough for Christians to preach the gospel, it is also necessary for them to be actively involved in transforming situations of poverty, hopelessness and oppression so that they more closely conform to what God wants for the world and the people that God has created:

> Theological ethics, therefore, adopts a world-transforming rather than a world-escaping approach to social and physical realities. This means that God's work of salvation is not to be restricted to a heavenly future. As our Creator, Lord, Saviour, Mother, Father, and Friend, God seeks us to engage us in the task of restoration and re-creation of the fallen and broken world in which we currently live (Kretzschmar in Villa-Vicencio 1994:22).

The book in outline

In this book we are entering into a discussion on some of the issues that we face. The purpose is not to provide facile answers, but to provide information and the means to judge the facts so that one can make informed and morally responsible decisions. We are not only talking about "abstract, good intentions ('ethics of convictions'), but of concrete, realistic responsibility ('ethics of responsibility')" (Moltmann 1989:40). With Moltmann, we regard morality as something that should be done as well as discussed. But we would like to take the idea of responsibility one step further. For us this means to follow H Richard Niebuhr in his view of what it means when we say we are to act responsibly: "Responsibility affirms 'God is acting in all actions upon you. So respond to all actions upon you as to respond to his action'" (Niebuhr 1963:126). We are therefore responsible before and to God for our actions. We are also answerable to ourselves and each other. What this means in concrete terms is not always crystal clear. The purpose of this book is to make a contribution towards making it clearer. The book is not to be seen as the last word in the discussion, but rather as the first word in an ongoing dialogue. It is both an effort to respond to the challenge thrown out by Dr Nxumalo and a means of empowering people to contribute to the moral reconstruction of our country as a tangible demonstration of their Christian faith.

We have structured this book so that people can enter the discussion at a number of different places and levels. In Part 1 we wish, particular, to engage those people who are involved in ethics in a professional way, ie those who wish to enter into dialogue with us about the necessity for and the substance of the discipline. It will nevertheless interest and inform all those concerned with life and morality. André van Niekerk considers whether we need morals systems at all, whether they are actually necessary in society. He concludes that we cannot do without morality, it serves both on the individual and societal level to provide meaning and cohesion. He also introduces a number of key moral issues. Len Hulley considers the use of the Bible in ethical endeavour and how we may use it responsibly. Neville Richardson argues that we need to take account of the African heritage to enrich our ethical thinking, which has largely been dominated by ideas which have emanated from Western philosophy and theology. Some Western philosophers and theologians are now also independently discovering the value of notions and practices that have served African ethical thought for generations.

Part 2 consists of more personal ethical matters, things that we encounter in our personal and community lives. Louise Kretzschmar examines the sensitive matter of human sexuality and a number of associated issues such as marriage, singleness, homosexuality and rape. In the light of the modern attitudes to human sexuality, Len Hulley considers the question of whether we in fact still need an institution like marriage. Matters such as the male-female relationship and divorce are considered from a biblical theological perspective. In 1996, the government passed a new law in which the previous strict provisions concerning abortion were considerably liberalized. In response, Kretzschmar and Hulley consider the matter of abortion and contraception arguing, among other things, that abortion is not to be seen as a belated alternative to contraception. Finally, they open up the world of medical ethics. This is a matter that involves each of us, more or less frequently. Here subjects such as artificial insemination, aborting malformed foetuses, access to medical services, and other health issues are touched upon so as to raise awareness concerning the range and type of modern ethical problems within the world of medicine.

In **Part 3** we consider ethical matters on an even larger scale. Here we discuss ethical concerns as they have a bearing on what happens in society. Most people are familiar with the world of personal, or individual ethics, but find it hard to relate these moral values to what happens in society at large. Mokgethi Motlhabi shows that because ethics needs to understand various aspects of society, it needs other disciplines to grasp and interpret society. Christian ethics is then able to provide practical guidelines for the well-being of society. Des van der Water argues that the Bill of Rights in the new Constitution provides us with ethical guidelines for our multi-faith and multi-cultural society. Nico Koopman reflects on racism to see to what extent we have overcome this problem in the new South Africa. He shows that it surfaces in subtly different forms, but that we can deal with it as we build a new, common history for ourselves. Another aspect of our historical baggage that burdens us in the present is the attitudes and practices in society as they affect women. Louise Kretzschmar examines some key issues in the gender debate such as culture, family, the economy and the church. Charles Villa-Vicencio, who has been intimately involved with the Truth and Reconciliation Commission as its Chief of Research, has written a theological evaluation of the question of guilt as it has emerged in the work of the Commission, and similar processes elsewhere.

We narrow the focus again in **Part 4**. Here the matter of ecology is considered by both David F. Olivier and David N. Field. Olivier looks at the Goldfields Faith and Earth Keeping Project and the religio-ethical issues raised by ecological matters. Field considers how we can achieve sustainable development, that is, development that does not destroy the environment. The next contribution, by Hulley and Kretzschmar, is a critical look at the government's Reconstruction and Development Programme and the role the churches can play in bringing its objectives to fruition. Business ethics, which some people may regard as a contradiction in terms, is the subject of the last chapter in Part 4. Hulley attempts to provide a model which will enable business people to make morally responsible decisions.

The concluding section, **Part 5**, is again by André van Niekerk. Having read the previous chapters, he confronts us with the question, "What will be required of moral systems in the future?" He affords some reason for hope, showing that there is light at the end of the tunnel, and he helps us to recognise what will contribute to providing us with viable ethical options in the future.

BIBLIOGRAPHY

Dimension August 1997

Moltmann, J. 1989. "Political theology and the ethics of peace", in Runyon, T (ed). *Theology, Politics and Peace*. Maryknoll: Orbis.

Niebuhr, H Richard. 1963. *The responsible self: An essay in Christian moral philosophy*. New York: Harper and Row.

Villa-Vicencio, C and De Gruchy, J (eds). 1994. *Doing ethics in context: South African perspectives*. Cape Town: David Phillip.

PART 1

What is ethics?

1

Morality and life

André van Niekerk

The question that I wish to ask in this introduction concerns the existence of morality: Should there be moral systems at all?

If we look at the widespread misuse of morality, we cannot evade this question. The wise know that when inquiry is denied at the door, doubt comes in through the window! To begin with, then, let me summarize a few accusations against moral systems:

- Do theoretical foundations for morality not justify existing unjust social relations?
- Isn't sexual morality created by a male paternalistic society to further male interests while treating women as commodities? (Feminists).
- Are moral systems' codes and signals not created to manipulate others rather than to inform them? (Dawkins and Krebs).
- Is morality not the big enemy of humanity because it condemns the basic instincts of life? (Nietzsche).
- Is morality not the main cause of neurosis in people because it suppresses natural responses? (Freud).

Although morality in general, and Christian morality in particular, have been heavily criticised, I want to defend the continued existence of moral systems in this chapter, while pleading for a thoroughly critical assessment of these systems in the last chapter of this volume.

In answering the question 'Should there be moral systems at all?' I wish to advance one basic argument: Morality is necessary because life without orientation is chaotic and even meaningless. The necessity for morality is essentially related to the reality of life.

The nature of human life demands some form of normative system. There is truth in evolutionary ethicists' argument that shared beliefs about right and wrong were necessary for the survival of human groups. Human society would not be possible were it not for moral codes which allow us to overcome, to a certain extent, our fundamental selfishness. But morality is necessary not only for the preservation of life, but also for the quality of life.

Morality is an orientation to life

To be without morality is like trying to find your way around a foreign city without a map. You don't know where you are, where you have come from, or to where you wish to go.

According to Küng (1987) the reality of life is ambiguous. We experience good and evil, success and failure, happiness and sorrow, meaning and meaningless. We need to be orientated within this ambiguous reality. Since the 1960s, there has been a decline in the recognition of traditions or institutions within the Western world which can be held onto for orientation. All forms of authority (eg political, academic, judicial and ecclesial) have been regarded with suspicion. Consequently, all values are regarded as suspect or even openly rejected. The process of liberation was necessary, according to Küng, but it went too far. To put it differently, authoritarianism was exchanged for relativism which frequently leads to nihilism. Küng (1980:14) said that the result was not freedom. The result was meaninglessness, practical nihilism, criminality, political and religious fanatism. These are consequences of an orientation crisis.

Voices from popular psychology are in agreement with Küng's observation of an orientation crisis. M Scott Peck (1992) and Stephen Covey (1994), to mention only two examples, observed this crisis among their higher and middle class clients. The crisis also reached students, youth groups, the unemployed, and people at the periphery of the market economy. Successful businessmen, executives and people at the top of the economic market experience "outer success" but an "inner emptiness" (Covey 1993).

The problem is not that there are no regulations and laws. The creation of laws and regulations do not give orientation. Actually they confuse the moral maze in which people are trapped. The ambiguity of reality forces us as people to have more than rules. We need a fundamental orientation. We cannot experience meaning without a basic orientation towards reality. If you are lost in a foreign city all the traffic lights, the opening hours of banks, and the procedures of the city council won't help you. All the electronic substitutes will rather aggravate your feelings of being lost. We need a basic orientation. Every human being needs a compass and a map to partake in the journey of life. In short, the first reason for the indispensability of morality is to give orientation and meaning to an individual's life.

Morality is the fabric of society

The second reason for the need for morality is because a society cannot function properly without it. Morality not only gives meaning and direction to individuals, it is also the fabric of society at large. Many people are convinced that we are experiencing a crisis in our societies today due to a lack of morality. By the term crisis, I mean that things have developed to such a stage that we face acute personal and social danger.

Violence

We must avoid the trap of simplistically recalling the "good old days". Nostalgia hides the many awful truths of the past and makes us pessimistic about the present and even irresponsible towards the future. There was certainly no time in history without violence. Our concern about violence is that it doesn't decrease. From history we learn that we learn nothing from history! The examples set by Hitler and Stalin did not prevent the genocide of the 1990s in Bosnia by the Serbs through their "ethnic cleansing", the bombing of Grozny by unwilling Russian soldiers under the power of politicians, or the carnage in Rwanda between the Hutu's and the Tutsis.

It is estimated that 500 000 people – mostly Tutsis, including women, children and babies were brutally killed during 1994 in Rwanda because they belonged to the "wrong" tribe. It was, however, not only a spontaneous eruption of ancient ethnic hate. It was rather carefully planned by people who feared the loss of their power. They were disinterested in the fate of those in the killing fields and did not lay down any rules of engagement for their soldiers. Millions fled to refugee camps where they suffered from malnutrition and cholera (Gibbs 1994).

But "Are we in South Africa really different from the inhabitants of Rwanda"? asks *City Press* (25 September 1994). Aren't we the nation who invented the gruesome necklace method to wipe out our political opponents? In our striving for political power we have slaughtered sleeping women and children and thrown innocent people out of moving trains. Probably the culprits were a third force, but that does not absolve us. We could, according to *City Press*, be called the dregs of the world.

Indications are that although the rate of violence dropped dramatically during the first democratic elections in April 1994 it has risen again to an unacceptable and very dangerous level.

According to police statistics, 11 919 people were murdered in South Africa from January–August 1994. This amounts to 56,5 murders for every 100 000 people per annum! In Russia, which is also in a time of political and economic transition, 18 murders for every 100 000 people were reported, while the number for the USA is 9,8 murders for every 100 000 people. Seven times more murders were committed in Johannesburg than in New York city, reputedly one of the most violent cities in the world! In the first eight months of 1994, armed raids rose by 17,59 % compared to 1993, rape by 16,44 %, car thefts by 26 %, and the hi-jacking of cars and trucks by 54 %! (Police figures as reported to the National Committee for safety and security, see *Beeld*, 2 November 1994). Nedcor's report on crime, released in June 1996, mentioned that 94 % of released prisoners immediately get involved in criminal activities again. An estimated 18 % of South Africa's population are directly hit by the crime-wave annually.

It is clear that we are heading for anarchy if our culture does not cultivate the conviction that the lives of human beings are sacrosanct. Without a revival of morality, more police, stricter courts and even the re-introduction of capital punishment, for which many people plead, would not curb the tide of anarchy.

Criminality

From the previous paragraph it may sound as though the only culprits are bandits and thieves – probably without a proper job. The truth is rather that a lack of norms is not only reflected in the aggressive feelings and frustrations of the jobless. It is also clearly reflected in the numerous cases of fraud that come to light everyday. White-collar crime has increased dramatically, both in the private sector and in the government. In 1994 it was discovered that Armscor planned to sell weapons to Lebanon: for the selfish short term profit advantage, weapons of death were to be delivered to an other country! The hearings of the Truth and Reconciliation Commission during 1996 and 1997 have revealed the most gruesome crimes against humanity frequently committed with the permission of high ranking civil officials. Truly – *corruptio optimi pessima est* – the corruption of the top is the worst.

Promiscuity, rape and AIDS

An alarming boom in prostitution is reported from all over the world. An investigation by *Time International* correspondents on six continents shows how prostitution debases women and children all over the world (Hornblower 1993). This "trading in flesh" is encouraged by massive socio-economic movements: the collapse of the Soviet empire, the increase in global mobility, and disparities of wealth all over the globe.

In South East Asia it is estimated that 30 million women have literally been sold to brothel owners throughout the world in less than twenty years. Most of them are minors – the sale of 14 year olds is "commonplace".

Indications are that more and more women in South Africa are turning to prostitution because of the economic situation. Although no exact figures are available, advertisements in papers (of call girls and escort clubs) give a clear indication that promiscuity is growing. According to police statistics a woman is raped every 18 minutes and 23 seconds in South Africa (*Beeld*, 2 November 1994). The sexual abuse of children is so common that the police have established a special unit to deal with this matter.

Globally, prostitution plays a significant role in transmitting the AIDS virus. Due to the brutal way in which these women are treated by their "owners", their lack of education, and language barriers, their AIDS awareness is nil. In Bombay, known for its brothels around the hospitals to which rich Arabs come for inexpensive medical treatment, the official number of HIV cases rose from 6 in 1986 to a million in 1993 (Hornblower 1993).

Data released by the Department of Health (1994) show that the AIDS virus continues to spread in South Africa. According to this data 4,25 % of the 12 360 people surveyed in 1993 were infected by HIV – a doubling of figures in just 13 months! (*Beeld*, 17 April 1997) reported that nearly 1 000 people a day become AIDS victims in South Africa. It is estimated that 15 000 AIDS babies are born in South Africa annually. In the province of Natal, 10 % of the people are believed to be carriers of the virus. A total of 2,5 million, it is estimated, will be carriers by 1997. It is clear from these alarming figures that HIV represents a serious threat to our country economically, socially and politically.

Suppression by laws alone would not be able to save millions of lives in the world. If the world's morals cannot be reformed and people's bodies continue to be viewed as commodities and objects of lust, one of humankind's greatest degradations will grow even worse in the 21st century.

Road accidents

The necessity of morality is not only shown in sensational examples like violence, rape and murder. Even everyday "innocent" actions, like driving a car, underline the importance of morals. Although most countries have a fairly similar traffic rule system, the accident and death rates vary greatly. Factors like education, the condition of cars and the state of the roads play a significant role. Fraud is also a contributing factor. It is estimated that there are 1,5 million illegal driver's licences in South Africa. Road cultures are decisively determined by the presence or absence of applicable moral values.

According to the International Road Federation (1993), South Africa has one of the highest road accident and death tolls in the world. For every 100 000 motorcars in South Africa, 2 084 injuries occur and 182 people die annually! Comparative figures for Australia are 230 injuries and 22 deaths. The figure for Egypt is 1 120 injuries and 222 deaths. For Germany it is 1 223 injuries and 25 deaths and, for the USA, 1 784 injuries and 22 deaths. For each 100 million kilometres travelled, 10,37 people die on South African roads while in Britain only 1,11 people die. The figure for the Netherlands is 1,38, but in Kenya 35 people die for each 100 million kilometres travelled.

Ecological facets

The moral systems of the developed countries are unable to preserve our planet in a healthy condition. We are technological giants, but moral dwarfs (Sider).

The rich, more developed countries of the Northern hemisphere – Europe, North America and Japan – consume an inordinate share of the world's resources. These countries are responsible for pumping the greater proportion of pollutants into the atmosphere, piling up vast amounts of waste and driving more species to extinction. The USA, for instance, produces 21 % of the world's carbon dioxide, while China – with 4,5 times as many people – generates only 11 % (Alexander 1994). Carbon dioxide and other greenhouse gases are responsible for the overall warming up of the planet which could result in droughts, melting ice caps, rising sea levels, coastal flooding, more severe storms and other climatic calamities.

In 1992, during the Earth Summit in Rio de Janeiro, a new bargain between the rich countries of the North and the poor developing countries was reached. The developing countries in the South would do more to protect their vast forests while the North would reduce energy use and provide technology and money to compensate for the loss of income from the sale of timber from the forests. Two years after the Conference (1994), Alexander reported that, due to the recession, the amount of money made available to the developing countries was even less than previously, and that 17 million hectares of tropical rain forest – an area about the size of Japan – are destroyed each year. The only real improvement in the past two years occurred in the manufacturing industry – probably because "green" products make for better profits!

It is high time that more altruistic motives rather than materialistic self interest guide our actions. Treaties between countries and state laws will not necessarily heal all our global ills. Morally responsible people on a large scale will.

Morality is indispensable for future life

We need a map if we want to find our way around our home city. But we need a map even more when we visit a unfamiliar city. Likewise, we need orientation to give us direction both in terms of our present and our future crises.

In 1970, Alvin Toffler dealt with the problem of change and how we adapt to it in his book Future Shock. According to him, rapid changes cause people to experience a "future shock". The creation of an environment that is too "ephemeral, unfamiliar and complex" for us to cope with, leads to future shock that Toffler defines as an "adaptive breakdown". One of the issues that he discusses is the implications of a rapid turnover of information. In a situation of "information overload", people are not able to take in new information without breaking down traditional world views and values. A serious result of the process of change and exposure to new things, places, people and value systems is the loss of moral values. For Toffler, values for orientation are a necessity to help people to adapt to the rapidly changing situation. He challenges the churches to "update" their values by facing the challenges of these rapid developments by providing a basic factor of permanence in the midst of change.

Toffler's observation is not to be restricted to the 1970s and to Western developed countries. It gives us a model to explain the vanishing of traditional values in Africa's processes of urbanisation, colonialisation and democratisation. Furthermore, it warns us that future changes could be unbearable both for individuals and for societies without moral systems. Let us take two examples of possible future crises for which we would need ethical guidance:

The population explosion

According to the population conference in Cairo during September 1994, the world's population will grow from the 1950 figure of 2,5 billion people to 12,5 billion people in 2050! Whereas in Spain it would take 433 years (at the present birth rate) for the population of 38,6 million people to double, in Zaïre, which has a similar population of 37,9 million people, the population could double in only 22 years! If we keep in mind that the world's resources are already over-exploited: that only 24 % people have enough to eat; that 1 billion people already live in poverty; that 2 billion people are already without potable water; that 960 million adults – two thirds of them women – are illiterate and thus difficult targets for birth-control campaigners, we undoubtably face serious problems in the future (cf Steen 1994; Usher 1994).

In South Africa, half of the population is under fifteen years of age. The average fertility rate is between three (for urban women) and six (for rural women). At the present rate, South Africa's population will double in 20–30 years. South Africa's arable land only consists of about 10 % of its surface area. Water is scarce and already under pressure. The causes of high population growth in South Africa are: a high illiteracy rate among women (two thirds of all the illiterate persons in the world are women); the low standing of women in society (they own 1 percent of property in the world); traditional culture (men may have more than one wife, and end up with 20 children to boast their virility and status); and poverty (the average of women's earnings in the world are 10 percent of wages earned by men) (Geach 1994).

It surely cannot be doubted that we need to refine moral principles to address this burning issue as Mothlabi does elsewhere in this volume.

Embryo engineering

In recent years, scientists have been capable of identifying genetic disorders in foetuses. Researchers Hall and Stillman from the George Washington University reported in October 1993 that they successfully cloned 48 human embryos from 17 embryos. This experiment was not genetic manipulation in the sense of the manipulation depicted in the film Jurassic Park, in which DNA material from a extinct dinosaur is nurtured and grown into a living replica. But the experiment nevertheless started the "fiercest scientific debate about medical ethics since the birth of the first test-tube baby 15 years ago" (Elmer-De Witt 1993). Although Stillman and Hall did the experiment as part of finding ways to help couples who have trouble in conceiving children, some people are worried that this was only the first step in what could become an "embryo factory" or a human "spare parts" division.

In March 1997, Scottish embryologist, Ian Wilmut and his colleagues announced that they had successfully cloned a lamb from an adult ewe's mammary gland. The lamb is a carbon copy, an identical twin, of her mother. Although it took the researchers more than 10 years to achieve their breakthrough, the process is so easy to master that the cloning of human beings could be possible for technicians in future. According to Arthur Caplan, a bioethicist of Pennsylvania, human cloning would be possible within a mere 7 years from the breakthrough in Scotland (Kluger 1997).

What the reaction to the experiment of Stillman and Hall and the breakthrough of Wilmut and his colleagues indicates, is the lack of ethical guidelines for the rapidly developing field of bio-technology. For future generations it is therefore necessary to have a more developed system of bio-ethics. Technology has a momentum of its own. Moral systems must be put into place to make timeous moral judgements in relation to the future possibilities within the field of reproductive technology: surrogacy, the freezing of embryos, the use of frozen human embryos as a legacy, and the possibility of an "embryo supermarket", where parents could pick and choose characteristics of the child they wish to have.

A summary of why morality is a vital necessity in our world

In the foregoing paragraphs, I have advanced three arguments for the necessity of morality. The first is that morality gives the individual person orientation and meaning in life. Secondly, I have argued that because morality provides a cohesive fabric for society, it presents a solution to present social problems like the growing violence, criminality, the high death toll on roads, and ecological disasters. The third argument for morality is that it is indispensable if we want to deal with life-threatening problems in the future.

BIBLIOGRAPHY

(Please note: The abbreviation JTSA refers to the *Journal of Theology for Southern Africa*).

AIDS ANALYSIS Africa. 1994. South African epidemic continues to spread 5(1).

Alexander, CP. 1994. "Two years after the Earth Summit it's time to take the Pulse of the Planet", in *Time International*, 7 November: 47–51.

Beeld. Anargie wag tensy misdaad deeglik bekamp word. 2 November 1994.

Beeld. In SA word meer as 600 mense elke dag met vigsvirus besmet. 23 November 1994.

Beeld. Vigs: Swart probleem of S A probleem? 17 April 1997.

Covey, SR. 1994. *The Seven Habits of Highly Effective People*. London: Simon and Schuster.

Department of Health (RSA), 1994. *AIDS Analysis*. Pretoria: Department of Health.

Elmer-Dewitt, P. 1993. "Cloning: Where do we draw the line?" in *Time International*, 8 November: 40–46.

Geach, B. 1994. "Population", in *New Ground: The Journal of Development and The Environment* 15:1–4.

Gibbs, N. 1994. "Why? The Killing Fields of Rwanda", in *Time International*, 16 May: 22–29.

Hornblower, M. 1993. "The Skin trade", in *Time International*, 21 June: 22–36.

International Road Federation 1993. *World Road Statistics 1988–1992*. Geneva.

Kluger, J. 1997. "Will we follow the sheep?" in *Time International*, 10 March: 55–58.

Küng, H. 1986. "What is true religion? Toward an Ecumenical Criteriology", in *JTSA* 11:4–23.

Küng, H. 1987. *Why I am still a Christian*. Edinburgh: T and T Clark.

Küng, H. 1980. *24 Stellingen over de vraag naar God in deze tijd*. Hilversum: Gooi en Sticht.

Peck, M Scott. 1990. *The road less travelled*. London: Arrow.

Steen, W. 1994. "Herausgefordert zu Frieden und Gerechtigkeit in der Welt", in *Materialdienst des Konfessionskundlichen Institut Bensheim* 45(5):87–92.

Toffler, A. 1970. *Future Shock*. New York: Random House.

Usher, R. 1994. "The One and the Many", in *Time International*, 19 September: 76.

2   What about the Bible and ethics?

Len Hulley

Why is biblical ethics important?

In the world of today there are many people who question the value of biblical ethics. These may be dismissed by some as people who do not believe in the Bible or the Christian message, and for that reason they can be ignored. But there are even some people within the Christian camp who say that the Bible is no longer useful in providing guidance in ethical matters. Some of them argue that the world of today is so radically different from that in which the Bible was written that we can get little, if any, guidance from its pages. If these assertions were true, it would mean that we would have no need to ever refer to the Bible. I find it instructive that even those scholars who question its revelance, or even reject it out of hand, still quote the Bible. It seems that even in their rejection of its relevance they still turn to it for support.

While it is important to take account of critical points of view, we are faced with the situation that the church, and by that I mean the whole fragmented church of Christ as we come across it in the world today, still regards the Bible as its charter document. The church is built on faith in Christ, but it is in the New Testament that we encounter both the writings which witness to the Christ event and the other records and writings of the early church which make up what the church regards as the Christian revelation. The church also regards the Old Testament, which is that part of the Bible we share with the Jews and in a sense inherited from them, as authoritative. The role that the Bible played and still plays in the church is decisive in this discussion. Above I used the words "revelation" and "authoritive". These terms are crucial in this discourse on the place and importance of the Bible within Christian circles.

Modern problems not addressed in the Bible

In our modern world we are faced with all sorts of problems, many of which are new and peculiar to our age. They are the products of modern technology and consequently we are left without direct precedents to guide us in our moral decision-making. Not only that, but the Bible does not give us any specific guidelines on how to deal with these matters. There are several examples that come to mind. We have in modern nuclear weaponry the ability to destroy large sections of the population in a matter of moments. One result is the destruction of people and property, another is the radioactivity which contaminates the area and is a threat to life for some time afterwards. The kind of warfare about which we read in the Bible cannot be compared at all with this situation. How then do we draw upon the Bible for in our ethical judgements?

In modern medical science the advances made often bring with them a host of new questions about what may and may not be ethical. The field of reproductive technology, sometimes spoken of loosely as test tube babies, fairly bristles with questions about what is right or wrong. It is commonplace in fertility clinics to carry out *in vitro* fertilisation[1] of the ova with male sperm and then to place the fertilized ova in the reproductive tract of the woman so that a "normal" pregnancy will follow. But this is just the start of our problems. Some people argue that we are bringing other people into the relationship between husband and wife. Where the ovum is that of the wife and the sperm belongs to the husband, often referred to as AIH (artificial insemination husband), we can argue that medical technology is merely helping them to fulfill their injunction to "go forth and multiply". But is this justifiable in a world faced with the problem of over-population? Or again, is it true to say that when the sperm comes from another man than the husband, the so-called AID (Artificial Insemination Donor), that we have a case of adultery? (This must be distinguished from the disease known as AIDS (acquired immuno-deficiency syndrome) – AID merely refers to insemination using donor sperm.) To make the matter even more complicated, sometimes the ova are donated and the husband's sperm is used to inseminate them, whereafter they are placed in reproductive tract of his wife who carries the babies until a normal birth. A final example from this field: some doctors have used this reproductive technology to enable women who are beyond normal childbearing years to have children. So, for example, a woman of 59 years had twins and another of 60 had a child. One could go on and discuss the use of donated tissue in transplant operations or euthanasia.

In these circumstances it is small wonder that in recent years medical bodies have debated the ethical issues involved and brought out guidelines for their members, or that governments have appointed committees to investigate the matters and have passed legislation to regulate aspects of medical science. I do not want to go into these matters any further, but have merely mentioned them so that I could highlight some of the modern ethical problems which are not addressed in the Bible. One must admit immediately that the problems addressed in the previous paragraph face those who are relatively well off. In poorer countries there are other problems facing people. Amongst the poorest survival is paramount, in some situations the political suppression and economic exploitation of the poor are ethical

---

1   *In vitro* literally means in glass. The ova and the sperm are mixed in a glass container before the fertilized ova are placed in the reproductive tract. They usually implant several ova to increase the possibility of successful impregnation.

problems of vast proportions. It is an interesting observation that these problems are among those addressed in the Bible itself. In poor countries one also finds "new" problems, for example, an explosive rate of population growth and the use of trees for fuel to such an extent that whole areas are denuded of trees. While issues like the chopping down of trees and rapid population growth are also related to poverty these are matters not so clearly addressed in the Bible.

The Bible as a source of moral guidance

Because the biblical record is regarded as divine revelation, it is accorded authority within the church. It is the written record of God's communication with human beings. In 1 Corinthians 10 Paul writes about what happened to the Israelites during the Exodus, drawing certain lessons from their experiences. Although we may not altogether agree with his method of exegesis in this passage, most would agree in principle with the conclusion he reaches, "These things ... were written down to instruct us" (1 Cor 10:11). After extensively examining the way the early church used the Bible when faced with ethical challenges, Allen Verhey states "the church has ... identified the Bible – and especially the New Testament – as the finally normative part of her rich tradition" (Verhey 1984:3). This holds true in the present as well. When one studies recent documents produced by the churches on moral issues, one invariably finds that a fundamental source of the ethical guidelines that they identify as relevant is the Bible. I want to provide some examples of this to substantiate my case. In 1974 the Dutch Reformed Church made the following statement in a document *Human relations and the South African scene in the light of scripture*, commonly known by its Afrikaans title *Ras, volk en nasie*: "In its consideration of relations between races and peoples, the Church must accept the Word of God as premise and norm" (DRC 1974:7). In fact, in the title of the document the point is already made that the scripture was regarded as a source of guidance in the matter of race relations. One can find fault with the arguments in the document and question the way scripture was used, but the point is made that the Bible is seen as a source of guidance on moral issues.

In a very significant study by the Roman Catholic Bishops in the United States of America, entitled *Economic Justice for all*, they say this:

> The fundamental conviction of our faith is that human life is fulfilled in the knowledge and love of the living God in communion with others. The Sacred Scriptures offer guidance so that men and women may enter into full communion with God and each other, and witness to God's saving acts. We discover there a God who is creator of heaven and earth, and of the human family. ... The focal point of Israel's faith – creation, covenant, and community – provide a foundation for reflection on issues of economic and social justice (O'Brien and Shannon 1992:585).

Here we find that the bishops take an intermediate step, they use the biblical concepts of creation, covenant and community as basic points of departure in their statement. In their search for guidance on economic and social justice they refer to many other scriptural passages and theological themes as well, adding that "These biblical and theological themes shape the overall Christian perspective on economic ethics" (O'Brien and Shannon 1992:593).

The last example I want to consider is not a denomination, but rather two South American ethicists who write from a liberation theology perspective. They argue that we cannot go to the Bible expecting to find a theoretical framework for Christian ethics. "The scriptures are not a recipe book, but they do contain the basic meaning of what it is to be human, since Christ is humanity in its fullness" (Moser and Leers 1990:37). The Bible is what they call the "deepest well of inspiration" for ethics. In the scriptures we meet Jesus Christ both as Lord and Saviour and we relate our questions and responses to him. They argue that "the basic criterion, the *norma normans*, is the following of Jesus Christ" (Moser and Leers 1990:67). My purpose in choosing these disparate examples is to illustrate the fact that Christians from a wide range of perspectives all look to the scriptures for guidance in their quest for moral counsel. I could go on giving further examples, but I think that the point has been made.

Biblical hermeneutics

There are some scholars who quite correctly warn us against a too facile use of biblical texts when considering modern problems. When attempting to use scripture for ethical guidance, Houlden says that we should ask ourselves whether we can isolate the proposed topic from the theological world of the New Testament without distorting it. While he is concerned in particular with the New Testament as a source of ethics, his views can be applied to the Old Testament as well. He says furthermore that one can hardly speak of a New Testament ethic because there are a number of points of view in the New Testament and we cannot merely assume that they are in harmony with one another. I may add that we cannot read the Bible and apply what we find there to our modern situation without taking into account the differences between the "then" of the biblical record and the "now" of our contemporary world. How does one bridge the gap? That is the task of hermeneutics, the attempt to interpret the Bible for our modern context. Earlier I made the point that we are often faced with matters not directly considered in scripture. We then have the task of employing theological themes derived from the scriptures that enable us to respond in terms of our faith, as the American Catholics bishops did. This raises the question about the way one considers that the Bible fulfills its function of providing guidance in ethical matters. Longenecker says that there are several approaches to this issue, we now turn our attention to them and examine some authors who use them.

A book of laws

The first of these positions which we will consider is that which considers the Bible to be a book of laws or codes of behaviour which we have to obey. People who hold this view consider that God has revealed his will clearly in both the Old and New Testaments in the form of commandments. These are clearly and objectively revealed and there can be no confusion in moral matters. This is a very old approach to ethics which was already found in Rabbinic Judaism. The rabbis codified the laws so that those who wished to adhere to them had ready access to them. Many sincere Christians today have the same approach to moral behaviour. An example of a noted ethicist who espouses this approach is Norman Geisler:

> Christian ethics is based on God's commands, the revelation of which is both general (Rm 1:19–20; 2:12–15) and special (Rm 2:18; 3:2). God has revealed himself both in nature (Ps 19:1–6) and in Scripture (Ps 19:7–14). General revelation contains God's commands for all people. Special revelation declares his will for believers. But in either case, the basis of human ethical responsibility is divine revelation. ... Since moral rightness is prescribed by a moral God it is prescriptive (Geisler 1989:23).

Later he argues for what he calls graded absolutism. By this he means that when we are faced with a clash of divine commands some are more important than others and we must subordinate "the lower duty to the higher one" (Geisler 1989:132). But those commands are nevertheless absolute and objective. Graded absolutism has certain characteristics:

> It stands firm on moral principles based on the absolute, unchanging character of God. These moral principles are absolute in their source, absolute in their sphere, and absolute in their order of priority. They are objective, propositional, and substantive in their content. God's moral laws are specific and known in advance of the situation. Furthermore, there are no exceptions to them (Geisler 1989:131).

The people who espouse this way of using the Bible in ethics may work with what has been called a canon within the canon. This merely means that they are selective in what they regard as authoritative and ascribe particular authority to specific parts of the Bible. This is not uncommon. An example of someone who functioned like this is the great reformer Martin Luther. Although Luther believed that the Bible had great authority, he was selective in what he regarded as authoritative. So we find that some people regard what Jesus said as having more authority than the Old Testament or Paul. Indeed it is almost impossible to attribute the same authority to all parts of scripture, that is, not be selective. This is the reason why Geisler holds that some injunctions carry more weight than others.

We must acknowledge that the Bible contains imperatives that are not optional extras for those who belong to the people of God. Jesus' summary of the greatest commandment, about loving God with our whole being, and loving our neighbours as ourselves is one such example. The same can be said about our concern for the poor. "With such moral imperatives there is no need to wait for a specific issue to arise. ... The moral imperatives made clear in the biblical witness are to be internalized as part of the basic identity of the community of faith" (Birch and Rasmussen 1989:193). As you can see, there is a close relationship between these moral imperatives and those values which we absorb in the process of character building. These "unconditional imperatives" become part of who we are and influence our ethical decision-making in that way.

Having said that I must nevertheless add a word of caution. We must be very careful about any attempts to endow biblical moral imperatives with such a high status. Before this can be done, one has to do careful exegesis of the passages involved and they must enjoy the support of the whole canon: "Only those concerns consistently identified throughout the Scripture as moral imperatives necessary to the authentic self-understanding of God's people can be claimed as necessary marks of faith on biblical grounds" (Birch and Rasmussen 1989:184).

Although it is important to remember that the Bible has prescriptive force, the New Testament portrays the Christian life as much more than following a set of rules. The New Testament uses various images to describe what happens to people who respond to Jesus Christ. Matthew sees them as disciples, John as having been born again, Paul as new creatures. Included in these terms is the idea that there is a radical moral change. This is very different from adhering to a set of rules. Keeping rules does not bring about a radical change in character, it merely inhibits people from engaging in morally questionable behaviour. Furthermore, having a set of rules means that you have to somehow interpret these rules for each new situation. These interpretations eventually solidify into a tradition which virtually displaces the original rules. We see this in the place accorded the rabbinic codifications, the role played by Roman Catholic Canon law, and the way some Protestant groups have certain codes of behaviour to which their adherents must conform. These interpretations start to carry more weight than the scriptures themselves.

There are several authors who use this paradigm for their ethical systems, most of whom come from the American evangelical tradition, Geisler being an example. Some of them even speak of objective divine revelation, as Geisler does. That implies that God's will and commands should, in principle, be visible to anyone who seeks to know them. The problem, however, arises when these scholars do not agree with one another on what they are so sure is the divine will. It also is significant that the strictest Protestant groups who function with this approach to rules usually confine themselves to the realm of personal ethics, as the rules approach lends itself to this. There is seldom any discussion on the very important area of social ethics because rapidly changing social circumstances make it difficult to function with a rules ethic. Above I mentioned several areas in which new problems have emerged that were not even thought of in biblical times. Operating with a rules ethic means that we are at a loss about what to do in such circumstances. The way they work in the courts of law in our country is in fact a very close parallel to having a rules ethic. In the supreme courts of the land, judges and advocates are engaged in the matter of applying rules, or laws, to changing circumstances. In a sense, the judge has a set of rules which have to be applied and has to determine whether in fact they are appropriate to the circumstances which apply to the particular case being heard. Where completely new circumstances emerge, for which there are as yet no rules, the judge seeks to decide what is just in the situation and decides accordingly. By doing so, new rules are created. But where we hold that the Bible is the only source of rules, we are faced with a finite number of rules while we are faced with ever new sets of problems.

Universal principles

At the turn of the century Adolf von Harnack,[2] a German scholar, argued that Jesus' message was not so complicated as was sometimes made out. He held that we could reduce it to three main points. He taught about: "(1) the kingdom of God and its coming; (2) God the Father and the infinite value of the human soul; and (3) the higher righteousness and the commandment to love" (Longenecker 1984:4). When one took these three together, one came up with a kind of humanism inspired by the teachings of Jesus Christ, its basic values being faith, hope and love.

In essence this means that we should not look to the scriptures for rules, but that we should derive universal principles from the values that underlie the laws and injunctions codified in the Bible. These will provide biblical norms which we can apply to the changing situations on the levels of both private and public morality.

I Howard Marshall, working from an evangelical perspective, argues that we must distinguish between the exegesis and application of a passage, trying to establish what it meant for the original readers and its significance for us. He further argues that the essence of the evangelical approach is: "When we come to a biblical exhortation we must inquire into the underlying theological and ethical principles which are expressed in it, and then proceed to work out how to translate those principles into appropriate exhortations for today" (in Wright nd:50).

Longenecker argues that deriving universal principles from the Bible is certainly useful, but one tends to end up with a philosophical system of morality divorced from biblical theology. Alternatively, one ends up with a natural law ethic in which the Christian content is minimal and humankind and human reason become the sources from which we derive values that guide our ethical decision-making. Against this, Marshall asserts that deriving principles from the Bible enables one to take the Bible seriously while at the same time being aware of the cultural differences between our contemporary society and that which we find in the relevant biblical passages. It further enables one to avoid the necessity of taking literally the commands in the Bible which are no longer applicable in modern society. The question arises whether using Marshall's approach we are not also in danger of ending up with a purely philosophical ethic based on certain principles as Longenecker

---

2   Adolf von Harnack is sometimes referred to in literature as Adolf Harnack, Longenecker being an example of this usage.

asserts. This is not likely. Whereas Marshall sees Christian ethics as an expression of the relationship between a believer and God, those for whom it becomes a philosophical ethic of some kind see ethics as an autonomous discipline not requiring a faith commitment of any kind.

An encounter with God

The third way of doing biblical ethics is that of an encounter between the reader of the Bible and the sovereign God through the Holy Spirit. In that moment, God reveals to the reader what is the ethical thing to do. There are several scholars who see ethics in these terms. Some also speak of the encounter as a response of faith, Emil Brunner being an example. In his *The Divine Imperative* he says:

> The Divine command gathers up into itself the meaning of all laws; likewise it implies this twofold demand: "Come to Me, in faith, and now take the next step, the first one you can see before you!" All the "Commandments" point to the one "Command": "Love God and your neighbour". But it is also law ... and I can only learn what it means at the moment at which God calls me (Brunner 1964:112).

Whereas others, like Dietrich Bonhoeffer, see the encounter as being directly between the believer and Jesus. Another exponent of the divine encounter ethic is Karl Barth. We will, however, give attention only to Brunner and Bonhoeffer. Brunner sees his approach to radical obedience as the alternative to legalism, and he also regards the use of ethical principles as a form of legalism. Here he joins hands with the existentialists and extreme individualists. He holds that:

> There is no Good save obedient behaviour, save the obedient will. But this obedience is rendered not to a law or a principle which can be known beforehand, but only to the free, sovereign will of God. The Good consists in always doing what God wills at any particular moment (Brunner 1964:83).

Bonhoeffer uses the story of the rich man in Mark 10:17–31 to make his point about obedience. The young man wanted to know what he had to do to inherit eternal life. But he was unprepared for Jesus' response:

> He stands face to face with Jesus, the Son of God: it is the ultimate encounter. It is now only a question of yes or no, obedience or disobedience. ... If, as we read our Bibles, we heard Jesus speaking to us in this way to-day we should probably try to argue ourselves out of it like this: 'It is true that the demand of Jesus is definite enough, but I have to remember that he never expects us to take his commandments legalistically. What he really wants me to have is faith' (Bonhoeffer 1976:67 and 69).

Bonhoeffer says that we start raising all sorts of problems, or giving all kinds of reasons why we should not be radically obedient, as he shows in the quotation above. We rationalise ourselves out of obedience. He even goes so far as to say that ethics is to be regarded as an alternative to obedience. In other words, we argue about and discuss the issues rather than being obedient to what we know is God's will.

This approach sounds very attractive because it is apparently straight forward and simple. I have, however, come across very sincere people who claim that God has called them to a specific course of action which for the life of me I could not reconcile with what I believed about God and the divine will. The danger is that with this view of radical obedience it can cut one off from the great Christian heritage of revelation about God. Rejecting any laws or principles can result in a purely individualistic ethic. Indeed one cannot reason with a person who claims direct divine revelation as the only ethical imperative. For anyone holding this point of view it would not then make any sense to study ethics or engage in ethical discussion.

Situation ethics

A fourth, and closely related, ethical approach to the former is what is known as situation ethics. This term is best known for its connection with Joseph Fletcher whose book *Situation ethics: The new morality* was very influential. In Paul Lehmann, Fletcher found a kindred spirit. They had similar ideas about the rejection of what Lehmann calls absolutist ethics and what Fletcher labels prefabricated rules. In essence, they both say that you cannot have absolute rules which you then have to apply "to all people in all situations in exactly the same way" (Lehmann 1963:125). In this quotation from Lehmann he uses the word "situation" although he prefers to speak of context. In other words, the various factors involved in a problem which may play a role in how it is judged ethically have to be taken into account. We discussed this point briefly above while considering a rules ethic. Situation ethicists hold that the situation is the primary factor in any ethical judgement.

Situation ethics has been a useful addition to the armoury of ethicists. For Fletcher the only valid ethical norm is love, agape. In every situation one has to exercise love, that alone determines what one ought to do. But this approach too has its problems. How does one decide what is the loving thing to do in an ambiguous situation? Reading Fletcher's book is not a great help because the examples he provides are based on extraordinary situations and are not conclusive. One could decide on another course of action than the one Fletcher proposes and still hold that it was motivated by love. For example, a woman in a concentration camp has sex with one of the guards in an effort to fall pregnant, because if she does she will be sent home. The argument is that she engages in sex because of the love she has for her family. That love, Fletcher argues, justifies her behaviour. But, one could equally say that in spite of the possibility of going home if pregnant, she decides that she loves her husband and family too much to engage in adulterous sex.

Lehmann holds that it is within a fellowship of Christians that we can determine what is right. He puts it like this: "it is from, and in, the koinonia that we get the answer to the question: What am I, as a believer in Jesus Christ and as a member of his church, to do?" (Lehmann 1963:47). This approach has much to commend it, and we shall return to it below, but anyone with a rudimentary knowledge of church history will know that the church has done some things one finds hard to reconcile with Christian moral values. In South Africa we have the example of apartheid which was justified by some churches as moral. The basic problem with situation ethics is that it is rather optimistic about the ability of individuals to act lovingly and to make good decisions.

As you can see, there are several options in the way we employ the Bible in Christian ethics. In practice we find that in doing ethics there is an interaction between the situation and the moral values we hold, whether we regard them as rules, principles or the embodiment of obedience to Christ or even trying to give expression to agape.

Do we start with the text or the context?

When we are faced with a moral problem do we start with the Bible, as do those who work with rules, or principles, or do we start purely with the context, as Fletcher suggests? How do we in fact recognise that something is a moral problem? Some scholars tell us that it is because we become aware that we are breaking certain rules or principles, whereas Fletcher says we discern that we are being unloving in the situation. Related to this problem is just how we come to the realisation that something we have been doing for some time without any pangs of conscience is wrong. In other words, we are faced with the fact that we have previously accepted what has been happening without having any moral qualms, but which we now start to question.

What brings about this change? My conviction is that we develop a set of values over a period of time, we could even say that our characters are developed in the environment in which we live. In the process we absorb various moral values from our surroundings, our homes, school and university or work setting, and during participation in church activities. These values are often, perhaps even usually, taken on board unawares. These values determine who we are. Within the Christian koinonia we would develop our character, a Christian identity. Out of this identity flows a certain style of behaviour, that is, who we are determines to a certain extent what we do. In that sense we are the products of our environment. Our characters are at least partly formed by the social processes to which we have been subject. This point of view is endorsed by the theories of the sociology of knowledge. Included in the values we develop are ideas of fairness, justice, integrity, love for other people – a particularly Christian value, kindness, an understanding of human dignity, and respect for others to name some of the more obvious ones. These values are part of what we find in the teachings of the Judeo-Christian tradition and we would absorb them from our earliest days in the Christian fellowship. This is a short description of what is often referred to as character-formation. I shall return to this matter below.

This discussion picks up an aspect of the value of koinonia we came across in Lehmann's thought. In this case, however, we do not necessarily go back to the koinonia to make our decisions, although this would be a good thing. Sometimes we are confronted with behaviour or action which we accepted unquestioningly in the past, only this time it bothers us. We may not know quite why we experience the niggling feeling other than an intuition that something does not quite add up. Here I think we could legitimately speak of the operation of the Holy Spirit. We become sensitive to the promptings of the divine Spirit, although we may remain unsure of what the implications of our feelings are. Over a period of time, perhaps with the help of the koinonia and a specific, directed study of the scriptures, we wrestle with the matter and come to the conclusion that we have been acting immorally in the past. What has happened is that we came to the realisation that those practices and attitudes which we accepted without question in the past were not congruent with our system of Christian values. Within the koinonia we become aware that the Holy Spirit is calling us to a new sphere of obedience. The old social norms or rules are seen to have been wrong. In a sense our characters have developed further in the direction of the Christian values we hold.

Such a change could be dramatic or slow. If one looks at the history of slavery, it took many centuries for people to become aware that slavery is wrong. All the while it was not in line with the ideas of human dignity and freedom which belongs to human beings made in the divine image, but people did not see it. In fact, sincere Christians defended it in terms of their faith. In recent years we have seen the same happening in the areas of discrimination against women and people of different races. Few people today defend racial discrimination as based on the teachings of the Bible, although there are many who still practice it and even exclude members of a different race from membership of their churches. This suggests that they are not yet convinced that it is wrong. We still find many people who continue to defend discrimination against women. So, for example, there are many theologians and practising Christians that argue that women may not be priests or ministers in the church. The ordination of women to the priesthood in the Church of England has caused some priests and members to resign in protest.

Is a biblical ethic individual or social?

Christians often limit the ethical role of the Bible to providing guidance in their personal lives. So, for example, during a mission in our church I participated in a group discussion in which we were asked to consider what being obedient to God meant for us. The leader of our group did not want us to "get involved in political issues" when being obedient in matters of social justice were raised. What she was concerned about was individual conversion and personal obedience, that is, obedience in the personal aspects of our lives. What does it mean when we are told to "strive first for the kingdom of God and his righteousness" (Mt 6:33)? In terms of this discussion group all it means is that I must be converted and have a "right relationship" with God. Is that adequate? Is God not also concerned with social justice? For me this discussion raises the question of the adequacy of conversion as understood in the conservative evangelical tradition and of individual versus social ethics, as though they are alternatives. I am not questioning the necessity of turning to God, or of faith in Jesus Christ as Lord and Saviour, but am asking whether we need to go further than personal and private matters in our obedience. Let us now examine that matter.

Part of the problem is that many people reduce the role of Jesus Christ to being their individual Saviour and personal Lord only whereas we are told in John's gospel that God sent his Son into the world because he loved the world. This tells us at least that God is concerned about the world out there and not only about whether we believe or not. Furthermore, when we confess that Jesus is Lord we are saying that he is the Lord of all life as well as our Lord. To take this argument a step further; when we pray that God's reign may come and God's will be done on earth as it is in heaven (Mt 6:10) we are also praying about what happens in this world. Discussing the nature of God's reign Küng states: "It will ... be a kingdom – wholly as the prophets foretold – of absolute righteousness, of unsurpassable freedom, of dauntless love, of universal reconciliation, of everlasting peace" (Küng 1978:215). Some may argue that here we are concerned about God's reign and will in the end time. That is true. But, can we say that we do not then have to be concerned about that will in the present? In examining this matter, Küng remarks: "If anyone wants to talk about the future in the spirit of Jesus, he must also speak about the present and vice versa" (Küng 1978:222). In the light of this discussion, we are not faced with a choice between individual morality and social ethics, but rather we should see them both as essential. It is often much easier to retreat into our private world where the choices we have to make are usually, but not always, simpler. To face the world and there seek for what we believe is God's will in the context is often a daunting prospect, but it is part of our calling as Christians.

The Bible and the Christian community

We turn now to the matter of the role of the Christian community and the Bible in the exercise of ethics. One writer says: "The Bible had its origins and received its final shape as the canon of scripture in the faith community. As a resource for the Christian moral life it can be appropriated only in the context of the faith community" (Birch 1991:30).

With such a strong emphasis on the relationship between the Bible and the faith community, we shall now examine the nature of that community and the role it plays in Christian ethics. We turn again to Lehmann who emphasises the role of the koinonia in Christian ethics. He argues that when speaking of Christian ethics one can speak of koinonia ethics because its nature is determined by the fact that the church is "the body of Christ". Analysing Ephesians chapters three, four and five he asserts that "the first point to be underlined is that the church, the fellowship which is the body of Christ, the koinonia, is the fellowship-creating reality of Christ's presence in the world" (Lehmann 1963:49). With that point of view few people can have any problems. He goes on to argue that "koinonia is always there in the community of faith where prophetic-apostolic witness to revelation and response of the fellowship in the Spirit coincide" (Lehmann 1963:50ff). As I understand it, what he is getting at is that within the fellowship of Christians one enters into the heritage of the teaching of the church on social issues which stretches back to the prophets and apostles. That heritage we find written up in the scriptures and when we respond thereto within the fellowship, guided by the Holy Spirit, in terms which faithfully reflect the message in the scriptures, the Christian community functions as a genuine koinonia. In terms of this concept of koinonia, responses which do not rightfully reflect the teaching of the Bible imply that the fellowship in which such responses took place are themselves not quite genuine.

I want to pick up a final point from Lehmann's discussion. The purpose of that fellowship is the building up of its members as mature Christians (see Eph 4:13). "Christian ethics aims, not at morality, but at maturity" (Lehmann 1963:54). Mature Christians can be relied upon to act in a responsible way in relation to God, before whom we are morally accountable. Bruce Birch (1991:31) summarises these points neatly as follows:

> The whole range of the church's activity as a moral community is in interaction with the Bible as a primary source of the church's identity and purposive action in the world. The church acts as the shaper of moral identity, the bearer of moral tradition, the community of moral deliberation, and the agent of moral action, and the Bible plays a central role in each of these activities.

Lehmann referred to the development of maturity among believers and Birch referred to the shaping of moral identity, whereas I mentioned character formation above. Essentially, these all refer to the same thing. It has to do with the being and doing of believers. In other words, who we are determines how we will behave. In the Sermon on the Mount in Matthew's gospel, the same idea is expressed in the well known saying "Every good tree bears good fruit, but the bad tree bears bad fruit" (Mt 7:33). How does this formation take place? In their book, Bible and ethics, Birch and Rasmussen (1989:190) explain it as follows:

> Character formation is the learning and internalizing of a way of life formative of our own moral identity. It is our moral "being", the expression of who we are. ... Character includes our basic moral perception – how we see and understand things – as well as our fundamental dispositions, intentions, and motives.

There are a host of factors that go into the making of our characters, but here we are concerned in particular with the Bible as an influence on our moral makeup. Within the Christian community the Bible plays a central role and it must therefore follow that it must also play a leading role in our formation as Christians. We absorb the biblical values as we are nurtured in the teachings of the Christian faith. Throughout this process we are exposed to those values the community has derived from the Bible and given expression to in its fellowship, teaching, preaching, liturgy and hymns. We of course also come into direct contact with the message of the Bible as we hear it being read. Perhaps one of the most significant ways in which we are influenced is by people who themselves have absorbed the ethos of the scriptures and who make a deep and lasting impression on us. Although this is an indirect influence it usually plays an important role in our spiritual and moral formation. There is, of course, what may seem the most obvious way in which the scriptures provide us with our moral makeup and that is when we "read, mark, learn and inwardly digest the scriptures", to quote an old catechism from memory. This may take place in individual Bible study, but often we come to new insights in the koinonia led the Holy Spirit. Here too we may seek guidance on how to act in particular cases. In terms of the earlier discussion, we may be struck by something that is bothering us morally and then we turn to the Bible and the fellowship of believers for help and guidance.

Do we still need to study biblical ethics?

Someone may ask "But is it necessary to study ethics, and biblical ethics in particular, when one can get guidance from the Holy Spirit and the Christian community?" It is necessary indeed. Not only does one become more aware of the content of the moral teaching of the Bible, on both the personal and social level, but you are taught certain skills which improve your ability to read and understand the ethical implications of the scriptures. You are taught how competent scholars have gone about using the Bible to provide guidance in moral matters. In the fellowship we are also helped to see social issues from various angles as we share insights with one another. What we have overlooked may be spotted by someone else. In my experience, this has enriched me immeasurably. In the end you can serve yourself and your fellowship, as well as society at large, more effectively by being better equipped in biblical and ethical disciplines.

In the final analysis we need to be able to be responsible in our use of the text and contextually relevant to the issues at hand. We must be equipped to adequately bridge the gap between the context from which we derive the biblical texts and our own day. The objective of biblical ethics is to do just that.

BIBLIOGRAPHY

Birch, CB. 1991. *Let justice roll down: the Old Testament, Ethics and Christian Life*. Louisville: Westminster/John Knox Press.
Birch, CB. and Rasmussen, LL. 1989. *Bible and ethics in the Christian life*. Minneapolis: Augsburg.
Bonhoeffer, D. 1976. *The cost of discipleship*. London: SCM.
Brunner, E. 1964. *The Divine imperative – A study in Christian ethics*. London: Lutterworth.
DRC 1974. *Human relations and the South African scene in the light of scripture*. Cape Town: Dutch Reformed Church Publishers.

Flechter, J. 1966. *Situation ethics: The new morality*. Philadelphia: Westminster Press.

Geisler, Norman L. 1989. *Christian ethics: Options and issues*. Grand Rapids: Baker Book House.

Houlden, JH. 1973. *Ethics and the New Testament*. London: Mowbrays.

Küng, H. 1978. *On being a Christian*. Glasgow: Collins.

Lehmann, P. 1963. *Ethics in a Christian context*. New York: Harper and Row.

Longenecker, RN. 1984. *New Testament social ethics for today*. Grand Rapids: Eerdmans.

Moser, A and Leers, B. 1990. *Moral Theology: Dead ends and alternatives*. Maryknoll: Orbis Books.

O'Brien, DJ and Shannon, TA (eds). 1992. *Catholic social thought: The documentary heritage*. Maryknoll: Orbis Books.

Wright, D (ed). nd. *Essays in evangelical social ethics*. Exeter: Paternoster Press.

3

Ethics in an African context

Neville Richardson

E thics as a distinct field of study, a discipline of its own, is a fairly recent concept. Until the modern era, even in the West (Europe and North America), the study of morality was seen as an aspect of a greater whole, together with such concerns as religion, law and politics. In Africa the separation of morality from the rest of life is even more problematic, as will be explained under the first of the headings to follow. This is one reason for a discussion on ethics in Africa being less straightforward than may be expected at first sight.

Further, the topic "ethics in Africa" could be approached in at least two ways. First, it could be seen as requiring a factual study of the moral condition of Africa. This would entail massive research on phenomena in African society deemed to be indicators of the moral state of that continent, or at least of certain parts of Africa. It would probably turn out to be an impossible task. Which parts of Africa would be studied, and why? Which phenomena should be selected, and on what basis – corruption, crime, witchcraft, AIDS, or more positive aspects such as generosity, compassion and care for the natural environment? If an acceptable selection of topics and an adequate study of them could be made, would the results not be significantly out of date by the time the vast study was completed?

Secondly, a study of ethics in Africa could be seen as a consideration of the ways in which moral reasoning takes place in Africa, of factors according to which moral decisions are made. This would entail a different kind of study from the first, but no less complex. A similar selection would have to be made of particular areas of the continent, but the study would then focus on why the people of the selected areas regard certain things as right and good and others as wrong and bad. The research task here would not be the gathering of social-anthropological descriptions as with the first type of study, but the explanation of moral thinking and acting. This is the approach which will be followed here, and the general geographical area in mind will be southern Africa, with specific reference to Zulu customs and patterns of thought.

This analysis of approaches indicates something of the complexity of our simple-sounding title in which the key terms, "ethics" and "Africa" are each complex in themselves. Does this mean that the task should be given up as hopeless before we begin? Certainly there are those who would offer such pessimistic advice. I see their point, and am even tempted at times to agree with them. After all, Africa is a vast continent covering almost one quarter (22 %) of the world's total land area, with about 11 % of the world's population, over 500 million people. At least one thousand languages are spoken and there are even more ethnic groups, some accounts recognizing over three thousand.

The practical implications of that viewpoint, however, seem to be highly undesirable – that it is not possible to discuss ethics in Africa as a whole, and that moral conversation between the various parts of Africa is not viable. It even suggests that the heterogeneity of Africa may render the concept "African" vacuous for all practical purposes. While it is true that precise studies of the anthropological kind are vital to an understanding of the many particular cultures of Africa, there is sufficiently wide agreement that there are indeed certain common features that go together to give substance to the term "African". Kasenene observes helpfully after noting a number of striking cultural differences in Africa:

> It would be misleading to overlook such cultural differences, but it would, however, be equally wrong not to recognise the common values and, at times, uniformity that exists within this diversity, south of the Sahara. There is a common Africanness, which must not be lost sight of (Kasenene 1994:138).

While there is no end to local variation, it is in respect of this "common Africanness" that we can consider ethics in its African context. Some of the main general features which should be noted in a consideration of the African context for ethics are: holism, vitalism, communality, authority-by-consensus, and ubuntu. Let us look at each of these in turn.

Holism

In order to appreciate this concept, it is useful to note its foreignness to Western minds. Western thinking is thoroughly dualistic, dealing almost instinctively in pairs of opposites – above and below, human and divine, physical and spiritual, sacred and profane, before and after, inner and outer, thesis and antithesis. A very long list of such opposites could be drawn up. With this pattern of thought, the tendency is to group things into categories in order to set them apart from and opposite to things in other categories. The effects of this pattern of thought on Western thinking and acting are very far-reaching. This dualism goes back to Greek philosophers such as Plato and Pythagoras and now, twenty five centuries later, is so deeply rooted in our thinking and our language that it seems to modern Westerners to be the natural way to think.

Traditional African thinking is not dualistic. It sees the togetherness of things rather than their separateness. It stresses interdependence and harmony among people, as well as between human beings and their natural environment. It is assumed that all things, human and environmental, are in a natural balance and that any disruption has a specific cause which can be detected and put to rights. The function of many traditional African rituals is the maintenance of the harmony or, if things have been disturbed, the redressing of the balance. These rituals may or may not be seen as religious. There is no way of distinguishing the religious from the secular, for there are no such separate categories of thought. They are taken most seriously, for they are the main means of communicating with the ancestors, and it is the ancestors, by and large, who control the harmony. Certainly, in moral terms, the observation of those customs which please the ancestors can only be regarded as good, because they make for the health, strength and prosperity of the community. That is for the good of all, and the social ethics of Africa is deeply concerned with the good of all.

Religious blessing of any kind is never regarded as being for the individual alone. The gospel of individual salvation to everlasting life is seriously at odds with African tradition and, one may add, is less than faithful to biblical tradition too! Salvation in African terms can only be for the community as a whole and should be reflected in its welfare. Further, the notion of only some spiritual part of a person being saved, a dualistic idea if ever there was one, is as incomprehensible to traditional African thinking as it was also to the Hebrew ancestors of Jesus. Such physical-spiritual dualism has crept into Christian theology through its keeping company too closely with classical Greek philosophy. The African understanding of holistic well-being seems much closer to the central biblical conviction of God's dealings with the people of Israel as a whole and, further, with Paul's view that salvation is not only for a certain group, nor even for human beings alone, but for the whole creation: "... the creation itself will be set free from its bondage to decay and obtain the glorious liberty of the children of God" (Rm 8:21, RSV).

The holism of traditional African thought militates against the isolation of morality as a topic separable from the whole life of the community. In African thought there are no departments of life. There is only life as a whole. Furthermore, dividing the subject matter of our discussion into sections and subsections seems artificial. Yet, for the sake of clarity, and mindful of the probable Western imposition on, and therefore distortion of, our African subject matter, we continue to make distinctions and follow headings as though African traditional life can be looked at in separable pieces. As we do so, however, we should be aware of the strangling effect of our rationalistic-academic line of thought. We do indeed "murder to dissect". To evoke the life of a community in written form is always a challenge to a writer. It is all the more so in the case of African community!

Vitalism

The natural harmony of things noted above was not considered to be a neutral or fixed static state. It was thought to be the very dynamic process through which the force of life itself was imparted. A person or group may have this life force in smaller or greater measure. Clearly, the ideal is to have as much of the life force as possible and this, while difficult to quantify precisely, is measurable in terms of the numerical, physical and economic strength of one's family or clan. When linked with the holism mentioned above, it is easy to see how my well-being and that of my clan is bound up with the well-being of others. In contrast to the 'winner-takes-all' approach so prevalent in modern Western society, there is in African tradition a strong inclination towards a 'let-us-all-win-together' approach.

Traditional rituals have much to do with the maximizing of the vital force. Before the birth of an individual, at key points throughout life, until after his or her death, certain rites of passage must be observed if the life force is to be fully available and properly appropriated. An example is the imbelego ceremony in which the name of the newly born, or recently born, child is communicated to the ancestors. The hope is that the ancestors will approve of the name and care for the child all through life. Names are of great historical significance in the life of a family. They signify an event or state of affairs. That is why a new child's name is believed to matter so much to the ancestors – a far cry from the modern Western practice of choosing a name simply because it sounds nice to the parents!

The general assumption regarding the life force is usually characteristically optimistic. In normal circumstances the life force should be freely available to all people. When it is seen to be diminished, through such eventualities as sickness, misfortune such as a car accident or lightning strike, depression, or the inability of a woman to conceive and deliver a healthy baby, the general assumption is that malevolence has been at work. The diminution of the life force has been brought about by the malicious ill will of some particular person or group – not total strangers – but someone who is in touch with the sufferer. Here is evil at work, and it must be countered in some specific way. The role of the ancestors is important here, not that they are thought to be the bringers of evil. On the contrary, they seek to protect and to increase the "abundant life" (cf John 10:10) of their descendants. At most they may challenge or warn and chastise, like any conscientious parent. The appropriate response is then that one or other of the rituals may well have been overlooked causing concern to the ancestors. Are they being forgotten or their importance downgraded? The ritual response is then one of reassurance and the re-establishment of the vital link between the living and their "living dead". Serious diminution of the life force, however, is not the kind of thing which the ancestors would visit on their descendents. Therefore, it is regarded as having its origin in the deliberate scheming of some person or group to bring about harm. The counter to this lies with the diviner, who has the skills to diagnose the problem, to identify its source, and to effect a cure.

Should the notion of life force seem strange to Western minds, they should consider Augustine's view in which goodness was identified with "enlargement". Augustine saw only goodness as real. Evil, serious though it was, was merely the absence of goodness. True enlargement, therefore, was an increase of goodness. James Gustafson uses Augustine's categories of thought effectively in a restatement of sin and salvation not far removed from African thought.

> If the human fault can be indicated by the metaphors of the contraction of soul and of interests, and its consequences as improper relations of ourselves and

all things to God, the correction can be indicated by an "enlargement" of soul and interests, and by a more appropriate alignment of ourselves and all things in relation to each other and to the ultimate power and orderer of life (Gustafson 1981:307).

We should not be surprised at this affinity between Western and African thinking. It comes after all from an African, albeit a North African!

Communality

This is widely recognised as being the central concept, as well as the determinative experience of African morality. The manner in which the above points, holism and vitalism, cohere in the notion and experience of communality makes it clear that we are not dealing here with three separate points, but with three facets of one point. The rituals also have as their purpose the physical survival, ongoing identity and social harmony of the community by which they are observed.

Two main considerations make African communality difficult for modern Western minds to grasp. First, since the Enlightenment, Western thought has been dominated by a confidence in the automony of the individual. The individual has become the focal point of our sense of identity and morality. How, we imagine, can the moral agent be anything but the reasoning individual? That which is right and good can only be that which is considered right and good by an individual, even if the individual's decision-making process involves consulting others. For example, if a Westerner is approached by an unmarried friend seeking advice because his girlfriend is pregnant and they are considering an abortion, the "advice" will invariably end with something like, "you must decide for yourself". Even if the friend in trouble then pleads for more decisive guidance, the last word will still tend to be something like, "you must do what is right for you." This may seem a case of abdication of moral responsibility on the part of the moral confidante, but it is in fact an indication of the entrenchment of the moral sovereignty of the individual in Western consciousness. We are reluctant to make moral rules and decisions for others. This has come to apply even in pastoral situations when a member of a religious group approaches an authority figure for moral advice. James Gustafson (1978:4–5), not without some humour, suggests the following responses: The Catholic priest begins his reply, "The church teaches that ..." The Jewish rabbi begins, "The tradition teaches that ..." The Protestant pastor offers lamely, "Well, now I think that ..." The indication here is that the rabbi and priest speak from a position of authority, which presupposes a community of some sort. The Protestant pastor, by contrast, has nothing to offer but his personal opinion, with the only authority coming from the force of his own personality, and no sense of community in operation at all. Of all the Western faiths, Protestant Christianity has been most fundamentally shaped by individualism. This is largely because the Protestant reformation occurred at a time when the European renaissance was in full bloom, human beings were seen as ruling over nature, and the individual, as exemplified in the humanism of Erasmus, was increasingly seen as being free from institutional bondage. It is an exaggeration, but one which contains some truth, that "Erasmus laid the egg, and Luther hatched it!" Later, in the Enlightenment of the seventeenth and eighteenth centuries, the individual came to the fore as an autonomous agent. Prior to the Enlightenment, the notion of the sovereign will of the individual was a rare thought. After the Enlightenment it became so widely accepted that it is now almost axiomatic. The impact of this individualism on the development of Protestant Christianity was profound. Salvation was conceived as being primarily a matter between the individual believer and God, and Christian morality was regarded as being the response of the individual believer to the direct guidance of the Word and the inspiration of the Holy Spirit. Goodness consisted primarily in the state of the individual's "inner life".

Secondly, Western minds find African communality difficult to grasp because traditional African community means more than belonging to a particular group of people who are alive at present. It encompasses those still in their mothers' wombs, about to be born, and also the ancestors. Ancestors *(amadlozi)*, play an active role in protecting and effecting the well-being of the community. While in theory they stretch back to the time of human origins, or at least the emergence of the particular clan, in practice they go back "three or four generations in the case of commoners and somewhat longer in the case of royalty" (Thorpe 1991:38). In the *ukubuyisa* ritual, observed approximately one year after the death of a family member, the departed one is "called home", not to some distant heaven, but to the everyday life of the family homestead. In this ceremony, the living are strongly linked to the dead, for mutual advantage, but what is not always seen is the power of the ritual to bind the living to each other in a vital family relationship.

Christians are sometimes dismissive of ancestors. They are concerned that merely to believe in ancestors and certainly the business of communicating with them smacks of the spiritualism, wizardry, and necromancy explicitly condemned in scripture (Deut 18:9–12). They regard "ancestor worship" as infringing on the belief in one God (monotheism) and the worship of that one God alone (monolatry). What is overlooked in this negative regard of ancestors is that the entire notion is seen and judged from a Western perspective. Once we begin to think in vitalistic terms, it becomes easier to think of the life force as extending beyond those presently living, and to regard them as still somehow sharing that life with us. Once the framework of our thought is holistic rather than dualistic, it can immediately be seen that the ancestors do not belong and have to be sought in another, supernatural realm. There is only one realm, and we all belong in that realm together. We, with them, are all part of one profound community. Our belonging transcends the superficial empirical realm, bounded as it is by the senses of sound and sight. The ancestors are present, but are merely unseen. Communing with the ancestors is not seen as worshipping them. Berglund explains:

> The shades are not worshipped. There is, rather, ukuthetha amadlozi, a speaking relationship with the shades. They are the seniors of the lineage, and with-

out communication with them there is a breakdown of normal and harmonious togetherness with them. Without their constant activity and nearness there cannot be a happy future (Berglund 1976:384).

It is important to recognise that the term used for relating to the ancestors is not *ukukhonza*, meaning worship, but *ukuthetha*, for which the most appropriate translation is communication. This is not far from the practice in certain Christian circles of engaging with and praying via the saints – it is important to note that this is praying through them not praying to them. At most they are venerated *(ukuhlonipha)*, not worshipped. The encouragement provided by the ancestors is similar to the New Testament notion that those who struggle and suffer to be faithful to the gospel are: "surrounded by so great a cloud of witnesses" (Heb 12:1). Who are these witnesses but ancestors in the faith?

Based on this strong, central notion and experience of community are two consequences of great importance for ethics. First, that which is right and good is not thus because it seems right and good to me as an individual. It is right and good only to the extent that it is right and good for the particular community to which I belong. In contrast to the Western ethical thought noted above, with its emphasis on the sovereignty of individual will, traditional African moral thought has the community at its heart. Secondly, the very identity of the individual is inextricably bound up with his or her particular community. Moyo states categorically: "There is no identity outside community" (1992:52). John Mbiti plays on Descartes' maxim, so influential in the development of Western thought, "I think therefore I am", when he says:

> Whatever happens to the individual happens to the whole group, and whatever happens to the whole group happens to the individual. The individual can only say: 'I am, because we are; and since we are, therefore I am'. This is a cardinal point in the understanding of the African view of man (Mbiti 1969:108–109).

It is clear that moral decisions in this context cannot be the decision of the individual alone, especially because such individualism is foreign to African tradition. The notion of the sovereign will of the individual is obviously very far removed from the view that one's very identity is known and expressed through one's belonging in the community. Once the moral agent is no longer the sovereign individual but the person-in-community, morality becomes translated into different forms. Were abortion to have been an option, the enquirer would have sought moral guidance through an authority figure, a senior member of the group, who in turn would have consulted other representative figures before a decision could be made.

The connection between personal identity and ethics becomes clear in the following statement by Mercy Odoyuye:

> Africans recognize life as life-in-community. We can truly know ourselves if we remain true to our community, past, and present. The concept of individual success or failure is secondary. The ethnic group, the village, the locality, are crucial in one's estimation of oneself (Odoyuye 1992:110).

The Shakespearian ideal "To thine own self be true" becomes, in this context: "To thine own community be true". There is no other self to be true to, except the communal self. The community, its continuing harmony and well-being, are the measures of what is good.

Authority-in-community

As indicated above in the illustration on abortion, the search for moral guidance in an African context is very different from the individualism of the West. In the moral tradition of the West the consultation of others is not essential to moral decision. It is enough for me to know my own mind. Although I may choose to refer to the opinions of others, or to have my moral sense illuminated by referring to written sources, including scripture, what is essential to morality is that I make up my own mind and stand alone as a responsible moral agent. In African tradition, consultation is essential to morality.

Secondly, in Western practice who I consult is also a matter of my own choice. If I choose wisely I shall receive advice that is helpful to me, especially in the business of making up my own mind. In Africa there are certain authority figures whom I am duty bound to consult if I am to be morally correct. If I break the pattern, I am acting out of keeping with the structure of the community and am consequently damaging the harmony and well-being of the community. There is a hierarchical order in the people to be consulted, with the general rule being that the younger consult the older in normal circumstances. The chief is normally considered the high point of reference. Whether or not he is in fact the oldest member of the community does not matter, he represents in his person the community in its entirety. Even higher than the chief, of course, are the ancestors. They are consulted by everyone, including the chief, especially in matters of great importance to the community. Not to consult them is to court disaster.

Further, it is assumed that the chief himself is not operating as a lone individual merely dispensing his own opinions. In all important decisions and matters of policy, the chief is part of a process of communal consultation. In this process the method of arriving at decisions is of great significance. Decisions are not arrived at by vote in which the greater number wins, even if the majority is a single vote. Rather, discussion and negotiations continue until consensus is reached. Naturally there will always be those who support a consensus more enthusiastically than others. The important thing is that every one supports the consensus to some degree, and that all agree in each case on the priority of the community over their own individual viewpoint. The way of consensus requires time, patience and great social skills, especially on the part of the leaders, but there can be no doubt that, as a decision-making method, it is far more community creating than an often divisive and sometimes community destructive majority vote. While it may lack efficiency in terms of time, which is such a vital factor in modern industrial society, it is a vehicle of great efficiency at another level, that of communal coherence and of ongoing community building.

One of the tension points in the youth movements against apartheid, such as the Soweto schools boycott of 1976, was that the youth took the initiative, often against the wishes of their parents and other seniors. The moral rationale, where it was considered, would be in terms of the abnormality of the situation – first, that the Bantu Education system directly affected those in the schools and that this was therefore a problem appropriately faced by the pupils themselves and, secondly, that the struggle against the oppression of apartheid in the 1970s was a moral extremity requiring abnormal action. It is interesting to reflect, in passing, on the way in which such exceptions shape the tradition, and sometimes even overturn the tradition and become newly accepted ways of behaving. As we are considering the connection between ethics and community, it is important to note that as the accepted morality and especially the methods of decision-making change, so the community changes too. Which change comes first, the change in ethics or the change in society, is a matter of debate – a chicken and egg case.

Ubuntu

Having referred above to communality as the central concept as well as the determinative experience of African morality, it is hardly surprising to find that mutual caring and sharing are high on the agenda of African social relations and social ethics. A key descriptive term for these social relations and ethics is *ubuntu*. Attempts to translate this term into English all fall short not only because of the lack of a precise linguistic equivalent, but because of the loss of the holistic social reality out of which the term springs. Close approximations, however, are "humaneness", "compassion", and "fellow feeling".

More concrete than the etymology of the term are the many instances of *ubuntu* – practical pointers to the moral centrality of the community in African tradition. One such practical pointer is the care of the handicapped and the elderly. Far from these more vulnerable members being separated into institutions and committed to the "expert care" of others, they were retained and cared for in their own community. This care was not reserved exclusively for blood relatives. Another practical pointer was the attitude to strangers. Strangers were welcomed and accorded hospitality. This hospitality was not superficial politeness, but intended to be lasting and of such a nature that strangers would be transformed into fellow members of the community. Indeed, it was not uncommon for a stranger to be given land to plough thereby becoming an economically productive member, and even for a stranger to marry within the family (see Moyo 1992:53). Land, livestock and other possessions, while often privately owned, were regarded as being available for common use. Those who had fallen on hard times were often loaned cattle and other means of subsistence and wealth production. There was no thought of demanding some form of payment or interest. The loans were long term and intended to restore the fortunes of the impoverished ones, not only for their own good but for the good of the whole community.

Conclusion

Under the above heading of holism it was noted that African social ethics was concerned with the good of all. Under the heading of vitalism reference was made to the "let-us-all-win-together" approach. Under communality it was seen that in Africa the good must by definition be that which is good for my community, and that any difficult moral decisions must be made in consultation with community leaders. The practical embodiment of this morality in communal practice is best described in the term *ubuntu*, which may also be a personal characteristic more evident in some individuals than in others. Of course, as will be evident by now, any evaluation of individuals can be made only in respect of their relation to their community. Each community was comprised not only of those presently living, but also of the ancestors. To understand the community and its morality, one must have a sense of the social harmony and wholeness in which all the people participate, and which they must maintain from generation to generation by the scrupulous observance of important rituals.

While these general observations in the context of a "common Africanness" may seem far removed from Christian ethics as it is known today, it must be remembered that modern Christian ethics is to a large extent the product of modern Western thought. The life of the kingdom to which Jesus and the communities of his early followers witnessed may well be seen as having more affinity with the African communality described above than with the individualism of modern "Christian ethics". Jesus and his earliest Palestinian followers, had they ever known of African ubuntu, would have recognised it as being similar in its community centredness to the Torah based ethic which governed their moral life. Deuteronomy 10:18–19, for instance, which urges justice for the orphan and widow, and food and clothing for the sojourner is representative of that biblical ethic, but is also very similar to an ethic of ubuntu. Both are thoroughly communal and both are expressions of profound religious convictions.

A critical epilogue

Three points bearing on the entire preceding discussion must be made.

Tradition in Africa is in an ongoing process of dramatic change. Often, in modern urban life, little more than the remnants of traditions remain (see the reference to the umemulo ceremony in Richardson 1996:39–40). Some traditions are virtually forgotten even in rural areas where they once held sway. An example is that of the Zulu rain queen, Nomkhubulwane, recently resuscitated through a university research project (Kendall 1996). Some practices are observed, but their origins are lost (see, for instance, the reversal of the clerical collar at some Zionist funerals as noted in Berglund 1976:365). References to African tradition must be seen as general and therefore open to debate and reinterpretation in the light of the ongoing findings of anthropological research.

The temptation to romanticise African tradition should be avoided. It is all too easy from a modern vantage point to regard the African past as an idyllic state of communal life contrasting with the individualism, social fragmentation and loss of communality of modern Western existence. It would be misleading to imply that traditional African life was without its problems, moral and otherwise. We would be mistaken to imagine that traditions could be easily resuscitated and imported into the modern urban life that is fast taking hold in Africa.

Those wishing to pursue further the topic of Christian ethics in Africa should be aware that it has its place against the background of the deepening debate on the relationship between Christianity and African culture. The initial uncritical applauding of the work of the Christian missionaries was countered in the condemnatory view of Majeke. For her the missionaries were the culpable agents of colonial oppression. Renowned scholars such as Kwame Bediako and Lamin Sanneh have taken a positive view of Christianity's role in Africa, especially in respect of the revitalising effect they perceive it to have had on Africa's own religious heritage. In an important recent article, Maluleke (1996) rejects these approaches and suggests that a thoroughly African critique of Christianity would be the best step towards the development of a genuine African Christianity, characterised by its vital link to living communities. In similar vein, Eric Anum (1997) criticises even the currently fashionable "contextual method" of doing theology which is reflected in our title. Contextualisation, he feels, is a means of allowing western theologians to feel comfortable when they consider Christianity in Africa. Instead, like Maluleke, he suggests that Christian faith having been planted in Africa, should be left to the African people to develop as they see fit, according to their own needs and concepts.

A Christian ethic in an African context, which fits the thinking of such scholars as Sanneh and Bediako is being challenged, through the critical work of scholars like Maluleke and Anum, to become an even more thoroughly African Christian ethic. Such an ethic, one should expect, may seem foreign to modern Western Christians and theologians, but it would be surprising if it did not embody many of the key characteristics of "common Africanness" described in this essay – a richly communal ethic, closer to that of ancient Israel and of the early people of "the Way" (Acts 9:2) that came to be called Christianity.

BIBLIOGRAPHY

Anum, Eric. 1997. Conversation with the author, 25 May.

Berglund, Axel-Ivar. 1976. *Zulu Thought-Patterns and Symbolism*. London: C. Hurst and Company.

Gustafson, James M. 1981. *Ethics from a Theocentric Perspective* (Volume One: Theology and Ethics). Chicago: University of Chicago Press.

Gustafson, James M. 1978. *Protestant and Roman Catholic Ethics: Prospects for Rapprochement*. Chicago: University of Chicago Press.

Kasenene, Peter. 1994. "Ethics in African Theology", in C Villa-Vicencio and J de Gruchy, (eds) *Doing Ethics in Context: South African Perspectives*. Claremont: David Philip Publishers: 138–147.

Kendall, KL. 1996. "Zulu Women Bring Back the Goddess." (Article in English with Spanish translation), in *Zebra News*, 27 May: 25–26.

Maluleke, Tinyiko S. 1996. "Black and African Theologies in the New World Order: a Time to Drink from our Own Wells", *Journal of Theology for Southern Africa* 96, Novembe:, 3–19.

Mbiti, John. 1969. *African Religions and Philosophy*. London: Heinemann.

Moyo, Ambrose. 1992. "Material Things in African Society: Implications for African Ethics", in JNK Mugambi and A Nasimiyu-Wasike (eds). *Moral and Ethical Issues in African Christianity*. Nairobi: Initiatives Publishers: 49–57.

Odoyuye, Mercy A. 1992. "The Value of African Beliefs and Practices for Christian Theology", in JNK Mugambi and A Nasimiyu-Wasike (eds). *Moral and Ethical Issues in African Christianity*. Nairobi: Initiatives Publishers.

Richardson, Neville. 1996. "Can Christian Ethics Find Its Way and Itself in Africa?" *Journal of Theology for Southern Africa*. 95, July: 37–54.

Thorpe, SA. 1991. *African Traditional Religions*. Pretoria: University of South Africa.

PART 2

Ethical, sexual and
medical questions

4 Human sexuality and ethics

Louise Kretzschmar

The aim of this chapter is to provide a general introduction to the field of Sexual Ethics. The reader will notice that some of the issues simply raised here are discussed in greater depth in other chapters (eg "To marry or not to marry" and "Gender, women and ethics"). Also, the fields of sexual, social, medical and biblical ethics cannot be neatly separated. Each impinges and throws light upon the other.

Sexual ethics, then, cannot be discussed in isolation since sexual perceptions are affected by social relations, developments in medical technology, and by changes in biblical interpretation. All of these, in turn, are influenced by changes in world views as well as by the life experiences of persons and groups. To cite a controversial example, the question of the validity of artificial means of contraception may be viewed very differently by a celibate cleric than by a poverty stricken woman expecting her seventh child. Precisely because sexual ethics is such a complex and controversial subject, it demands both honesty and a careful analysis of varying views. In a few short pages, the entire field of sexual ethics cannot be comprehensively covered. My aim is simply to seek to introduce the reader to some of the main issues raised by this field of study and intimate human experience.

What constitutes human sexuality?

Some definitions

A distinction is commonly made between sex and sexuality. According to James Nelson,

> Sex is a biologically-based need which is orientated not only toward procreation but, indeed, toward pleasure and tension release. It aims at genital activity culminating in orgasm. While sex usually is infused with a variety of human and religious meanings, the focus is upon erotic phenomenon of a largely genital nature (Nelson 1978:17).

Sexuality, on the other hand, is a much wider term which goes beyond and need not even include genital sex. It is a very basic element of our humanness and is closely tied to our self-understanding and the way in which we relate to others and the world around us.

Our sexuality is a basic fact of our existence as males and females. As humans we are female or male embodied, relational beings. Put differently, "our sexuality is a basic datum of our existence as individuals. Simply stated, it refers to our way of being in the world and relating to the world as male or female" (Grenz 1990:8). The longing for relationship, epitomised by Adam's longing for a companion and partner (Gn 2:18–24) is a human characteristic, an inescapable aspect of our sexuality. Thus, whether persons adopt a married or single state, they need to experience unity and relatedness in one form or another. Human sexuality, thus, includes at least two vital elements: identity (who we are) and relation (how we relate).

In this regard, the distinction between genital sex and affective sexuality is a very useful one. Genital sexuality refers to the biological function of sexual intercourse, while affective sexuality encompasses "the emotional and psychological dimensions of our sexuality, [which] lie behind the mystery of our need to reach out to others, and is the basis for affection, compassion, tenderness and warmth" (Grenz 1990:5). This implies that there are many different expressions of sexuality including a smile, the touch of a hand, a hug, the ability to love, care, relate and listen, in short, the capacity for human relationship and intimacy. As Dominian puts it: "the experiences of touching, watching, talking and listening are the foundations of physical intimacy, the infrastructure of human attachment and therefore of affection" (Dominian 1977:33).

Some common myths

Before moving on to a description of various historical perceptions of sexuality, it is useful to briefly examine a few of the myths surrounding human sexuality.

The first of these is the perception that there are only two options: either giving oneself over to sexual desire or the complete repression of sexual desire. As indicated above, the distinction between genital sex and affective sexuality reveals that this perception is a gross oversimplification. While we cannot fully repress or escape from our sexuality, we need not go to the other extreme of abandoning ourselves to licentiousness. For though we certainly are sexual beings, there are other dimensions to both our identity and our relationships.

A second common myth is that the self and the body can be separated. There are those who view sexuality largely as an activity in which the body engages without such engagement having any effect on the self. A biblical ethic, by way of contrast, insists that the self and the body cannot be separated. As psycho-somatic beings (a unity of soul/spirit and body) we need to realise that the sexual appetites of the body cannot be given expression without affecting our very selves, nor can the actions of persons be separated from their commitment to God (1 Cor 6:15–20). Sexual permissiveness, argues Nelson, results in increasing personal and spiritual alienation and disintegration (Nelson 1978:37ff).

A third myth is that one's sexual relations are one's private affair. This is a mistaken perception because it assumes that what affects the individual affects that person only and not also that person's relationships. The error of this perception is indicated by the fact that all societies have some sexual taboos. Sexuality, precisely because of its power to affect lives, has always been regulated in one form or another. Even in our permissive age, rape, incest, and sexually expressed violence, for example, are regarded as unacceptable by the vast majority of people. The fact is that sex cannot be limited to the actions of "two consenting adults". The relatives, friends and children of those who engage in sexual relations, indeed the entire society, are influenced in some way. Thus, the increase of sexual permissiveness, sexually transmitted diseases, family strife, and marital breakdown affect society as a whole. In other words, sexuality is not a separate, private world; it impacts on the rest of reality and the rest of reality impacts upon our experience of sexuality:

> Sexuality is core to relationality, mutuality, intimacy. Hence the politics of sexuality are the politics of the family and locate themselves at the heart of social and spiritual identity (Armour 1991:162).

The historical and modern contexts of sexual ethics

It is important to consider the contexts within which sexual morality is debated because the moral principles used by ethicists to guide human behaviour must be related to changes in personal and social contexts in order to be meaningful and effective. For instance, Roman Catholic sexual morality has for centuries centred around procreation as the purpose of sexual relations within the context of marriage. Modern forms of contraception, however, greatly lessen the possibilities of children being conceived and, consequently, the effectiveness of the traditional insistence that sexuality (and marriage) be understood solely in relation to procreation.[1] This raises several questions: what is the purpose and proper context of sexual intercourse and what meaning has marriage for a post-contraceptive generation?

A stress on the influence of the social context does not mean that we need to conform to any and every changing social perception. Biblical norms and theological morality cannot simply be discarded because certain individuals or groups find them unacceptable. Nevertheless, ethicists need to evaluate why certain norms or moral standards are regarded as acceptable as well as ensuring that the moral standards which Christians espouse are enunciated in such a way that they are comprehensible and convincing.

What, then, have been some of the dominant perceptions concerning sexuality in the past and how have these changed during the 20th century?

Old and New Testament context

It is impossible to note all the elements of the many biblical teachings concerning sexuality. However, a few central elements may be noted here.[2]

---

1 For a discussion of these see Dominian 1977:59–65 and Kosnik et al. 1977:102–152.
2 For a detailed discussion see Kosnik et al. 1977:7–32.

The origins of humanity and sexuality (Gn 1–3); the emphasis on cultic purity (Lev 15 and 18; Deut 21–22; 24 and 27); spiritual and sexual fidelity (Is 1:21; Jer 3:6; Hos 2) and the joy of sexual love (Song of Solomon) are all stressed in the Old Testament. In the New Testament, Jesus stresses that morality was not to be restricted to externals, but to be practised also in the realm of thoughts and intentions (Mt 5:8, 27–28; 15:1–20). Paul, too, insisted upon purity and fidelity and he upheld both the married state and celibacy (1 Cor 7:1–40).[3] The desires of the flesh are contrasted with the desires of the Spirit (Gal 5:16–26).[4]

Radcliffe (1986:308–310) argues that both extreme asceticism and promiscuity are based on a despising of the body, whereas the heart of Paul's sexual ethic is an affirmation of our God-given bodies. Thus, immorality is a sin because the immoral person sins against his or her own body. This means that "a proper sexual ethic is one which helps one to live by the truth of what one does with one's own body" (Radcliffe 1986:311). A Christian sexual ethic maintains that one's body cannot be separated from one's relation with one's own self, other people, the Church as the body of Christ, and God. As Paul puts it:

> Or do you not know that your body is a temple of the Holy Spirit who is in you, whom you have from God, and that you are not your own? For you have been bought with a price: therefore glorify God in your body (1 Cor 6:19–20).

From the early Church up to the 16th century

Grenz (1990:xii–xiii) has argued that during the early centuries of its existence the Church affirmed sexuality within the context of morality. Against the Gnostics, the Christians taught that the material and sexual was good and God-created. Sexual distortions only occurred when this gift was abused and persons sinned against themselves, others and God. According to Price, what set Christians apart from the pagan world in the first few centuries of the Church's history was their sexual austerity. For the few who chose celibacy, a total renunciation of sexual relations was expected, for the rest, an insistence on marital fidelity and concord. In addition, they rejected adultery, fornication and homosexuality (1990:258).

Cecil Cadoux has shown how from CE 110 onwards, celibacy was increasingly viewed as preferable to marriage, though both remained central to the Church's teaching concerning sexuality, together with a rejection of practices such as sex outside of marriage, the abortion or exposure of offspring, prostitution, divorce, and remarriage (Cadoux 1925:191–196, 281–283, 443–446, 596–600). In either event, purity of heart, soul, mind and body was what distinguished Christians from "the world" and gave them their single-mindedness:

> To maintain her own integrity as a heavenly society that was only sojourning on earth, the Church needed members whose own bodies stood apart from the

---

3 From the Latin *coelebs* (a bachelor), celibacy means a renunciation of sexual relations, a decision to live a life of chastity.

4 The Greek *sarx* (flesh) does not refer to the physical body as such but the evil or sinful nature.

blurring and contamination, the loss of personal integrity and bodily vigour, brought about by easy sexual relations (Price 1990:273).

St Augustine, partly as a result of his own struggles with sexual purity, introduced a negative attitude to sex in the Church which has persisted up to the present day. Both in some of his own writings and in the selective use of these writings by subsequent writers, sexual pleasure itself was regarded as something to be frowned upon and marital sex perceived as having value only because it leads to procreation. Many of the early Church Fathers, precisely because of their own struggles with celibacy (together with the effect of the contrasting extremes of asceticism and eroticism within their social contexts) viewed sex in a pessimistic manner. An exception is the teaching of Clement of Alexandria (c 150–215) who argued that the purpose of marriage is not simply procreation, but includes "the mutual love, support and assistance that the partners extend to each other" (Kosnik et al. 1977:34).

By the early 4th century the Church had become the recognised religion of the Roman Empire. As a consequence of this, "virginity and the ascetic life replaced martyrdom as a way to complete Christlikeness" (Kosnik et al. 1977:35). Thereafter, a double standard became more evident: virginity and celibacy for a few, marriage for the majority, with the former being regarded as a sign of greater dedication to God, a result of which was the increasing insistence, in the Roman Church, on the celibacy of all priests.[5] During this time, celibacy was elevated above marriage.

Modern readers, living in an age in which sex is greatly over-emphasised, may find this celebration of celibacy peculiar. Within this context, however, asceticism (rather than materialism) was greatly valued. Furthermore, particularly for women, this was virtually the only means of choosing a life other than marriage shortly after puberty, followed by a succession of childbirths (if one survived), together with the life-long responsibilities of a family and home with virtually no access to the public sphere. Christian missionaries were accused of encouraging women to "reject the marriage bed" but, "what the women were rejecting, and the menfolk were defending, was not so much the sanctity of sex as the subjugation of women to their husbands" (Price 1990:268). Subsequently, a compromise was made between the medieval Church and the surrounding society:

> The government of the Church by a celibate elite, unique respect accorded to monks and nuns safely shut away in monasteries, while the traditional family under its male head remained the basic social unit in the outside world (Price 1990:268).

During the early and late Middle Ages (6th–15th centuries) both positive and negative perceptions concerning sex and sexuality were put forward. However, the pre-

---

5 In the Eastern Orthodox church celibacy was not insisted upon except for bishops. (Priests and canons could marry before, but not after, ordination). Significant declarations concerning celibacy in the Roman Church emerge from Councils in 306, 451 and 691. Priestly celibacy only became common after the Gregorian reforms of the 11th century. The Church of England abolished the obligation to be celibate in 1549.

vailingly pejorative perceptions concerning women (eg as seductive and inferior beings), concerns about ritual purity, and a mistrust of pleasure meant that sex was generally viewed with suspicion and pessimism (Kosnik et al. 1977:38ff). This is a striking contrast to our own age, where we have seemingly gone to the other extreme, according to sex an importance that far outweighs its actual value and also reducing it to considerations of physical performance rather than its meaning within the total personality, inter-human relationships and in terms of the injunction to "glorify God" with our bodies.

The effects of the 16th century reformation

After the 16th century Protestant reformation, marriage was again seen as the norm for the majority of people within Protestantism and priests or ministers were free to marry. However, within Catholicism, priests and nuns were still expected to take vows of celibacy.

This rejection of compulsory celibacy by the Reformers had a number of significant effects. First, it meant that marriage and marital sexuality were re-affirmed as valid expressions of human sexuality; they were not to be despised as inferior to celibacy. Within Lutheranism and Calvinism and amongst the Anabaptists, ministers of religion were free to marry if they so wished. Many former monks, priests and nuns renounced their vows of celibacy and married. Amongst Protestants generally, and particularly amongst the English and American Puritans, a positive view of sexuality was put forward, as long as it was practised within the context of monogamous marriage.

Despite these positive developments, however, the picture was less rosy for women. Despite the Protestant affirmation of the "priesthood of all believers", only men were permitted to be ordained ministers and, thus, women were denied access to the official religious ministry. Thus, whereas women had previously exercised many varied and influential ministries within their nunneries and the parish as a whole, Protestant women were now largely excluded from the public sphere and from religious leadership. Their role was limited to child-bearing and rearing, household duties, and a supportive role in the Church.[6] Not until the missionary movement of the 19th century and the movement for the ordination of women in the 20th century were Protestant women, both married and single, again able to "officially" discover, develop and use their spiritual gifts in a variety of ways, including those of teaching and leadership within the churches.

The 16th century to the present day

Between the 16th century and our own century, a number of fundamental changes have had a profound impact on sexuality in general and the family in particular.

6　The English phrase, "Children, Kitchen and Church" comes from the German "Kinder, Küche, Kirche" (or "Kinders, Kombuis en Kerk" in Afrikaans).

These include industrialisation, urbanisation, secularisation, new medical technologies, the emancipation of women, and "scientific" studies of sex.

Industrialisation meant that from the 1700s onwards many families in Europe no longer made a living within the context of the home (as craftsmen and women or as farmers), but went out to work in factories and offices. One consequence was that fathers (and often mothers as well) went "out" to work, leaving the rest of the family at home. In South Africa, especially after the mid 19th century, the high incidence of migrant labour meant that black men were away from home not simply during the day, but for as many as 11 months of the year. In recent decades this separation of the family amongst all race groups has become so acute that some speak of the "absent father syndrome" and of "working mothers", the negative effects of which may be greater family instability and lack of security and discipline in the children.

As a consequence of urbanisation, many people left not only the land, but also the family homestead, the extended family and the village community. Thus, families became separated, individuals and families moved around in search of work, and ties with family members and old friends were difficult to maintain. This resulted in greater isolation, stress and loneliness. In such a context, moral standards and discipline are difficult to maintain and there is greater opportunity for extra- and non-marital sexual relationships in the anonymity of the city.

Secularisation could be defined as "the decline of religion" or, more specifically as the process by which "religious institutions, actions and consciousness, lose their social significance" (Wilson 1982:149). The incidence of secularisation has meant that the connection between sexuality and religious morality has been undermined. Thus, religion is relegated to the fringes of life, and many people no longer have a religious worldview that is all-encompassing, affecting every dimension of their personal and social lives. Thus, a separation between religious commitment and sexual behaviour is created, permitting a separation and compartmentalisation of peoples' psyches and lives. Another significant factor during our century has been the development of medical technologies, particularly those affecting conception. This has given those who have access to this technology a degree of control over reproduction undreamed of by previous generations. This raises the issue of the use to which such medical technological innovations are put. On the one hand, it has freed married couples, particularly wives, from the fear of falling pregnant yet again and of being physically, emotionally and financially exhausted by a succession of births. On the other hand, such innovations have made it possible for persons to engage in sexual intercourse outside of marriage with little fear that conception will take place.[7]

It is doubtful whether the "swinging sixties" that characterised certain sectors of society during the 1960s in the West would have occurred without the combination

---

7 For a discussion of the debate concerning contraception see N Anderson 1977:59–84 and Kosnik et al. 1977:44–52.

of the contraceptive "Pill" and an increasingly permissive morality. During what has been termed the "sexual revolution", traditional moralities were discarded by many as repressive and outdated in favour of the pursuit of sexual freedom, whether in the form of couples "living together" or the form of the search for a succession of sexual partners. Since the 1990s, however, this attitude of sexual licence has begun to give way to a greater emphasis on caution and commitment, possibly as a result of both the threat of sexually transmitted diseases and the increasing awareness of the psychological damage caused by the impermanence and distrust engendered by transitory sexual relationships. Nevertheless, the advertising industry as well as a great many books, television, radio programmes, and magazines still promote the view that "free" sexual expression should be encouraged.

Another factor that has influenced late 20th century sexual perceptions is the greater emancipation of women. In the so-called "first" world, and amongst certain sectors in the rest of the world, women no longer spend most of their lives bearing and raising children. Such women are better educated, more affluent, and they have smaller families. They no longer perceive themselves simply as agents of procreation or objects of male pleasure. This frees them to develop other aspects of their personalities and to engage in a variety of activities outside the home. Consequently, they are no longer entirely financially dependent on fathers, uncles, brothers and sons and they are increasingly critical of the theoretical and practical restrictions of patriarchy.[8] On the other hand, a much greater percentage of the world's population of women are neither affluent nor educated. They have little opportunity to question their "lot" in life, to become educated, trained, or to break out of the cycle of multiple births and poverty. Such women remain largely dependent on the male members of their family and destitution may result at any time if their male protector deserts them, divorces them or dies.

One final factor can be mentioned here, namely the collapse of the taboo of silence and the "scientific" study of sex. Whereas in previous centuries, the Church's view of sexuality was the dominant one, a range of views are today propagated by the media, conflicting schools of psychology, the entertainment industry, and sexologists. The views of Sigmund Freud, Havelock Ellis and Alfred Kinsey have done much to challenge the Church's traditional teachings about the nature and purpose of human sexuality (Mace 1971:220–232).

The South African context

Within the South African context, all the factors described above have had an impact. In addition, white conquest, colonialism and the subsequent entrenchment of Apartheid resulted in the serious dislocation of traditional African life. The loss of land, poverty, migrant labour, and political exploitation engendered by these social forces and structures, profoundly affected African social and family life.

---

8 Literally "the rule of the fathers", patriarchy refers to the fact that society is largely dominated by male perceptions and is organised to suit male interests.

Thus, in South Africa, all the issues already discussed have been aggravated by the complexities of racial, class and cultural differences. Black South Africans have sought to protect what is best in their own cultural heritage from the onslaught of Western culture. But because of the massive impact of white settlement upon their lives since 1652, African culture itself is in a state of flux. It is no longer what it was even a century ago, nor has it totally embraced Western values (or lack of values). Amongst white families, too, domestic strife or violence, divorce and even family murders occur to a greater or lesser extent. While living in Africa, few whites feel entirely comfortable with black African culture. Yet neither are whites born in South Africa over several generations any longer fully "English" or "European". To add to the complexity of the picture, the "Coloured" people and the "Indians" bring their own distinctive identities and histories to bear.

Within this situation, young people are marrying much later, or not marrying at all, certain couples are having fewer children, increasing numbers of teenagers engage in sexual relations (and often fall pregnant), some marry while others "live together". Certain women have children without ever intending to get married, the divorce figures increase yearly, and the phenomena of "blended" families, consisting of adults and children from various previous relationships living under the same roof, are becoming more common. All of these factors, together with a period of intense social transition following establishment of a new government in 1994, create a complex and explosive whole.

Singleness

All persons initially experience themselves as individuals and sexual beings within the context of singleness. Furthermore, some may never marry while others may experience the loss of a spouse (eg through death or divorce). In all these instances, singleness is a common experience.

There are at least four forms of singleness. There are the "young singles", that is, those between puberty and possible marriage. Then there are those who some call the "unchosen singles", that is, those who for one reason or another have not married even though they may have wanted to do so. A third category is that of "chosen celibate singleness". This phrase refers to those who deliberately choose neither to marry nor to engage in genital sexuality. Such persons are often driven by some form of altruism and this group includes priests, nuns, missionaries and various professionals such as social workers and teachers. The fourth category, that of "post-marriage" singleness, refers to those who are single as a result of separation, divorce or the death of a spouse.

Within the Bible, both marriage and singleness are to be found. Although prophets such as Jeremiah were single, prophets and priests were not required to be single. In the New Testament, singleness was given a new emphasis. John the Baptist, Jesus and probably Paul were all single. The latter even argued that a single person can dedicate themselves more fully to "the Lord's affairs" (1 Cor 7:

32–35). Singleness was not, however, required of Christians (1 Tim 3:4–5, 12).

There are many different perceptions of singleness. Some may view it as a form of failure, while others perceive it either as a form of dedication to God or to an ideal or simply as the exercising of a personal choice. In contexts where the role of women is perceived only in terms of getting married and having children, a single woman is a failure. In cultures such as that of ancient Israel and traditional Africa, where marriage was the norm, singleness was extremely rare. In Europe, celibacy and the single life, especially for those called to the religious life, has been a persistent, although not universal theme. There too, until very recently, marriage has been regarded as the path that the majority will follow. Thus, there are different perceptions of singleness, depending on a variety of socio-cultural expectations.

In recent years, greater numbers of people are single. Some people deliberately choose singleness, others may be single by default. Certain men and women have dedicated themselves to their careers, deliberately deciding not to get married. Others "live together" but remain legally single. Others remain single but have regular or occasional "affairs". Some women have engaged in temporary relationships in order to have children but refuse to get married. This has become possible since certain women are now economically independent; they are no longer entirely dependent on a father, brother, husband or lover to survive. Certain women and men enter into homosexual relationships (some have publicly "married") rather than entering into a heterosexual relationship or marriage.

As indicated above, not all single persons are celibate. For those who choose celibacy, this choice need not result in the person denying their sexual identity. Celibate, single persons are no less masculine or feminine because human bonding and the forming of close relationships is not dependent on genital sexuality. But, as Grenz points out,

> the bonding indicative of the single life is, of course, quite different from marital bonding. It obviously does not take the form of a permanent, monogamous relationship between husband and wife entered by public covenant and nurtured by covenant renewal in the sex act. Single bonding is neither permanent nor one-person centered, and it is seldom entered through formal covenant (Grenz 1990:168).

Amongst Christians, this single bonding takes place in three main ways: relationships with the extended family, relationships formed within the community of the church, and close friendships. As a result of economic prosperity and education among certain classes, together with the high rate of divorce, there are a great many more single people in the world who do not have any particular calling to a celibate life. Many such people drift into what Turner calls "limited engagements" with members of the opposite, and sometimes, the same sex.

In this regard, the entire subject of non-sexual friendships has been much neglected. The Greek philosopher, Aristotle, argued that a friend is "in a sense another self: friendship exists between those who are both good and alike with respect to virtue. Friendships are carefully chosen, preferential, and limited in number" (E Turner in P Turner 1989:152). Four characteristics of friendship are:

> To desire what is good for the sake of the other; to desire that the other live for his own sake; to enjoy passing time with and choosing the same things as the other; and to share the other's sorrows and joys (Turner 1989:154).

Although often marked by affection, intimacy and passion, true friendship is a non-sexual relationship since it involves the meeting of souls rather than **bodies.**[9]

Marriage, divorce, re-marriage and parenting

Any contemporary discussion of marriage cannot proceed without a consciousness of the fact that certain people remain married while the marriages of others end in divorce. Further, the degree of marital happiness experienced differs widely and all married couples experience marital difficulties and crises. Marital "success" or "failure" cannot be simplistically defined. This state of affairs makes any discussion of marriage a complex matter, people have had diverse experiences of marriage, either their own or the marriages of their parents, family members and friends. Thus, in addition to discussing marriage, divorce, re-marriage and parenting also require mention. However, as another chapter in this book deals specifically with marriage, it is only briefly discussed here so as to highlight some of the ethical issues surrounding marriage.

What is marriage?

How, then, can marriage be defined? According to Jack Dominian, marriage is a re-lationship

> ... of love which aims to foster sustaining, healing and growth and that these characteristics need continuity, reliability and predictability, in other words, permanency. Within permanency, the couple attempt to reach the whole of each other as persons and to do so in a manner that serves their realisation of their potential, their movement towards perfection (Dominian 1977:61).

Writing from his experience as a psychologist, he argues for marital commitment and permanence because there can be no emotional sustaining if there is no securi-ty in the relationship. There can be no deep healing of our wounds if there is no trust, security or encouragement, nor can there be psychological maturation if the relationship is based on doubt and uncertainty. It is on the ground of promoting love in terms of sustaining, healing, and growth that marriage as a permanent rela-tionship should be advocated by the churches.

This understanding of marriage as a relationship varies greatly from that which regards the basic purpose of marriage as procreation, a definition which has been pre-valent in Western theology until very recently. It is also very common within tradi-

---

9 See also CS Lewis' discussion of *philia* in *The Four Loves* (Glasgow: Fontana Books, 1960).

tional (and modern) African thought. Thus a "barren wife" could be returned to her family in disgrace or be expected to encourage her husband to marry a second wife.

In addition to definitions such as these, certain other key elements of marriage can be mentioned. These include courtship, betrothal, the public wedding ceremony, promises of permanency and exclusivity, the legal implications, consummation, co-habitation, procreation and parenting.

Although societies all over the world have sought to in some way regulate sexual relations and the rearing of children by means of marriage, this social institution has taken on more than one form. Monogamy (one husband, one wife) and polygamy are the two major forms. Technically poly (many) gamy (marriage) can refer to either one husband and many wives, or to one wife and many husbands, the more common form is polygyny (many wives) rather than polyandry (many husbands). In traditional African societies, but to a lesser extent today, the close involvement of the extended family in courtship and marriage meant that strong ties were created between the relevant families. Other variations include marriages in which couples remain legally married but engage in extra-marital activities or what is termed serial monogamy (where a second or third monogamous marriage follows divorce from the earlier partner). There are also increasing numbers of "informal" marriages in which the couple appear to be married in all senses except the legal sense. In recent years this phenomena has been termed "living together," an option often followed as a result of their rejection or fear of a legal and public marriage.

This raises the question of what is love. Scott Peck offers a very insightful critique of the myths surrounding the phrase "falling in love" pointing out that love is not a feeling. Nor is it a form of dependency or destructive self-sacrifice. Instead he defines it as "the will to extend oneself for the purpose of nurturing one's own or another's spiritual growth" (1978:85). It involves the exercise of the will, the taking of risks, the combination of proper self-love and love for others, and commitment. For a Christian, genuine love always involves the interplay between love for God, love for one's self and love for one's neighbour (Mk 12:28–34).

Divorce and remarriage

The Catholic view of marriage as a sacrament and its notion of the indissolubility of marriage means that it does not permit divorce, though it does permit separation. Only if a marriage has been officially annulled, is re-marriage allowed. By way of contrast, some traditions within Christianity do permit divorce and church-blessed re-marriages. Why is this so? As is often the case, much of the debate centres around the interpretation of the relevant scriptures and their application to contemporary circumstances.

Some of the key texts in this debate are: Deuteronomy 24:1; Malachai 2:10–17; Matthew 5:32 and 19:3–12 (esp vv 8–9); Luke 16:18; Mark 10:10–12; and 1 Corinthians 7:1–40 (esp vv10–15). While all are agreed that divorce is a sin, some hold that the marriage bond can never be broken while others argue that the evidence around us shows that it can be broken. Much depends on the definition of marriage (eg as a sacrament, a covenant or a human relationship). Also, the *porneia* clause which occurs in Matthew 19:9 is of importance here. While many Catholics interpreters regard this reference to porneia (which means unchastity, fornication or habitual immorality) as a later scribal addition, other interpreters regard it as an authentic part of Jesus' argument. According to the latter, Jesus allows the "injured party" in marriage, that is, the spouse who has suffered as a result of his/her partner's unfaithfulness, to seek a divorce. They regard this as a legitimate cause for divorce since infidelity constitutes a breaking of the bond of marital intimacy. Further, they argue, Paul allows divorce in the case of the desire of the "unbelieving" partner wishing to leave a marriage in which the other partner has become a Christian. There are also those who argue that physical, emotional or sexual abuse within a marriage also constitute legitimate grounds for divorce since such behaviour amounts to a violation of the marital framework given in Ephesians 5:21–31. Thus, though some Christians would argue in favour of divorce in certain circumstances, few would want to follow the frivolous approach to marriage and divorce so common in our societies today. Those that permit divorce also tend to permit re-marriage, while those who do not accept divorce naturally regard re-marriage as unacceptable. For the latter, persons who have been brutalised in marriage may separate, but not re-marry, unless they are able to obtain an official annulment of their marriage by the Church.

Parenting

Given the poor state of marriages today, it is to be expected that inadequate parenting is a major feature of many societies, not least in South Africa. Christian commentators have always held that parenting is an awesome God-given responsibility (see Anderson and Guernsey 1985:55–82). In effect, our children are not "ours" in the sense that we can do what we like with them, instead, we are accountable to God for the way in which we bring them up. Parenting, thus, is a process in which both parents are expected to meet the spiritual, personal, physical and social developmental needs of the child. As the child grows up, a variety of needs (eg attachment, differentiation, individuation, constancy and generalisation) need to be recognised and met.[10] The parents' authority over their children is relative, not absolute. But, if the parents themselves do not learn to give and receive love, they cannot show genuine love towards their children. Arguably, churches need to provide much more assistance to families in the area of marriage and parenting than is often the case at present.

Homosexuality

What, then, of the controversial matter of homosexuality which has given rise to very diverse reactions from within the church and society? Technically, a distinction

---

10 Respectively: a sense of belonging and care; allowing the child to receive a proper amount of meaningful outside stimuli; avoiding excessive dependency; the experience of permanence and trust; and exposure to mutual dependence (see Anderson and Guernsey 1985:79–81).

can be made between homosexuality (between males) and lesbianism (between females), but often the term homosexuality is used to refer to both forms. Essentially it refers to "same-sex" attraction or relations rather than "opposite-sex" attraction or relations.

While some Christians and theologians have adopted a pro-homosexual position, others have insisted that homosexuality is contrary to Christian faith and practice.[11] All are agreed, however, that ignorance, prejudice and fear are inimical to a Christian approach to homosexuality.

Despite the heat generated by the modern debate, fuelled in part by the gay liberation movement and the high incidence of AIDS (Acquired Immune-Deficiency Syndrome) amongst homosexuals, this is not a new issue; homosexual practices were known in the ancient world, especially in the Greek and Roman cultures.

There are a number of issues that characterise the modern debate. These include how homosexuality is best defined, how many people are homosexuals, what the causes of homosexuality are and whether homosexuality should be regarded as a sin or a valid alternative lifestyle.

With reference to the *definition* of homosexuality, there is some debate as to whether it should be understood in terms of an activity or an inclination. In other words, is a homosexual someone who performs genital sexual acts with someone of the same sex or is a homosexual someone who feels attracted to someone of the same sex? The importance of this distinction is that according to the first definition (act centred) while someone may, at a particular time in their lives, eg during adolescence, have felt an attraction to someone of the same sex, this does not mean that they are homosexuals. There may be a variety of reasons for such an attraction. Only persons who actually perform genital sexual acts, and continue to do so, and feel no attraction to the opposite sex, could be termed a homosexual.[12] In terms of the second definition, anyone who feels sexually inclined towards someone of the same sex could be regarded as a homosexual. This broad definition, however, does not adequately account for the varied reasons for such an attraction, nor the fact that such an attraction may be temporary and/or never lead to actual genital sexual relations.

Another reason why this matter of definitions is so crucial is because, so certain psychologists assert, immature sexuality or the lack of proper parental nurturing may lead a young person to feel homosexually inclined. Subsequently, however, such persons may "grow out" of this stage. Those who regard homosexuality as a valid alternative lifestyle find this notion offensive. For such persons homosexuality is not to be perceived as immaturity or perversion, but as inversion, that is, a permanent personal orientation or a definite preference towards persons of the same sex.

---

11 Nelson, Kosnik and Montefiore adopt a more positive position while Keysor, Grenz and White adopt the view that homosexuality is not a valid expression of human sexuality (see bibliography).

12 According to this definition, an isolated same-sex genital experience does not constitute homosexuality nor does "situational" homosexuality, as practised, for example, in prisons or hostels.

In addition to the matter of how homosexuality can best be defined, there is the issue of *how many people* have a homosexual orientation or commit same-sex acts. In the late 1940s and early 1950s, Albert Kinsey conducted a number of surveys in the USA, as a result of which he reported that 1 in 10 persons were homosexuals. Since the persons whom he interviewed were largely drawn from boarding-houses, prisons, tertiary colleges, mental asylums or were hitch-hikers, many have questioned whether his sample can be regarded as representative of the population at large.[13] A recent study conducted by a team from the University of Chicago has reported very different findings concerning sexual practices. Concerning homosexual genital relations, "only 2,7 % of men and 1,3 % of women report that they had homosexual sex in the last year". 7,1 % of men and 3,8 % of women reported that they had had sex with someone of their same gender since puberty. 6,2 % of men and 4,4 % of women reported that they felt sexually attracted to people of the same gender (*Time Magazine*, 17 October 1994:56 and 59). This is significantly lower than the 10 % estimated by Kinsley. However, the accuracy of such surveys cannot be absolute, nor can the figures for one country be assumed for another country. Finally, the numerical incidence of homosexuality is not, in itself, an argument in its favour any more than the incidence of murder is an argument in its favour.

A third important issue is that of the causes of homosexuality. In other words, is one born a homosexual or does one become a homosexual? Sometimes characterised as the "nature vs nurture" debate, it concentrates on the issue of whether homosexuality has biological or genetic causes (eg an excess or deficiency of sex chromosomes) or sociological and psychological causes. Some regard homosexuality an inherent sexual orientation (biological or genetic causes), whereas others regard it as a learned preference (sociological or psychological causes). It has been argued that the nature of persons' relationships with their parents, particularly their fathers, have a major impact on the way in which individuals perceive and experience their sexual identity. In addition, the experience of actual sexual distortions, such as rape and child abuse will almost certainly affect persons' sexual feelings and actions. According to Hettlinger:

> It is possible that some inherited characteristics may render a man susceptible to homosexual deviation; but without the contributing influences of inadequate family relationships and cultural pressures, these potentialities do not become decisive. Most authorities attribute the homosexual condition to a combination of psychological and sociological factors which prevent the individual from achieving full and free personal relationships with the other sex (quoted in Grenz 1990:202–203).[14]

How, then should one respond to the homosexual debate? Is it a sin or a valid alternative lifestyle? Within the Church, moral theologians have traditionally argued

13 See *Time Magazine* 17 October 1994, pp 54–60.
14 Richard Hettlinger, *Living with Sex* (New York: Seabury, 1966) p 11.

that the Bible condemns homosexuality. More recently, these interpretations of the relevant passages have been questioned. The key passages are: Genesis 19:1–29 (Lot and Sodom), Judges 19:22–23; Leviticus 18:22 and 21:13 (the Holiness Code) and New Testament teaching in Romans 1:26–27, 1 Corinthians 6:9–10 and 1 Timothy 1:9–10.[15]

It has been argued by those who adopt a more positive attitude to homosexuality, that the Greek, Roman and Hebrew civilisations did not know of homosexuality as a lifelong sexual orientation. The biblical texts are thus, not condemnations of this form of homosexuality, rather they condemn attempted rape, lack of hospitality, idolatry, pederastry and homosexual prostitution. Some biblical commentators argue that in the case of Sodom, the sin was not homosexuality, but threatened "homosexual anal violation as a reminder of subordinate status". By way of contrast, other commentators hold that the texts in Leviticus clearly refer to homosexuality as a perversion of the created order (see Kosnik et al. 1977:186–218 and Grenz 1990:203–209). Other debates centre around the terms *malakoi* (male prostitutes) and *arsenokoitai* (homosexual offenders) used in the Corinthian and Timothy passages: do these terms refer only to pederasty or to sexual relations between men in general? Is Paul's condemnation in Romans 1 referring to pederasty and rape or to homosexuality and lesbianism? Is homosexuality natural or is it an "unnatural" distortion of God's creation of humans as either males or females? (See Greenlee in Keysor 1979:81–114).

The modern debate concerning homosexuality, not least within the churches, remains a complex and controversial one. In general terms, those who argue in favour of homosexuality say that homosexuality is a natural sexual orientation and that the biblical texts cannot be used to condemn homosexual orientation or practice. (Suggit in Hulley et al. 1996:230–240). They further argue that as long as homosexual relationships are faithful and permanent, they are morally valid. By way of contrast, there are those Christians who believe that one cannot be both a Christian and a practising homosexual (Keysor 1979 and Grenz 1990). In general terms they argue (and I would largely agree with this approach) that while the surrounding Assyrian, Greek and Roman cultures widely practised homosexuality (and often affirmed it as a valid lifelong preference) both Jews and Christians did not. Not only are there both Old and New Testament texts that reject homosexuality (according to this view the texts cannot be reduced to definitions such as rape, pederasty, violation of hospitality or homosexual prostitution), but the whole tenor of the Christian scriptures affirm marriage between a man and a woman as the only valid framework in which sexual intercourse ought to be experienced. This approach often draws on the creation narratives (which stress the creation of humanity as male and female, and not also a "third sex") and on natural law arguments (which argue that "same sex" sexual relations are contrary to nature). It ought to be added, though, that a rejection of

15 Concerning male cult prostitutes see Deut 23:17; 1 Kings 14:24, 15:12 and 22:46.

a homosexual lifestyle does not encourage homophobia (fear of homosexuals), nor does it promote the condemnation of homosexual persons.

To conclude this section, it would seem that the key issues in this debate are how we perceive homosexuality in the light of the Bible's emphasis on the creation of male and female and the institution of marriage. Further, the interpretations given to the key biblical texts already cited are crucial to the debate. In addition, definitions of what constitutes homosexuality, the possible causes of homosexuality, and whether stable, faithful forms of homosexuality can be regarded as legitimate expressions of Christian love are central to this contentious debate.

Rape and battering

Rape can be defined as the "forced penetration of the penis or any object into the vagina, mouth or anus against the will of the victim" whereas battering can be defined as "physical, verbal and/or emotional assault within the home by family members" (*Towards a Theology of Sexuality* 23). In the vast majority of cases, women or children are the victims of rape and battering. (The rape of men by men occurs, for example, in prisons.)

In South Africa today, the estimates of rape and battering are frighteningly high. It is estimated that in South Africa 1 000 women are raped every day, 33 % of married women are beaten by their husbands, 10 % of young girls are sexually harassed in their families and only 1,3 % of the men who rape women are ever convicted or charged (*ibid*. 23). There are various other estimates of the incidence of such crimes, but it is difficult to know with certainty how often such brutal acts are committed as many are never reported.

There are a number of texts in the Bible which deal with the subject of rape. These include: Genesis 34:1–31; Deuteronomy 22:23–29; Judges 19:10–30; 2 Samuel 13:1–39. A number of ethical issues arise from the foregoing. These include the biblical perception that rape (or any other form of violence) constitutes a violation of a person whom God has created and for whom Christ died. The entire teaching of the Bible and the Church concerning the value and sanctity of the human person is contradicted and desecrated by such actions. Further, the emphasis of liberation theologies, in particular, on Gods' special concern for the weak and powerless (eg Isa 1:16–17 and Luke 4:18–20) is of marked relevance here. Also of vital importance are the many instructions to husbands to love and cherish their wives (Eph 5:21–33; 1 Pet 3:7). Our bodies are temples of the Holy Spirit and should thus not be abused or used to abuse the bodies of others (1 Cor 3:16–17 and 6:19–20). It is also important to ask why emotionally, physically and sexually abusive persons engage in such acts. Condemnation alone, necessary though it may be (and how reluctant many churches are to face these issues) is not sufficient in itself. The spiritual, psychological and sociological causes need to be analysed so that such practices can be rooted out rather than ignored or excused.

Child abuse

Finally, there are also many distorted expressions of human sexuality such as *incest and child abuse* that are evidenced in our world.

In recent years, increased attention has been given to the whole matter of the sexual abuse of children, whether it occurs within the immediate family (incest) or whether such children are abused by family "friends", or other people who have contact with the children. This is a particularly horrifying example of a completely distorted and destructive expression of human sexuality. While it is a mistake to believe that such practices are peculiar to our own age, it is true that much that was previously hidden is now beginning to be exposed. European and Middle Eastern history, for example, attest to the fact that pederasty (men having intercourse with young boys) and child prostitution were known. Even today, there are regular reports that young persons, even children, are involved in prostitution and child pornography. Often they are forced to have sex with adults or with each other and are virtually imprisoned. Individuals and groups that have been particularly vulnerable throughout history are those who have been sold into slavery, the poor, orphans, runaways, refugees, abandoned children, and anyone else finding themselves alone and unprotected in the world. This does not mean that abuse only occurs in families lower down the social and economic ladder, sexual abuse (as well as physical and emotional abuse) occurs across the social scale. It has been reported on national television that it estimated that, in South Africa, one out of every three girls and one of every six boys is in some way sexually abused. This means that female children experience twice as much abuse and the perpetrators are generally men. Women who actively practise sexual abuse are in the minority, but it is true that they acquiesce to it; often allowing it to happen and failing to report the abuse of their own or other people's children by fathers, husbands, boyfriends or brothers. Often those who acquiesce to or actively perpetrate sexual abuse were once themselves victims of physical, sexual or emotional abuse. This means that very often sexual abuse runs in families (and amongst those associated with such families), whereby the patterns of abuse are repeated in a seemingly endless cycle. Only when the deeds committed in secret can be confessed or exposed can the possibilities of justice and healing for the victims (and for abusers who confess their evil deeds and seek treatment) emerge.

These matters of child abuse draw attention to the broader issue of children's rights. With the exception of animals and the rest of creation, perhaps no other group is as vulnerable to neglect and abuse. Millions of children all over the world desperately need basic things such as food, water, shelter, clothing and medical care. Furthermore, they need to be protected, nurtured, loved and educated. In addition to the comments already made above concerning parenting, the strict prohibition against incest (sexual contact between close relatives) in Leviticus 18:6–18 is of relevance here. As is the instruction to fathers, which indicates the limits of their authority, not to provoke their children to anger (Eph 6:4). Adults cannot escape responsibility for the children that their sexual relationships bring into the world. In this regard it is striking that some of the sternest words of judgment uttered by Jesus were directed towards those who in any way neglect or hurt children (Mt 18:6; 9:42 and 17:1–2).

Some concluding remarks

Despite the length of this paper, the reader will notice that only the surface of this complex subject has been scratched. In conclusion, however, a few key perspectives can be reiterated.

The longing for relationship is a human characteristic, an inescapable aspect of our sexuality. Therefore, human sexuality needs to be defined more broadly than genital sexuality. Affection and intimacy are essential to humanity, whether one is married or single. This need for intimacy has not always been recognised and some have even seen sexuality as evil in itself, or at least regarded sexual pleasure as wrong. But it is not pleasure that is evil, but the abuse of our bodies and the obsession to extend sexual experience beyond the bonds of what God has willed for our good. To deny our bodies affection and intimacy is to repress our sexuality entirely and to turn ourselves into lonely and fear-filled persons. But it does not follow that we can go to the other extreme and abandon ourselves to sexual promiscuity without doing damage to our deepest selves. We are a unity of body and soul.

Consequently, the tradition of Christian ethics (and other religious and moral traditions) seeks to control or limit the sexual drive precisely because it is so powerful and potentially both harmful and healing in its effects. These groups do not do so because they are kill-joys. It is often forgotten that sexual promiscuity and hedonism are based not on the simple pursuit of pleasure, but on the fear of emotional attachment. Such relationships are characterised by the minimum of engagement and the maximum of haste and disengagement. The "one-night-stand" is a good example of this approach to human sexual relationships.

Finally, our sexuality is not simply a private matter. It has family and social consequences and cannot be separated from our relatedness to God. Humans need to have an openness to life and the integrity to exercise self control in the interests of inter- and intra-personal wholeness and the willingness to live their sexual life in terms of their love for God. To refuse to do so is to destroy what God has created.

BIBLIOGRAPHY

Anderson, Norman. 1977. *Issues of Life and Death*. Downers Grove, Illinois: InterVarsity Press.

Anderson, Ray S and Guernsey, Dennis B. 1985. *On Being Family: A social theology of the Family*. Grand Rapids: Eerdmans.

Armour, Mary. 1991. "Forbidden Agendas: Feminist Theology and the Politics of Sexuality", in D Ackermann, et al. (eds). *Women Hold Up Half the Sky: Women in the Church in Southern Africa*. Pietermaritzburg: Cluster.

Cadoux, Cecil John. 1925. *The Early Church and the World*. Edinburgh: T and T Clark.

Dominian, Jack. 1977. *Proposals for a new Sexual Ethic*. London: Darton, Longman and Todd.

Dominian, J and Montefiore, H. 1989. *God, Sex and Love*. London: SCM Press and Philadelphia: Trinity Press International.

Grenz, Stanley. 1990. *Sexual Ethics: A Biblical Perspective*. London and Dallas: Word Publishing.

Hulley, LD and Mofokeng, TA. 1982. *The Ethics of sexuality, marriage and family life*. Study guide for TEB 200–C. Pretoria: UNISA.

Hulley, LD, Kretzschmar, L and Pato LL. (eds). 1996. *Archbishop Tutu: Prophetic Witness in South Africa*. Cape Town: Human and Rousseau.

Keysor, Charles W (ed). 1979. *What you should know about Homosexuality*. Grand Rapids: Zondervan.

Kosnik, A et al. (eds). 1977. *Human Sexuality: New Directions in Catholic Thought*. London: Search Press.

Livingstone, EA. 1977. *The Concise Oxford Dictionary of the Christian Church*. Oxford and London: OUP.

Mace, David R. 1971. "The Sexual Revolution: Its Impact on Pastoral Care and Counselling". *The Journal of Pastoral Care* 25:4. Dec 1971: 220–232.

MacQuarrie, John (ed). 1967. *Dictionary of Christian Ethics*. London: SCM.

Nelson, James B. 1978. *Embodiment: An Approach to Sexuality and Christian Theology*. New York/Philadelphia: Pilgrim Press.

Peck, Scott. 1978. *The Road Less Travelled*. London: Arrow Books.

Price, Richard M. 1990. "The Distinctiveness of early Christian Sexual Ethics". *Heythrop Journal* 31 (1990): 257–276.

Radcliffe, Timothy. 1986. "'Glorify God in your bodies': a Pauline basis for a sexual ethic", *New Blackfriars* 67:793/4 (August 1986): 306–314.

Turner, Philip. (ed). 1989. *Men and Women: Sexual Ethics in Turbulent Times*. Cambridge, Mass: Cowley Publications.

White, John. 1977. *Eros Defiled: The Christian and sexual guilt*. Leicester: Intervarsity Press.

Wilson, Brian. 1982. *Religion in Sociological Perspective*. Oxford: University Press.

Towards a Theology of Sexuality c 1993. Umtata: Umtata Women's Theology Group Bible Series.

Time Magazine 17 October 1994, pp 54–60.

5

To marry or not to marry: that is the question

Len Hulley

Introduction

In this book we are concerned in particular with an understanding of various issues from the perspective of Theological Ethics within the Christian tradition. We shall therefore examine marriage in terms of Christian convictions. It is however important to remember that marriage is a much wider phenomenon – persons other than Christians also get married. This may seem a trite statement, but it is very important for several reasons. The marriages of persons who do not subscribe to the teachings on marriage which are generally accepted within the church, if there is such a consensus at all, are no less real than those who accept them. To deny this would be to say to those people who are not married in church only think that they are married, but that they are in fact "living in sin". Their children would similarly be regarded as illegitimate. This would include people who belong to other faiths as well as people who have been married in court rather than in a church. How ought one to regard people who choose to get married in a church because it is traditional to do so rather than as an expression of their faith? One couple chose a particular church because it would provide an attractive backdrop for the wedding photographs! These questions form the wider background against which marriage will be discussed from a Christian perspective.

Is marriage outdated?

Marriage as an institution is being questioned in many circles. There have even been suggestions in some circles that it is outdated and that it will soon disappear from the scene. I believe that those who hold to this view are writing the obituary of an old and honourable institution too soon. There are nevertheless large numbers of people who are experimenting with alternative relationships. It is said that these alternative relationships are so significant that they are questioning the monogamous marriage relationship long considered to be the norm in mainline Western churches. Most of us have come across people who have chosen to "live together" rather than get married. This is not questioning monogamy, but the necessity of "getting married". People enter into such arrangements for various reasons. Sometimes young people feel that they are not yet ready to make a public commitment and get married, so they live together. Some do indeed get married after a while. Some couples who intend getting married say that it is cheaper to live together and it allows them to save some money for their home. I find this argument unconvincing, it suggests that while they are living together they do not have a home. But this phenomenon of living together is by no means limited to young people only. One often comes across people who have previously had unsuccessful marriages and now are not prepared, or not yet ready, to get married again. They are afraid that the marriage may fail yet again. They nevertheless find having a live-in partner convenient. Such arrangements may last for any length of time, from a few months to several years. As a marriage officer I have been involved in the marriages of several such couples, one of which had been living together for seventeen years. The break up of such relationships does not entail going through a divorce, but is often traumatic nonetheless.

There are several other alternative lifestyles. These include single parents, usually as result of a death or divorce, but sometimes due to extramarital pregnancy, and single people who for various reasons do not get married. To back up the argument that marriage is being questioned on a large scale and that we are moving to other types of being family, Nelson (1978:131) provides statistics which he maintains shows that in the United States no one type of family "is statistically normative". While that is strictly true, I find that his categories are misleading. His figures are as follows:

> Nuclear families (both parents and their children in one household), 37 %; single adults without children, 19 %; single parents (usually divorced or separated) with children, 12 %; remarried couples with children, 11 %; childless couples or couples with no children at home, 11%; experimental family forms, 6 %; and three-generation households, 4 %.

I suggest that Nelson's figures are misleading because he implies that because the nuclear family is not statistically overwhelming, marriage is under threat. Of these figures, only those engaging in experimental family forms clearly opt for a different way of life. Single adults without children may choose not to marry or may yet marry so that the figure probably needs to be reduced. All the rest, 77 %, apparently believe in marriage, although their marriages may have failed – the single parent group – or they may have chosen not to have children. People who remarry are not opting for an alternative lifestyle, they believe in marriage and are willing to try again even if their previous marriages were not successful. The small number of three-generation households clearly believe in the importance of families and married life. In Africa, especially in the rural areas, the incidence of multiple generation households is very common. To say that this calls marriage into question would be incorrect. In fact, the extended family system is often a guarantee that people who get married are strongly committed to making a success of their marriage. The relatives of both the husband and wife are concerned to make the relationship work. My analysis of Nelson's figures makes them look rather different. This also shows that statistics must be handled rather carefully. But this is not to suggest that everything in the garden is rosy, there are major problems. We now turn our attention to some of these problems.

Sex and marriage

Ross (1994:163ff) says that in earlier generations many of the young men among the upper classes sowed their wild oats before settling down to life in respectable society. The women with whom they consorted usually came from the lower classes who turned to prostitution as a means of making a living. One of the factors that has influenced sexual morality this century, and seems to have accelerated in the last few decades, is the rejection of the traditional values in sexual matters. This was due in part to the upward mobility of the middle classes who started to engage in the kind of behaviour previously the preserve of the upper classes. The ideas emanating from social anthropologists and Sigmund Freud were popularized in the 1920s. With the increasing levels of education in the 1920s and 1930s, particularly in Western Europe and the United States, many young people began to question social conventions previously accepted. In this intellectual ferment, the idea of "free love" began to emerge. It was held that human sexuality had been inhibited by confining it to relations between married couples. Sex came to be regarded as something pleasurable which should not be repressed. The advent of effective contraceptives, which removed the threat of unwanted pregnancies, made the sexual revolution of the 1960s possible. It also meant that young women who were previously restrained from sexual experimentation for fear of unwanted pregnancy now joined the sexual revolution. Recreational sex, engaged in by couples merely for the pleasure of it, and premarital sex, engaged in by couples who may intend to get married, became the norm rather than the exception in many circles. It was popularly believed that there was a great deal of adultery committed by married men and women. This idea was fueled in part by the statements contained in the Kinsey report on human sexual behaviour in the United States in the 1950s. In a comprehensive National Health and Social Survey published in a book entitled *Sex in America: A definitive survey*, these findings were found to be inaccurate. Most married people remain faithful during marriage. More than 80% of women and 65 to 85% of men reported remaining faithful, with figures varying through the age range (Laurence 1994:16). This high level of faithfulness between spouses also raises the matter of sexual intercourse being regarded as a symbol of the union between the spouses which may not be violated. The idea of symbols will be discussed in more detail later.

There is nevertheless a popular perception abroad in the media that recreational sexual encounters are acceptable. We see the results of this change in attitude in films and television, where sexual relations between people are now portrayed as an integral part of acceptable social behaviour. Ross (1994:165) comments:

> While the family is still regarded as necessary for those who wish to have children, the emphasis on mutual sexual satisfaction ... has been an added factor in the breakdown of marriages. The number of marriages ending in divorce is on the increase, and the incidence of extramarital sexual liaisons is high. Widespread adulterous behavior forms an additional cause for the increase in divorce.

The fact that marriage is regarded as necessary for those who wish to have children also raises the matter of the significance of symbols. The symbol of making a public statement that a couple is married, the wedding service, is noteworthy.

In South Africa we are subject to all these factors emanating from Western Europe and North America, but we have problems peculiar to ourselves. The problem is largely limited to African society and has to do with the still widespread practice of migratory labour, although it is no longer the result of government policy, the pass laws and influx control measures which forced people to become oscilating migrant workers have been removed from the statute books. The practice still continues because a whole social and economic system was built around the migratory labour system. Men usually came to live and work in the mines or factories to earn money to send home and were accommodated in single-sex hostels for extended periods of time. They returned home for three or four weeks a year to their wives and families who remained in the rural areas. Even now, when it is possible for families to come to the cities, many choose to remain in the rural areas because if they move they lose their rights to the land which they cultivate and on which they graze their livestock. Another factor is, of course, the shortage of suitable and affordable housing. With the improvement in road transport, taxis and buses serve to connect some of the rural areas with the cities, people can now return home for a weekend or a few days more easily than before, if they can afford the fares. It is obvious that these long absences are not conducive to healthy marital relations. The men in the cities often acquire another wife and family, and because they have to support them financially, the rural family is neglected. The women in the rural areas are also deprived of the sexual relationship of their husbands and may enter into sexual liasons with other men. Another important phenomenon arising from migrant labour is that some women, many of them well educated, are not prepared to get married. Marriage to an absentee husband only entails obligations with no advantages. They therefore prefer to remain unmarried, but choose to have children. Because they are not married, the fathers of the children have no say over them and they are reared as part of the mother's extended family. This is a significant variation from what is the rule among whites where single motherhood is frowned upon and seldom intentional. This whole discussion raises the matter of sexuality to which we now turn.

God created humankind

The news and entertainment media have emphasised the genital aspects of sex to the extent that people could be excused for thinking that sexual intercourse is all there is to a human sexual relationship. While I think that this is a gross distortion of human sexuality, I do not want to create the impression that sexuality is something negative. Some people read about the "sins of the flesh" in Paul's letters and immediately jump to the conclusion that he is referring exclusively to sexual misbehaviour. We read as follows in Galatians 5:19–21: "Now the works of the flesh are obvious: fornication, impurity, licentiousness, idolatry, sorcery, enmities, strife, jealousy, anger, quarrels, dissensions, factions, envy, drunkeness, carousing, and things like these".

It is quite clear from that list that sexual sins are included among the sins "of the flesh" but so are other forms of misbehaviour which we often regard as less serious. Such misreading of the Bible, together with the teaching that sexual intercourse is related to original sin, an idea that goes back at least to Augustine in the 5th century, means that many Christians have a negative view of human sexuality. That negative view is however also a product of a poor doctrine of creation.

Referring to the Genesis accounts of creation, White comments: "The fact of creation by male and female and the biblical concept that all creation, including human bisexuality, was good allowed the Hebrews a very positive approach to sexual matters" (White 1965:9). When one reads the creation stories one is struck by the "essentially complementary character of man and woman" (White 1965:11). In the first creation story, Genesis 1:1–2:4a, this complementarity is clearly expressed. We read "God created humankind in his own image, in the image of God he created them; male and female he created them. God blessed them, and God said to them,'Be fruitful and multiply, and fill the earth and subdue it'". You may have noticed that I have quoted from a new revision of the Bible which uses non-sexist language. Here in particular it reflects the meaning of the original, especially since the "man" of the earlier versions included both man and woman. This description of the creation of humankind or the blessing which follows leaves no room for discrimination or claims for precedence of one sex over the other. Indeed two great theologians, Nicolas Berdyaev and Karl Barth, argued that it is only as male and female together that we reflect the image of God. One without the other would in some way be deficient. (This of course raises the issue of the divine image in single people, but to go into that at this stage would be to digress.)

The second creation story, Genesis 2:2b–25, adds some interesting ideas. After God had created the man we are told that God was not quite satisfied with what had been created. "Then the Lord God said, 'It is not good that the man should be alone; I will make him a helper as his partner'" (Gn 2:18). The idea of complementarity again comes to the fore, man on his own was not the divine plan, he needed someone else with whom he could fulfill God's purpose. Thielicke says that the Hebrew text could be translated as "I will make him a helper as his opposite" (Thielicke 1964:4). When I first considered these ideas, I consulted an Old Testament scholar and we came up with the idea that the word "counterpart" would capture the meaning of the original very well. A counterpart, as can be seen from its etymology, is something which in some sense is an opposite and yet completes. Man could not enter into an intersubjective relationship with the rest of created nature, but now an I-Thou relationship was possible. In the narrative we are told that when faced with this new creature man breaks forth, "This at last is bone of my bone and flesh of my flesh" (Gn 2:23). The man felt that this was a fellow-creature to whom he could relate because they were two of a kind. When considering the implications of a doctrine for creation for sexuality, Thielicke (1964:18) comments:

> [Humanity] in all its dimensions ... can be understood only in relationship ... to God, and ... sexuality cannot be excluded from this. This means that the biological side of sex cannot be isolated and viewed as autonomous. Rather it is only a mode of being and functioning of the one, whole, indivisible man, who is this one, whole indivisible man is from God, to God, and under God.

In the second creation story there is also no evidence of a superiority-inferiority relationship where men dominated. According to the narrative, such domination only came about as result of the fall, it was a product of sin and not part of the divine plan of creation (see Gn 3:16). This is rather significant because the creation passages were written in a strongly patriarchal society. They therefore represent a departure from the accepted views of the day.

What we can conclude from the foregoing is that according to Christian doctrine, marriage is a divine institution created for mutual companionship and care. The man and the woman needed one another, one without the other was not quite adequate. The relationship itself is important but we have yet to discuss the implications of the injunction to "be fruitful and multiply" within marriage as well as other elements of marital sexuality. Let us now examine that issue.

Is marriage only for procreation?

Part of the companionship between spouses is expressed in sexual intercourse which was also the means of procreation, but I believe that procreation is not its sole purpose, as Augustine, taught. This latter view is still to be found in much Roman Catholic literature and reflects the Church's official position, see for example the views expressed by Pope Paul VI in *Humanae Vitae*. In that encyclical he rejects "any action, which either before, at the moment of, or after sexual intercourse, is specifically intended to prevent procreation" (Horgan 1972:41). The argument is that all sexual intercourse between spouses must be open to conception. The only permissible means of preventing pregnancy is to abstain from intercourse during the fertile period of the wife's cycle. I do not want to get caught up in a discussion of contraceptives and will not discuss it any further here, it is discussed elsewhere in the book. The point about intercourse and procreation has however been made. What happens when we reduce intercourse in marriage to a means of procreation is that we diminish it to a biological function. The spouse is regarded as a means to an end, for the functional aspect of intercourse becomes paramount. If sexual intercourse between spouses is not merely for procreation, what is the role it fulfills in marriage? In response to that question I want to quote two scholars because their views taken together capture what I believe to be a crucial part of this discussion. First a Roman Catholic scholar, Bernard Haring (1970:21):

> It must be fully realised that the real measure of virtue or sin in married life is the degree of expression or denial of affection, respect, and encouragement of

the unique and whole personality of the other, created by God, chosen as the companion on the way to salvation and as the co-parents of one's children.

We turn next to a Protestant scholar with Dutch and North American connections, Pieter de Jongh (Wynn 1966:78).

Sex is human only if it is more than a biological function or a requirement for reproduction. It has to be part of an interpersonal relationship which concerns the whole of life. … Not until a woman is respected as a creature with equal rights, not inferior to man, can we speak of a truly interpersonal relationship between the sexes and between husband and wife in particular.

I and Thou

These quotes both make the very basic point, touched on in some measure earlier, that the relationship between the spouses is the primary issue in a marriage. All else in that relationship is at the service of that union. The relationship covers all aspects of their life together. De Jongh, in particular, states unambiguously that for it to be an interpersonal relationship in the fullest sense of the word there has to be equality between the spouses. This is what I call an intersubjective relationship. What I mean by that is that it is a meeting of two subjects, two people who do not objectify one another, do not treat each other as objects or things, nor merely as means to ends. In his famous book *I and Thou*, first published in German in the 1920s, the Jewish scholar Martin Buber expresses this idea in a singular way. "The primary *I-Thou* can only be spoken with the whole being. … I become through my relation to *Thou*; as I become *I*, I can say *Thou*. All real living is meeting" (Buber 1966:11; see also Buber 1966:60). In Buber's philosophic way, he is saying much the same thing as De Jongh. When we encounter someone as *Thou* we meet that person as another subject and do not treat them as a thing. Furthermore, it is only as I encounter you as a person, as *Thou*, that I truly find myself as a person. As I understand it, this is also what the Nguni word *Ubuntu* means. It is a difficult word to translate, but I have found it explained as follows, "I am because of others and I am for others". What this means is that only in relationship Im am fully a person, and I express my humanity in serving others.

What this has to do with sexuality? The issue of interpersonal relationship is, I believe, a crucial aspect of a sexual relationship for it is only when we encounter one another in this way that the sexual relationship becomes an expression of that relationship and contributes to it. Because we do not see the other person as merely a means to an end, the sexual encounter is not merely an attempt to satisfy our own desires. If we merely want to satisfy our desires, or lusts, what we are looking for is something to serve our ends. I have deliberately used the word "some*thing*" because it reflects the objectifying aspect of that approach to a relationship.

Furthermore, "If love is fundamentally linked with satifying performance, then I always have the right to withdraw my commitment and love when I am not satisfied" (Moore 1987:31). Grenz makes a similar statement, "Sex without commiment leads to a reduction of one's sexual partners, and thus, of others in general, to objects that move in and out of one's life" (Grenz 1990:96; see also Thielicke 1964: 23). Whereas Moore's statement has to do with the way others meet my desires in general, Grenz narrows this down to the sexual. Both cases link the relationship with treating the other person as the bearer of a function which serves my requirements. If the functional end is not met, any commitment which may have existed simply evaporates and another person, if "person" is the right word in this context, is used to serve that purpose. Kierkegaard, the Danish theologian, said that where people used marriage, or marital sex, for the wrong reasons, it amounted to adultery. As I understand him, what he means is that when sexual intimacy between the spouses is not the expression of the relationship, but merely a means to an end, the identity of the sexual partner did not really matter. This is the equivalent of adultery. But the treating of a spouse as a person, not as a means to an end, is here linked to the commitment I have to that person. We therefore turn our attention to the idea of commitment.

Commitment

Commitment is a significant aspect of a relationship between spouses. In contrast to the references in the previous paragraph which have a purely functional approach to sex, the report of the Church of England commission on the Christian doctrine of marriage entitled *Marriage, divorce and the Church* (1973:17) properly places sexuality within the committed relationship:

> Once the sexual act is recognised as the means of declaring the deepest and most complete personal exchange of love, its significance can best be experienced and expressed in a lifelong commitment. ... Within this ... commitment ... it can strengthen and enhance the very relationship which it expresses.

In recent years there have been many types of relationships that have developed. This has made it possible for people to study what happens in so-called open relationships. The results have surprised even those sympathetic to this lifestyle. Achtemeier quotes from a study by Carl Rodgers on commune life in the United States. He found that whatever people profess, they experienced hurt and jealousy whenever relationships changed. This was not merely related to sexual behaviour, but also loss of closeness in the relationship. Rodgers come to the following conclusions:

> Jealousy is often an underestimated problem which can undermine a group. Indeed, I wonder whether jealousy is simply conditioned by the culture or actually has a basic biological foundation, like territoriality. ... Related to this is, I believe, a similar underestimation of the need of each person for a reasonably secure, continuing, one-to-one relationship. This need seems to run very deep and may be considered too lightly (Achtemeier 1976:46).

Fidelity

What this suggests is that the traditional Christian conviction that a married couple should keep exclusively to one another in sexual matters reflects a deep need in human marital relationships. In Afrikaans the word for marry is "trou". But this word also has another meaning, fidelity. This is, I think, a most appropriate ambiguity. There seems to be a need in humans for a particular relationship which is wholehearted and dependable. The marriage partnership provides for the need for intimacy, closeness, and trust. On the other hand the self-giving love, agape, which a couple have for each other can come to its highest expression in the intimacy of their union, "when aided by other kinds of love and kept constant by fidelity" (White 1965:31). Our need to love and be loved is admirably fulfilled in a healthy relationship between spouses. The orthodox Christian view that the Creator intended human beings to have monogamous marriages, therefore, has support both from human experience and Scripture. Jesus, in his response to a question about divorce, expressed it clearly that he regarded it as God's intention that there should be an exclusive relationship between a wife and husband (Mt 19:4–6). "Fidelity ... emphasizes the importance of reciprocal relationships among humans and the coincidence of give and take" (Grenz 1990:96). This view reflects not only a human need, but is also widely reflected in practice contrary to what is often implied in the media. I quote again from the authoritative study done in the United States which shows that "more than 80 percent of women and 65 to 85 percent of men remaining faithful, with figures varying through the age range" (Laurence 1994:16). These figures are very significant because, with the effectiveness of the latest forms of contraception, the possiblility that an extramarital affair could end in an unwanted pregnancy to "complicate" matters is virtually eliminated. What we are finding therefore is that for most people the idea of marital fidelity is still central to their understanding of marriage. Why is it so important? I believe that there are certain symbols that signify important aspects of a marriage relationship, and we now direct our thoughts to this matter of symbols.

Symbols

Why is sexual intercourse regarded as so important? So important, in fact, that when people speak of making love they mean sexual intercourse. It is indeed part of human sexual behaviour, but still only a part. In the entertainment media, particularly television, sexual encounters have been trivialised. In many television serials men and women engage in sex as an apparently normal part of social behaviour. However, sex still has a kind of mystique. In the advertising world it is used to try to convey that which is desirable. It is something that people try to get by deception or force. The media has also created the impression that it is an end in itself, and yet when treated in this way it does not provide the fulfillment that people are seeking. They try again and again, but by treating it as an end in itself, and the sexual partner as a means to that end, sex leaves the sexual partners with a feeling of the superficiality of it all.

Tillich speaks about a symbol which not only symbolises something but participates in the reality which it symbolises (Tillich 1964:196). The symbol does not point to itself but points beyond itself to that which it symbolises. The sex act between husband and wife fits this exactly. It is indeed part of the relationship, and is an expression of that union, but points beyond itself to the relationship which it symbolises. It also expresses the intimacy and vulnerability of the couple to each other as they relate on the I-Thou level. They are both figuratively and literally open and naked before each other. White makes much the same point when speaking of the one flesh idea: "This does not mean that the sex act comprises the whole of the one-flesh concept, but it is the *basic symbol*" (White 1965:14). This is why couples will often tolerate overt flirtation by their spouses in company, but infidelity which includes sexual intercourse will not be tolerated. It often leads to the break-up of the marriage. What has taken place is that the act which symbolises the marriage has been engaged in outside the marriage. "It is a destruction of the thing the symbol stands for and serves, the marriage relationship. The fidelity and trust intrinsic to a marriage has been betrayed" (Hulley 1982:86). This view echoes what we find in Matthew 19:9, viz that "unchastity" is a justified cause for divorce. The original Greek word is *porneia*, which is almost impossible to translate; most translations however suggest that it refers to serious sexual misconduct.

Above I referred to another symbol of a marriage when Ross made the point that people who live together generally get married if they decide that they would like to have children. They wish to make a public statement of their commitment to one another. What happens when people "get married"? In a civil marriage, two people stand in front of a marriage officer, in the presence of witnesses, and say that they take one another as husband or wife. In a church wedding, they pledge themselves to each other in the presence of a minister of religion and "before God and this congregation". They are then publicly declared to be "lawfully married". Does this mean that anything has changed between the couple, or that something has taken place? Most of their friends who were invited to their wedding knew that they were committed to each other before this event took place. Apparently all they were now doing was to make a public declaration of the fact. But that public declaration is a very significant event, it is the symbol of a new relationship between them. Whereas previously they had had a relationship which for all practical purposes was a marriage, the level of commitment which is expressed in marrying each other publicly is absent. Young couples find that public statement threatening, and previously divorced couples are not yet ready to do that which they find takes their relationship too far. It is too final and reminds them of the failure of their previous marriage. That public statement symbolised a level of commitment which such couples are not yet ready to make.

Some of you may be surprised that I have not emphasised the marriage service and the fact that a couple gets married "before God and this congregation". Or again, that I did not emphasise the "one flesh" aspect spoken of in both the Old and New Testaments. The former I see as part of the commitment to which they give expression in the act of publicly getting married. The latter is part of the sexual consumation of a relationship. Indeed, if we accept what Paul said in I Corinthians 6:16, people who engage in a genital sexual relationship have in a sense become one flesh. It may surprise many to learn that during the first few centuries, the church was not involved in legitimating marriages, it had no legal standing in society and could not solemnise marriages. The Church of England report states that "It was only after five to ten centuries of the Christian era that the Church 'moved in' to marriage in an authoritative way, first liturgically then juridically" (1973:45). Before that, a couple went to communion together and then consumated their marriage. The remnants of this are still visible in the canon law of the Roman Catholic Church. If a couple have not consumated their union there is no problem in annulling their marriage, declaring in a sense that it never took place. What this says in a way is that couples who live together are "one flesh" as it is understood by Paul, even if they have not been publicly married. When such couples break up it is still traumatic. This was clear to me when a fellow student in Holland came back to the programme in which we were involved having asked her live-in friend to leave. She was in a considerable state of shock. They had to divide their common household with little help from outside after their relationship had come to an end.

After that short excursus we turn again to the question of commitment. What happens when people shatter the symbol of their fidelity by being sexually unfaithful to their spouses? Often one partner accepts that it is a momentary lapse and forgives the other. It is, however, often a long time before the trust which is an expression of the acceptance of the other's fidelity is re-established. Sometimes the breaking of that symbol is so traumatic that the relationship is destroyed. There need not however be sexual unfaithfulness for spouses to come to the conclusion that their relationship has come to an end. The commitment which was symbolised in the public marriage service no longer exists, they are merely living together. Their thoughts and actions now turn to divorce.

Divorce

I do not wish to go into an extensive discussion of divorce. When you recognise that sometimes the central symbols of a marriage relationship can be shattered, what are the options? Some churches do not recognise the possibility of divorce, notable among these are the Roman Catholic Church and the Anglican communion. They base their complete rejection of divorce on Jesus' prohibition in Mark 10:9: "What God has joined together, let no one separate". In some marriage services I understand they have removed this statement because of the high divorce rate. It is suggested that it is an impossible ideal and we should not burden people with additional guilt by quoting it. This is, I think, to misunderstand what that statement is, and it also suggests that we should not have high ideals against which to measure reality. Montefiore argues that the statement is not legislation, Jesus did not come to give new laws, it rather represents "the pure will of God in instituting marriage"

(Montefiore 1973:82). White expresses a similar view:

> [Jesus'] concern was to show the demand of God, not to accomodate his ethic to human ability. Yet he was always concerned with and conscious of human weakness. Hence, what Jesus presented in his teaching was the ideal life in the presence of God (White 1965:93).

The purpose is not to minimise the demand of Jesus that we should be obedient to the divine intention, it rather accepts that human beings are sinners on the way to salvation. It accepts that divorce is breaking the will of God and must be regarded as sinful. The point I want to make is that divorce should not be regarded as an unforgivable sin, because that is the implication of holding that if a person gets divorced there is no possibility of remarriage, and any remarriage is to be seen as an adulterous relationship. When a marriage has broken down we must start where people are. To quote Montefiore again:

> The pure will of God makes no compromise with frailty, sin and error; and it may not be set aside lightly or without moral distress. In an actual human situation, however, where marriage has already broken down, people have to go on from where they are (Montefiore 1973:89; see also White 1965:111).

Such an attitude towards the breakdown of marriage and subsequent divorce is in line with the attitude Jesus showed in the Gospels, it is not playing fast and loose with his teachings. There are several incidents recorded in the Gospels that one could quote. I shall mention only two. When Jesus encountered the Samaritan woman at Jacob's well, he was more concerned about her future than with condemning her shady past (John 4:7ff). We find the same attitude in the story of the woman taken in adultery (John 8:3ff). Here Jesus made it clear that one could be forgiven even for adultery. This is very significant. If we accept the principle that we must start where people are and that there is forgiveness even for adultery, we can argue that the marriages of divorced people may be legitimate before God. While this is not true to the letter of the "law" laid down by Jesus, if it is such, it is nevertheless true to the whole tenor of the Gospel, that is that God's forgiveness and grace are available to sinners. This means that God's grace can be operative in the marriage of a couple in which one or both partners were divorced. In their study, the Anglican bishops (1973:122) capture this view in the following quotation: "It is compassion, together with a lack of illusion about life and sex, that opens the eyes of clergy and laity on the healing possibilities of a new and different marriage".

Concluding remarks

The arguments in this chapter largely represent my understanding of marriage and divorce, although I believe them to be well reasoned and to have the sanction of scripture. They also have support from other ethicists. The views are clearly not prescriptive. You may well come across other views taken by ethicists. One should consider whether they have the support of scripture, understood in terms of the teaching of the Gospels and Epistles – this is largely an argument from the New Testament – rather than proof texts standing alone. One also needs to be informed by the teachings of the tradition to which one belongs. What I am concerned about is that we have a flawed understanding of Christian marriage which, in turn, results in a too ready acceptance of divorce.

Humankind is capable of both reaching great heights and sinking to great depths, of being saints and sinners. Nowhere is this more obvious than in the sexual realm. Love between the sexes has given rise to some of the greatest art and poetry and yet when human sexuality is distorted and exploited one finds the most inhuman behaviour as shown in the modern sex trade where women are trapped into prostitution in foreign countries by unscrupulous people. Sexual intercourse can be the expression of the tenderest love and also reveal hatred and oppression such as in rape.

The prophet Hosea saw the relationship between husband and wife to be so significant that he used it as a symbol of the relationship between God and the people of Israel. In Ephesians, the love between spouses is likened to the love Christ has for the church. Yet, the church often neglects to pay sufficient attention to sexuality which is such an important aspect of the love relationship between spouses. This chapter is intended to help fill that void.

BIBLIOGRAPHY

– 1973. *Marriage, divorce and the Church*. London: SPCK.

Achtemeier, E. 1976. *The committed Marriage*. Philadelphia: The Westminster Press.

Buber, M. 1966. *I and Thou* (2nd ed). Edinburgh: T and T Clark.

Haring, B. 1970. *Married love: A modern Christian view of marriage and family life*. Chicago: Argus Communications.

Horgan, J (ed). 1972. *Humanae Vitae and the bishops*. Shannon: Irish University Press.

Hulley, LD. 1982. *Ethics of sexuality, marriage and family life*. TEB200–C. Pretoria: Unisa.

Laurence, C. 1994. "Startling findings in new US sex survey", in *The Sunday Times*, 16 Oct 1994, Johannesburg.

Moore, JF. 1987. *Sexuality and marriage: A Christian foundation for making responsible choices*. Minneapolis: Augsburg.

Montefiore, H. 1973. "Jesus on divorce and remarriage", in *Marriage, divorce and the Church*. London: SPCK.

Nelson, JB. 1978. *Embodiment: An approach to sexuality and Christian Theology*. New York/Philadelphia: Pilgrim Press.

Ross, JJ. 1994. *The virtues of the family*. New York: The Free Press.

Tillich, P. 1964. *Systematic Theology*. Vol. One. Welwyn: Nisbett.

White, E. 1965. *Marriage and the Bible*. Nashville: Broadman Press.

Wynn, JC. (ed). 1966. *Sex, family, and society*. New York: Associated Press.

6 Contraception and abortion

Louise Kretzschmar and Len Hulley

The debate concerning contraception and abortion is not restricted to South Africa; it is hotly pursued world-wide. In a country which is already experiencing difficulties in supplying food, water, housing, employment and education to millions of its people, the matter of population growth is not a purely academic one. However, the heat of the debate is not generated simply by its practical economic and ecological dimensions, it impacts very deeply on the religious, moral and cultural psyche of a great many people. For this reason, some recent SABC television debates on abortion have been characterised by emotion, invective and accusations as well as by reasoned arguments based on both principles and pragmatism.

The view adopted in this chapter is that the matters of abortion and contraception need to be discussed together and that there are instances in which both contraception and abortion can be defended on religious and moral grounds.

Some definitions and the context of the debate

Contraception can be defined as the use of natural or artificial means to prevent conception occurring as a result of sexual intercourse. Abortion can be defined as "the enforced removal of a foetus[1] from the womb of a woman to present a pregnancy from resulting in a live birth". Both contraception and abortion achieve the limitation of births, but in completely different ways and, often, for different reasons. While the former is concerned with the *prevention* of contraception, the second involves the *termination* of conception. While a great many people favour contraception, fewer are in favour of abortion, especially unrestricted abortion.

Contraception can be achieved by both natural and artificial (often chemical) means. The official teaching of the Roman Catholic church accepts only natural means such as abstinence and the rhythm method (restricting sexual intercourse to the "infertile" periods of a woman's menstrual cycle). Another natural method is commonly called by its Latin name, *coitus interruptus*, which refers to the withdrawal of the penis prior to ejaculation. Artificial means include the use of injections, condoms, the Dutch cap/diaphragms, and various types of pills. Some reject the use of intra-uterine devices (the loop or Copper T), which prevent the fertilised egg from attaching itself to the womb, because conception has technically already taken

---

1 Some writers use the American spelling "fetus", others refer to the conceptus.

place. The sterilisation of either the man or the woman is, of course, the most effective method, its only drawback being that it is irreversible.

Religious views with respect to contraception have significantly changed during the course of the 20th century (see Anderson 1977:58–84). In previous centuries, contraception was certainly not unknown (Riddle and Estes 1992:226–233), but contraception was viewed in a very negative way because its means (eg the use of certain plants) were virtually indistinguishable from abortive practices. Consequently, contraception was simply condemned along with abortion. In the modern context within which we live, three factors have radically changed: the first is that medical science has made it possible for contraception and abortion to be radically distinguished. Secondly, the world in which we live can no longer support unlimited population growth and, thirdly, increasing numbers of women are better educated and desire to exercise roles other than, or in addition to, the roles of wife and mother. For such women, the limitation of births is a necessity if they want to pursue a career outside the home environment.

Another reason why contraception was viewed with hostility in the past centuries, was that these means were most often used by prostitutes and adulterers, whereas in the modern debate, the vast majority of people using contraceptive means are married persons. There are those who would argue that it is only morally right for married persons to use contraceptives. Thus, as sexual intercourse has possibilities for both procreation and intimacy, these aims must not be separated or threatened. Further, long term responsibilities ought not to be forgotten in the heat of the moment. In short, contraceptives ought not to be used by those who wish to avoid the consequences of pre- or extra-marital sexual relations. Others would argue that although it is wrong for non-married persons to use contraceptives, it is a lesser evil for those engaging in pre-marital or extra-marital intercourse to use contraceptives than it is for them to bring an unwanted child into the world, or resort to abortion, and bring even further turmoil into their respective families. In common parlance, "if you can't be good, be careful".

A further reason for a rejection of contraception was as a result of the views of influential theologians with respect to sexuality in general. Augustine, for example, regarded the aim of procreation as the only valid reason for sexual intercourse. Simple sexual enjoyment, release and communion between married persons, without the fear of producing yet another child, were not part of his understanding of marital sexuality.

In the 20th century, the notion of responsible parenthood has been emphasised more strongly than in the past. Further, Christians now give greater theological support for programmes aimed at population limitation on the basis of the doctrine of creation. In other words, all the species have a right to exist in interdependence with each other – the human species ought not to expand so rapidly so as to destroy the other species that God has created.

In the modern context, it is significant that it is within the Catholic church, where the celibacy of the priesthood is still insisted upon, that a rejection of artificial (and more effective) means of contraception is still official policy. Amongst the Protestant churches, where the majority of clergy are married (and women are now slowly entering the ranks of ordained ministers), there is a common acceptance of the value of contraception. Unofficially, of course, Catholic lay persons have made their own assessment of the situation and many make use of artificial means of contraception despite what the Pope and Vatican have decreed.

Contraception: Is it ethical?

In what follows, the case in favour of contraception is presented over against the argument against contraception.

Contraception is not incipient murder

Some regard contraception as indistinguishable from murder. Such a view completely misunderstands the purpose of contraception; it constitutes the prevention of conception, not the destruction of what has already been brought into being. This means that a clear distinction needs to be made between contraception and abortion. It is also the case that if contraceptive means were more widely employed, there would be a radical reduction in the number of calls for abortion.

Contraception and the Bible

It is sometimes argued on the basis of Genesis 1:28 and Genesis 38:6–11 that contraception is against the will of God. Genesis 1:28 states: "be fruitful and multiply and fill the earth and subdue it". On the basis of this text it is argued that as there is a divine command to pass life on, contraception is wrong. However, it is necessary to ask to whom was this text addressed and what does it actually mean? Geisler argues that the text is addressed to the people of Israel in general and not to each specific person (Geisler 1971:213ff). This means that it is not commanded that each person should produce as many offspring as possible – if this were the case then celibacy would be wrong and clearly it is commended for certain persons whose calling it is (Mt 19.12; 1 Cor 7:25–35).

It is also necessary to ask within what context this text was written. While it is difficult to date this text or firmly establish its oral roots, the context which it addressed was certainly not one in which the earth was being "filled" to the extent that is the case today. In fact, someone was once heard to say that this is the only commandment that we humans have managed to obey!

Concerning passages such as Psalm 127:5, which stress that children are a blessing from God, it needs to be stated that a text such as this does not specify how many children constitute a blessing. Even one child constitutes a blessing to parents whereas, for a poor and struggling couple, the continued arrival of children does not constitute blessing.

With regard to the case of Onan (Gn 38:6–11), it is wrong to argue that this passage is indicative of a negative view regarding contraception. Onan's sin lay not in contraception, as it is understood today, but in his deliberate refusal to follow the levirate custom whereby he was expected to impregnate the wife of his deceased brother so as to continue the family blood line. This means that the story of Onan cannot be used as a "proof text" against contraception.

Contraception, the political interests of black people and African tradition

In the past, it has been argued that contraception is contrary to black political interests and African tradition. These arguments were used as a means of ensuring the political and cultural survival of black people in a context of oppression. Whether this was a valid argument then, is debatable, since both British imperialist and white South African rule survived for over 300 years despite being vastly outnumbered by blacks. Arguably, it was not vast numbers of people that brought the demise of Apartheid, but the effective and orchestrated resistance of a relatively small number of people. However, within the present governmental dispensation it is doubtful whether this argument still has any political merit. In terms of culture, however, the argument is still relevant.

In the traditional African set-up, contraception was not deemed necessary. Wealthy men usually had more than one wife, but polygamy was not that common amongst the poorer sectors of the society. The practice of women not weaning their children until they were 2–3 years old meant that breast-feeding women did not soon fall pregnant again. Additional factors that limited population growth were a relatively high infant mortality and the death of significant numbers of adults from disease or war. Further, the land was relatively sparsely populated and pastoralists were able to move between areas of winter and summer grazing. For both pastoralists and agriculturalists, the possession of a large number of wives and children to till the fields and watch the herds was an advantage, rather than a liability.

The problem has arisen in South Africa because traditional African thinking and practices are not fully suited to a modern, urban and industrial life-style. Because white power has already done much to alter, even destroy, aspects of traditional culture, there is a tendency for some to cling to traditional culture which provides a sense of community identity in an often hostile world. However, not all aspects of either African or Western culture are right or good. White South Africans, by and large, no longer have large families. While their forebears did have large numbers of children, today even a family of 4 children has become the exception rather than the rule. In 1993 it was estimated that the total population growth was 2,5 %. The White fertility rate was 1,9 %, the Indian 2,5 %, the Coloured 2,9 % and the Black rate was 4,6 %. The teenage pregnancy rate was estimated to be 20 % (Population Conference Report 1993).

This raises the issue of the status and education of women in general. In those instances where women have more education and better prospects in terms of personal freedom and employment, they tend to have smaller families. In most cases, given a choice, women will have smaller families. The point is that the vast majority of women in South Africa are not given a choice. In a largely male-dominated society, the views, rights and choices of women have not been high on the agenda.

Contraception in the context of: the family, society and creation

It is argued by many parents that it is better to have a limited number of children, for which one can care properly, rather than to have many children for which one cannot provide adequate food, clothing, emotional nurture or education.

Governments may feel that a completely uncontrolled population growth may make it impossible for them to meet the needs of the citizens of that country. Thus, countries like China have strictly enforced population controls. In South Africa, politicians have been very reluctant to grasp this political "hot potato", but they surely cannot be unaware of the social dangers of a huge, needy population. Thus, in 1993 it was estimated that each day 1 400 unskilled people sought to enter the labour market which was only able to absorb 300 workers. Further, each day 3 500 babies were being born (Population Conference Report 1993). Presently, it is estimated that 60 % of the South African population is under the age of 30.

Furthermore, within the framework of humanity's stewardship of creation (as opposed to notion that humans are free to dominate and abuse the earth) humankind is required to rule responsibly over the earth on behalf of God. To destroy natural habitats, vast myriads of animal and plant species, and to pollute the earth, sky and water as a result of the abuse of our power and our uncontrolled human population growth cannot possibly be conceived of as a proper exercise of this stewardship. A further issue is that of the "rights" of nature, in other words, the human species does not have an unrestricted "right" to propagate. The other species which God has created cannot simply be eradicated to make room for more and more humans.[2] Furthermore, this generation of persons have no right to destroy the natural heritage of the next generation nor to threaten their very survival.

As over-population was not known in biblical times, it was not an issue that the biblical writers addressed. This means that there are no direct references to deliberate contraception upon which we can draw. We have to draw conclusions from general moral principles (eg the purpose of marriage, the importance of parenting, and the inherent value of all the species which God created) and it is at this point that disputes arise between Christians.

Abortion

Turning now to the issue of abortion, two major lines of argument are commonly advanced. The first is that abortion should be used as a means of *birth control*, the second is that abortions may be performed on the basis of therapeutic reasons, ie

2 See the chapter on Ecology by D Field in this volume.

the physical or emotional health of either the foetus or mother. In my view, the first line of argument is morally indefensible as it would result (as was the case in the Soviet Republic where contraceptives were not available) in the indiscriminate slaughter of foetuses. A large variety of methods of contraception are available as a means of family planning or birth control. It is these methods, which hold virtually no risk to the mother's health and involve the prevention of conception rather than the removal of an already living foetus, that should be used as birth control measures. The second line of argument, namely abortion for therapeutic reasons, is more widely accepted. It was on this principle that the previous South African abortion legislation (1975) was based.

Why, then, were there calls in South Africa for this law to be radically revised, if not discarded altogether? One of the primary reasons that was advanced was based on the high incidence of dangerous backstreet abortions. This was contrasted with the relative ease and safety with which it is possible for a medical practitioner to remove a foetus from a woman's body.[3]

Statistics concerning "backstreet" abortions are obviously difficult to obtain, but in 1992, Prof Mokgokong was reported to have stated that at least half of all the patients admitted to the gynaecological emergency section of the Ga-Rankuwa hospital were the result of something going wrong in "backroom" abortions (*Vrye Weekblad* 1992:19). In 1993 it was stated that at Baragwanath hospital just outside Soweto, "some 300 women a month are treated for failed or life-threatening abortions" (Cleminshaw 1994:171). This figure obviously did not include the "successful" illegal abortions, the number of which was estimated to be between 42 000 and 200 000. In a great many cases, these operations leave the women seriously damaged internally. Some die, while others are rendered permanently incapable of bearing a child. In the face of this alarming situation, many argued that the only solution was to liberalise the South African law so that any woman in the country could request that a safe, medical abortion be performed if she did not wish to bear the child she was carrying.

The situation is further complicated in South Africa by the following factors. It is estimated that over 50 % of black and coloured women have not been legally married, 50 % of the present population is under the age of 18, and there are 3 323 births a day in South Africa. Further, HIV and tuberculosis are spreading rapidly, and reported cases of rape, child abuse and child abandonment are increasing. Also poverty, unemployment, illiteracy, the breakdown of family and community life and the oppression of women are rife (Cleminshaw 1994:171–172). This means that ethicists cannot only take into account the issue of the sanctity of life, they also need to take cognisance of the issue of the quality of life.

---

3   The debate about legal abortions is thus but one of a number of other medical issues that have arisen as a result of advances in medical technology. Others include organ transplants, euthanasia, genetic manipulation and surrogate motherhood (see the chapter on Medical Ethics).

Abortion and South African law

Prior to the recent "Termination of Pregnancy Act" (1996), the South African Abortion and Sterilisation Act of 1975 permitted an abortion in the following five instances:

1. If the continued pregnancy constitutes a threat either to the life or the physical health of the pregnant woman.
2. If the pregnancy constitutes a danger of permanent damage to the pregnant woman's mental health.
3. Where it is likely that the baby will be born with serious or uncorrectable deformity or handicap.
4. Where the pregnancy is the result of rape or incest.
5. Where the pregnant woman is mentally sub-normal and therefore unable to give informed consent to intercourse.

Furthermore, three medical practitioners were required to agree unanimously that at least one of these conditions existed before a legal abortion could be performed.

It could be argued that the problem with this law was not so much in its limited provisions, but in the fact that so few black women had access to the medical facilities that could have made a greater number of legal abortions possible. However, the fact of large numbers of unwanted pregnancies (due to the unavailability of contraceptives, lack of information or negligence) exerted enormous pressure on parliamentary legislators. Despite a prolonged furore, the new Bill was passed into law, according to which:

1. A pregnancy may be terminated –
    (a) upon request of a woman during the first 12 weeks of the gestation period of her pregnancy;
    (b) from the 13th up to and including the 20th week of the gestation period if a medical practitioner, after consultation with the pregnant woman, is of the opinion that –
        (i) the continued pregnancy would pose a risk of injury to the woman's physical or mental health; or
        (ii) there exists a substantial risk that the foetus would suffer from a severe physical or mental abnormality; or
        (iii) the pregnancy resulted from rape or incest; or
        (iv) the continued pregnancy would significantly affect the social or economic circumstances of the woman;
    (c) after the 20th week of the gestation period if a medical practitioner, after consultation with another medical practitioner or a registered midwife, is of the opinion that the continued pregnancy –
        (i) would endanger the woman's life; or
        (ii) would result in a severe malformation of the foetus; or

(iii) would pose a risk of injury to the foetus.

(2) The termination of a pregnancy may only be carried out by a medical practitioner, except for a pregnancy referred to in subsection (1)(a), which may also be
carried out by a registered midwife who has completed the prescribed training
course.

Two case studies

Because of the widely varying reasons why women desire to have abortions performed, it is necessary to bear these different contexts in mind. This can be illustrated as follows:

> *Case study 1:* A black woman is living in a rural area in South Africa. She is 40,
> poor, a subsistence farmer, already has 6 children, and her husband is a
> migrant labourer. During one of his brief visits home (1 month out of every 12)
> he discovers that she has obtained contraceptive pills from the local clinic. He
> accuses her of infidelity while he is away and of depriving him of sons. He
> throws the pills away, sleeps with her and, later, goes back to his job at the
> mine. Later she discovers she is pregnant yet again. Should she be permitted
> to have an abortion?

> *Case study 2:* A young teenage girl and her boyfriend lead an uncaring and
> promiscuous lifestyle. She discovers she is pregnant and decides to have an
> abortion. Is her decision ethically justifiable?

Because of the varying contexts in which women seek abortions, the Anglican statement on abortion highlighted the sociological background of this issue:

> In particular black women suffer extensively from the lack of reproductive
> health education and facilities, the non-availability of contraception, male atti-
> tudes to sex and contraception, and extreme poverty (*CPSA Abortion* 1996:1).

This suggests that, whatever one's views regarding abortion, there is an important
educational and social task which faces society, namely, education about reproductive health and contraception and the making available of acceptable contraceptive
means.

What does abortion involve?

Abortion is an old procedure, and it is thought that it was practised over 4 500 years
ago as a means of birth control (see Silk 1994:32; Rosner and Bleich 1979:26, 119–
124):

> The safest and quickest method of abortion, if a pregnancy test is positive and
> it is less than seven weeks from the last menstruation, is called a vacuum aspi-
> ration or *mini-abortion*. In this procedure a tube with a suction device is insert-
> ed through the cervix into the uterus. (Dilation is usually unnecessary.) Within
> one or two minutes, the lining on the uterine wall and the conceptus are suc-
> tioned out. Cramping, nausea, and faintness may be experienced by a woman
> undergoing this procedure. It is commonly performed in the medical office.

If the pregnancy is terminated between the 7th and the 12th weeks, a *suction abortion* or *curettage* is performed. The procedure is similar to the mini-abortion. In the medical office or clinic, a local anaesthetic is given and the cervix is dilated to permit the suction and scraping of the uterine lining. In a hospital a general anaesthetic is used. Cramping, nausea, and vomiting usually follow the procedure. The patient can go home about two hours afterward.

The period of 12 to 16 weeks afford few safe methods of abortion, because the foetus is too large for a suction abortion and there is insufficient amniotic fluid for a saline injection. During this time, two methods are the use of repeated vaginal or intramuscular administrations of prostaglandins, which encourage expulsion of the conceptus within 10 to 15 hours.

The saline injection is performed during the 16–24th weeks of gestation. The procedure involves withdrawing between 50 to 100 cc of amniotic fluid through a needle and syringe. Approximately 200 cc of saline solution is then slowly injected into the remaining amniotic fluid. This procedure brings about a normal labour and delivery of the foetus within 18 to 20 hours. The same procedure is followed to instil prostaglandins into the amniotic sac, except only a small amount of amniotic fluid is removed. The results are the same. These procedures can be performed in a hospital and require 1 to 3 days stay.

In very few cases a hysterectomy or mini-caesarean section is performed to remove the foetus surgically. This is considered major surgery, requiring six to eight days' hospitalisation and a longer period of recuperation than any other method. It is usually performed only in the case of uterine abnormalities.

Generally, the later an abortion of any type is performed, the greater the risk. Psychological and physiological difficulties can and may accompany any method of abortion (Lewis and Warden 1983:166).

Three different views concerning abortion

With regard to this debate concerning abortion, essentially three basic views can be identified: those that adopt the "pro-life" view; those that adopt the "pro-choice" view; and those that argue for limited abortion on specific, morally defensible grounds.

The pro-life position

What is the pro-life position? Basically this approach takes its name from the view that the life of the child (usually the word foetus is not used) must be preserved at all costs. Those that hold this view argue that abortion is nothing but murder because from the moment of conception the child is a human being which has a right to life. One of the arguments used by those holding this position is that because a fertilised ovum already contains the complete human DNA, it must be regarded as a human being. Abortion, for whatever reason, is rejected by many theologically conservative Christians and it is also the official view of the Roman Catholic Church.

An example of this viewpoint is the statement issued by the 1995 KwaSizabantu Minister's Conference concerning the legalisation of abortion:

> It is not acceptable that unborn babies should be killed in the womb while murderers are not executed. We maintain that anyone who robs a person of his most precious possession, his life, is a murderer (KwaSizabantu Conference 1995:2).

The strength and value of this position lies in its affirmation of the importance of the sanctity of life and it constitutes a severe critique against those who believe that abortion on demand carries no moral or religious censure. Reference is often made to verses such as Ps 139:13–16; Is 44:24; Job 10:8–17; and Jer 1:45 which stress God's involvement with persons even before their birth.

Furthermore, those that hold the pro-life position are totally against the use of abortion either as a means of population control or for any other reason. Intercourse, they say, cannot be embarked upon lightly. Like any other human behaviour, it has moral and practical implications which cannot be ignored. Finally, the pro-life position illuminates the reason why so many women who have had abortions, often experience intense feelings of guilt afterwards. For all these reasons, many people have an inherent conviction that abortion is wrong.

The pro-life position also has several weaknesses. Firstly, it is overly simplistic. To say that abortion is in all instances nothing but murder, is to close one's eyes to the complexity of the moral issues surrounding abortion. For example, what if the life of the mother is directly threatened by the continued existence of the foetus? Furthermore, even recent South African law, which adopted a fairly conservative position when compared to abortion legislation elsewhere, permitted abortion in instances such as rape, incest and when the physical or mental health of a pregnant woman was threatened.

Secondly, the pro-life position does not consider the complexity of the term "murder". Do all forms of killing, including self-defence and war constitute murder? Did those who today adopt a pro-life position support conscientious objection during the Apartheid era? Do they now oppose the death penalty? Further, are they doing anything to prevent the many deaths that occur each year in our country as a consequence of child neglect or malnutrition? In many cases these questions can only be answered in the negative. This being the case, one must ask on what basis abortion is singled out as being subject to the command not to kill (Ex 20:13)?

A third weakness relates to the issue of spontaneous abortions, or miscarriages. These are not regarded as death by the law or medical profession, society or even the church. In cases where the pregnancy is far advanced and a miscarriage occurs, the church seldom provides pastoral help or offers to hold a proper funeral. This betrays the fact that we do not regard a miscarriage as a death. Many of these spontaneous abortions happen when the foetus is malformed. It would seem, then, that abortions of severely malformed foetuses could be regarded as correcting an error in nature. That conviction is, in fact, the basis for many surgical interventions.

A fourth point that can be made with regard to the pro-life position, is that their arguments are purely deontological in nature (ie concerned with norms of right and wrong) and they usually ignore teleological ethical considerations (ie considerations regarding good or bad motives, goals and consequences). This means that arguments concerning the sanctity of life (the latter being understood simply in terms of physical existence) are stressed, whereas those concerning the quality of life – physical, emotional, social or mental – are generally ignored.

The pro-choice position

This approach emphasises the pregnant woman's right to choose whether she wishes to give birth or not. Women, the argument goes, should have absolute control over their own reproductive capacities. No-one, not their husbands, the doctors, or the law should be able to make this choice on their behalf.

The value of the pro-choice position is that it emphasises the role of the woman concerned and the right of a woman to have control over her own reproductive capacities. Within a context where women have for centuries had little or no choice in this vitally important area of their lives, many people have a lot of sympathy for this approach. Given the patriarchal and male-dominated contexts in which so many women all over the world live, this position asserts that the rights and views of women must be acknowledged. After all, they are the ones that will carry, give birth to and, over many years, rear the child. Millions of women all over the world throughout history have experienced both joy and grief, pleasure and suffering as a result of bearing, or not bearing, children. Equally, much of the responsibility for child care has fallen upon women, thus, the wishes and life circumstances of women cannot be ignored in the debate concerning abortion.

Further, this emphasis on the right of women to choose highlights a number of issues relevant to the life experiences of women in South Africa namely: their access to education and health; their lack of self-esteem and empowerment; the social and moral context in the country; their vulnerability to rape; the lack of privacy; and the shortage of employment (see the *Women's Charter for Effective Quality*).

Despite these arguments, it is our view that the pro-choice view stresses the rights of the woman at the expense of the rights of the foetus. A foetus is not simply a "lump of tissue" that can be removed. Though dependant upon the woman for its continued existence for several months, it is wrong to regard a living foetus as a mere appendage which a pregnant woman can get rid of at will. When all is said and done the foetus, whatever the debates about its humanity, viability and personhood, is a potential human being. Consequently, only in the event of special circumstances, should abortion become an option. Anyone who has witnessed the performance of an abortion or can imagine the sight of countless pulsating foetuses lying in buckets waiting to be incinerated, cannot but regard the indiscriminate practice of abortion as a very real evil. Thus, the decision to abort or not, cannot be made purely on the basis of the rights, wishes or whims of the pregnant woman. From a Christian perspective, abortion on demand is often based on a purely secular, selfish and materialistic ideology.

The pro-choice argument is taking individualism to a point where it becomes problematic. It ignores any interest or concern on the part of the father, the family or the community. While individuals have the right to make choices, abortion on demand suggests that the community has no right to question personal actions. The point is that the community feels that it must guard the interests of the foetus which cannot fend for itself. Along the lines of the principle which one finds in the Hebrew Scriptures (much emphasised, in another context, by liberation theologians) that God has a special concern for those who are unable to defend themselves (Deut 10:18 and parallels), one cannot simply disregard the rights of a foetus, even though it may be regarded as nascent life or a potential human being rather than fully human.

A further severe weakness, in our view, of the pro-choice position is that this approach seems to assume that the problem of unwanted pregnancies can be solved by replacing one law (which restricted abortion) with another law (which permits abortion on demand). Neither are adequate in themselves since they do not address the following fundamental issues: why are there so many unwanted pregnancies and why have the relevant sexual partners not used (or had access to) contraceptives? At the end of the day, the huge problem of unwanted pregnancies cannot be solved through abortion, but through the exercise of moral responsibility, respect for human dignity and life, and adequate, morally founded, sex education.

Limited, selective abortion

In the case of abortion, we are dealing with an issue of *grenzfall* ethics, that is, borderline ethics. Only in relatively exceptional cases, for therapeutic reasons, where a morally defensible case can be advanced, should abortion be permitted. This is the approach followed by those who argue for limited, selective abortion.

This third approach to the issue of abortion adopts a position between the pro-life and pro-choice approaches. It seeks to maintain an emphasis on the rights of the foetus as well as asking whether there are some legitimate instances in which abortion can be justified. In this sense, it employs the argument of the lesser of two evils and is a teleological or consequentialist argument in that it seeks to identify mitigating circumstances in which abortion could be morally justified.

The starting point of this approach is that abortion is not simply a medical or legal issue; it is very definitely a moral issue. This is reflected in the long history of the rejection by the churches of abortion on demand. It argues that abortion, because it involves the destruction of life, can only be permitted on the basis of a higher ethical motive. Despite the invective that is sometimes heaped upon the heads of those who argue for this third position (by the pro-life lobby), this position bases its views on moral grounds. Unlike the extreme pro-choice position, it maintains that a potential human life cannot be destroyed at whim or for any reason other than a moral one.

This approach takes the position that abortion cannot simply be equated with murder. In the Old Testament, for example, if in the case of a fight between two men, a pregnant woman was injured resulting in a miscarriage, "and yet no harm follows", the one who injured her is fined rather than executed (compare Ex 21:22 and Ex 21:12). Here infanticide (see also Ex 1:66ff) is defined as the killing of a child which has been born.

Nevertheless, a foetus is a potential human being, it is neither fully human nor is it sub-human, it is "in the process of becoming a human being" and God is at work in this process (Ps 139:13–15). Christ was the God-man from conception (Lk 1:31–32). Thus, abortion is not murder, but neither is it ever to be undertaken lightly, no one has the right to interfere with the process of the development of a person unless some other moral purpose can be put forward. In other words, the sanctity of life ought to be preserved, but not at all costs.

When is abortion justifiable?

Those who argue in favour of selective abortion point out that when the procreative aspect of sexual intercourse is not controlled, it can lead to negative consequences. On the macro level it leads to over-population, with adverse social and ecological consequences. Within marriage it can lead to unplanned pregnancies and even unwanted pregnancies. While one cannot approve of the use of abortion as a family planning measure, it is important that careful use be made of medical resources that prevent pregnancy. This implies both an educational programme and the supply of contraceptives. Although unplanned pregnancies are not always disasters, as many families can testify, in poor families it can have serious negative consequences, leading to intense hardship. In the case of women, it can lead to loss of employment. The main sufferers in this respect are black women. The arrival of another child in a household where the resources are severely stretched could create a very real problem, and could even be seen as the last straw. Such women may indeed feel that abortion is the lesser of two evils. It may even be regarded as the only solution in an impossible situation. Such women, and they are generally those who have to bear the burden in difficult circumstances, are prepared to sacrifice what they possibly regard as "something not yet fully human" for the sake of the living. Here they use a logic similar to that which has been used by ethicists to justify an abortion which threatens the life of the pregnant women, sometimes referred to as therapeutic abortion (see Gill 1985:495). In "therapeutic abortion" it is argued that one can justifiably sacrifice the "life" of the foetus for the life and health of the pregnant woman and her family. Although there are divided opinions even here, there seems to be fairly widespread acceptance of this argument among people in the field of ethics. What we have here is that the interests of the pregnant woman, and of others affected by the pregnancy, are regarded as having precedence over any putative rights of the foetus.

Those who argue in favour of selective abortion state that one must consider the context in which events such as the pregnancy occur, because it is relevant when one has to come to an ethical decision. This approach reflects a concern for the people involved. A good example of this is the following statement in the CPSA document:

> Morally speaking, not all abortions are the same; the self-indulgence of a rich girl buying an abortion for superficial reasons is clearly more culpable than the desperate act of an impoverished rape victim (CPSA 1996:2).

One of the reasons for justifying a departure from the prohibition on abortion has already been mentioned, that is, where the life or mental health of the mother is in danger and an abortion is carried out for medical reasons, so-called therapeutic abortions. In cases where women have fallen pregnant as a result of being victims of rape, many ethicists would argue that an abortion is justified. They hold that to deny an abortion to a pregnant rape victim is to condemn her to a constant reminder of her ordeal. It may also lead to a child born as a result of rape being ignored or badly treated. Although there is divided opinion on this, the weight of opinion would be on allowing an abortion to take place.

Another justifiable instance is where the foetus is diagnosed as being severely malformed or handicapped. These justifications for abortion are regarded as having some moral standing and they are widely, although not generally, accepted. These "exceptions" were catered for in earlier South African legislation. Abortion was seen as an unfortunate necessity in these particular circumstances.

A more problematic area is when pregnancies occur out of wedlock. In many such cases, these young women are still studying, either at school or college or university. Together with their boyfriends, they have engaged in "recreational", premarital sex. The sexual relationship is not an expression of a long-term relationship which includes a significant level of commitment between the partners. When these young women fall pregnant, it often means the end of their studies and they frequently have to rear their children with little or no help from the fathers of the children. The young men often run away and usually get off scot-free. They assume no obligations and carry no stigma, they merely carry on with their studies or careers, while their girlfriends are left with all the anger, problems and rejections which result from such pregnancies. In such situations, the temptation to procure an abortion is great. It would seem that an abortion would solve all the problems which have been caused by the pregnancy. In this instance, the interests of the pregnant woman are taken into account, whereas the interests of the foetus are not recognised at all. Such pregnancies are regarded as an inconvenience which can be dealt with by having an abortion. This raises the question of whether these situations can be regarded as ethically justifiable instances for abortion.

In essence, then, this third position argues that abortion on demand for reasons of convenience and birth control are wrong. However, in certain instances, abortion can be justified on the grounds that it is the lesser of the two evils. This third approach asks the question: given that abortion involves the taking of a life, under which special circumstances could abortions be permitted? While the pro-life approach uses purely deontological arguments (based on the norm of the sanctity of life) and the pro-choice approach uses purely teleological arguments (based on consequences in terms of the quality of life), this third approach seeks to combine the deontological and teleological ethical criteria.

This third approach, like the pro-life approach, also stresses that there are options other than abortion, especially in the case of pre-marital pregnancies. These include: giving birth to the child and allowing it to be adopted or giving birth to the child and keeping it, knowing that "good can come out of evil". While some parents would insist on a "shotgun" marriage, that is, a young couple are forced to get married, other parents have assumed responsibility for the child, arguing that they do not wish their daughter to marry a man who does not care for her or the child he has so thoughtlessly conceived. It is seldom the case that the parents of the "boyfriend" assume responsibility for the unborn infant.

The weaknesses of this third approach to abortion, in terms of legislation, are as follows. It requires that structures be set up according to which the decision is taken whether the abortion is morally justified or not. Aside from the difficulties of deciding on the necessary criteria and appointing the necessary personnel (eg doctors, ministers, church workers, psychologists and social workers), such a system would be very expensive and difficult to implement. The advantage of the new South African legislation lies in its simplicity – it places the moral responsibility for the decision in the hands of the individual woman. The disadvantage is that the State assumes no moral responsibility and is not compelled to exert itself to provide the infrastructure to ensure that sex education or effective methods of birth control are provided.

In a context where abortions are now freely available up to 12 weeks, some may suggest that a clear distinction should be made between what Christians regard as *morally acceptable* reasons for abortion and what the law of the land finds *legally permissible*. Christians make the same distinctions, for example, with regard to adultery. It is not a criminal offence, but Christians would regard it as morally wrong.

However, although this seems to be an attractive option, it is not without its problems. We suggest that Christians should hold the position that the law of the country and the secular authorities ought to provide for the welfare of the whole society on the basis of equity, justice and fairness. This is in line with the whole prophetic tradition in the Hebrew Scriptures and with the prophetic role of the church in contemporary society. To do anything less would be to abandon the prophetic ministry of the church. After a thorough examination of the whole matter, churches ought to arrive at a considered, mutually agreed upon position with respect to abortion.

Conclusion

This discussion has shown that Christians are divided in relation to the matters of contraception and abortion. While some churches have issued official statements in relation to contraception and abortion, their conclusions are not the same. For this reason it is necessary for ethicists and church leaders to seriously note and evaluate on what basis conclusions are reached with regard to these sexual and medical debates. Only when we can agree to the ethical criteria to be used in making ethical assessments, will it become possible for Christian churches to reach agreement within their own ranks and present relevant and credible ethical pronouncements to the country at large. If we are not able to do so, and if we are not prepared to involve ourselves in a practical way with the problems presented in this chapter, our witness will be significantly weakened – if not demolished.

BIBLIOGRAPHY

Anderson, N. 1977. *Issues of Life and Death*. Downers Grove: InterVarsity Press.

Camp, S Talcott. 1995. "Why have you been silent? A brief look at the church and the abortion ban in South Africa", *Journal of Theology for Southern Africa* 91: 59–74.

Cleminshaw, Dot. 1994. "Abortion", in C Villa-Vicencio and J de Gruchy (eds), *Ethics in Context*. Cape Town: David Philip pp 166–173.

Geisler, N. 1971. *Ethics: Alternatives and Issues*. Grand Rapids: Zondervan.

Gill, R. 1985. *A textbook of Christian Ethics*. Edinburgh: T and T Clark.

Lammers, S and Verhey, A (eds). 1987. *On Moral Medicine*. Grand Rapids: Eerdmans.

Lewis, MA and Warden, CD. 1983. *Law and ethics in the medical office, including bioethical issues*. Philadelphia: FA Davis Company.

Macquarrie, John. 1967. *A Dictionary of Christian Ethics*. London: SCM.

Riddle, JM and Estes, JW. 1992. "Oral contraceptives in Ancient and Medieval times", *American Scientist* 80: 226–233.

Rosner, F and Bleich, JD (eds). 1979. *Jewish bioethics*. New York: Hebrew Publishing Company.

Silk, MJS. 1994. "Abortion: from the first month after conception through to the first month of separate life". Unpublished Theological Ethics assignment, Unisa.

Weeks, JR. 1978. *Population: An introduction to concepts and issues*. Belmont: Wadsworth.

DOCUMENTS AND REPORTS

Vrye Weekblad 7–13 February 1992, pp 18–19

Statement from the *KwaSizabantu Conference* 6–9 March 1995, 4 pp

Methodist Church of South Africa: 1995. Annual Conference. "Statement on Abortion"

CPSA 1996. *Abortion*. Photocopied report.

Women's Charter for Effective Quality (Issued by the National Women's Coalition)

Population Conference Report: Population Realities and the Future South Africa September 1993, compiled by the Chief Directorate Population Development

Choice on Termination of Pregnancy Act, 1996. Government Gazette 22 November 1996, 5 pp.

7 Some key issues in medical ethics

Len Hulley and Louise Kretzschmar

The issue of medical ethics is a prominent one in our contemporary world. Whether one thinks of medical ethical issues that feature conspicuously in the so-called First World or whether one stresses Third World issues, medical matters are never far from the ethical agenda. Because health is crucial to human well-being and survival, the ethical issues that arise from matters relating to health include the following: "Who is healthy?", "Why do certain individuals and groups not enjoy health care"? or "What is adequate health care?"

According to the World Health Organisation, health must be defined not simply as the absence of disease, but as a state of "complete physical, mental and social well-being" (Lawrence 1994:162). This is an important definition, because it stresses that health ought to be seen not simply in relation to disease but in a more holistic manner. Holistic in the sense that it relates to human well-being at a variety of levels. Looked at theologically, there is a close connection between this definition of health and the Old Testament concept of shalom. In an article entitled "Creating Newness: the spirituality of reconstruction" Liz Carmichael refers to Isaiah 65:17–25 and says:

> In Isaiah's vision there is "shalom" that enfolds the whole of life, a state of material and spiritual peace and fulfilment: housing and health, employment, good crops, reconciliation between former enemies, the ending of violence. There is joy and rejoicing (Carmichael in Hulley et al. (eds) 1996:184).

The context of medical ethics

As indicated above, when one speaks of medical ethics, there is a vast difference between the issues raised in a First and those raised in a Third World context (or, more properly, the Two-Thirds World as recent commentators have referred to the under-developed world). In general terms, the term "the First World" is understood to refer to Europe, North America and Japan whilst the term "the Two-Thirds World" refers to Africa, Latin America and large parts of Asia. Countries such as Korea, Russia and Australia are more difficult to place. In essence, though, "First" World refers to the more industrialised areas whilst "Two-Thirds" refers to the less industrialised areas of the globe. Whatever the complications of nomenclature are, there is obviously a vast difference between the nutritional and medical needs of the Two-Thirds World and the high demand for organ transplants (eg of the heart, liver or kidneys) in a First World medical context. Another factor that indicates the great difference between First and Two-Thirds World medical contexts, is the fact of unequal access to medical facilities. Thus, for example, some persons have to walk many kilometres to a rural medical clinic staffed by a nurse, whereas other persons can choose which of a possible 10 doctors in a five kilometre radius they wish to consult. In South Africa, both First and Third World contexts are to be found.

It is also important to note the distinction made between preventative medicine on the one hand and curative medicine on the other hand. Preventative medicine is based on the premise of providing basic health care and nutrition to the community at large so as to prevent disease. Curative medicine tends to be more highly centralised and focuses on relatively expensive treatment of diseases which have already been contracted. Thus, for example, to prevent cholera is vastly different from treating an outbreak of cholera in a particular community. All that is required to prevent an outbreak of cholera, is the provision of clean drinking water.

One final matter to illustrate the importance of the context of medical ethics relates to the type of medicine to which one is referring. Modern Western medical practitioners sometimes forget that centuries of human beings survived using their own herbal and other remedies, long before modern Western medicine developed. Presently, in South Africa, there is a debate as to whether Medical Aid schemes ought to cover the costs of "traditional" African healers (such as herbalists) and homeopathic practitioners in addition to doctors registered with the Medical and Dental Council of South Africa. In other words, the term "medicine" can refer to a range of medical approaches.

Some key issues in medical ethics

There are a great many issues that arise within the context of the ethical debates about medicine and health. Below we simply discuss a few of these to illustrate to readers the wide range of medical ethical matters.

Nutrition

As already mentioned, nutrition is a vital issue of medical ethics within a Two-Thirds World context. In fact, it is also an important factor among sectors of the First World population. Not every one in a First World context is well nourished. The importance of nutrition within the context of medical ethics lies in the fact that unless one receives proper nourishment, serious problems may result. Malnourished, or ill nourished, people are also more susceptible to diseases. TB (Tuberculosis) has sometimes been called the disease of the poor. As unemployment and poor nutrition increase, so does the incidence of TB. The provision of insufficient amounts of protein affect small children detrimentally, they develop kwashiorkor. This disease can mean that the development of their brain capacity is affected. They can thus be impaired for life.

The inadequate provision of nutrition is also obviously related to levels of poverty in a particular community. Where communities or families within particular communities are unemployed and do not have access to agricultural land, seeds, water, technical knowledge and implements, they are clearly not in a position to provide sufficient nutrition for their families. The matter of the necessity of clean water has already been mentioned above. It is no accident that the minister of Water Affairs, Mr Kader Asmal, has stated that, in South Africa, the provision of clean water is a socio-political matter. Without adequate water, communities cannot thrive nor can there be any possibility of such communities growing vegetables or other crops for themselves on a regular basis.

Population growth

Another matter which has proved to be something of a political "hot potato" is the matter of population growth. Politicians appear to be loath to mention the issue in public, but it is quite clear to any thinking person that a vastly increasing rate of population growth cannot but prove fatal to both individuals and the country as a whole in the future. It is simply not possible to provide sufficient food, water, housing, medical facilities, education and employment for an ever-growing population. The country is presently unable to provide for the basic needs of the existing population, let alone several million more.

This does not mean that the recently passed Termination of Pregnancy Act (1996), discussed elsewhere in this volume, ought to be regarded as the solution for all population ills. As is argued in the chapter on contraception and abortion, abortion ought not to be regarded as a means of birth control. There is no moral basis upon which abortion can be used as a means of limitating population growth. This means that the problem of population growth can only effectively be dealt with through extensive educational programmes (which include a proper moral foundation), wide access to contraceptives, and the socio-economic and educational improvement of the lot of women in our society. Studies in other countries have clearly shown that the rate of population growth only significantly drops as the educational level of women improves. When women are well informed about their reproductive capacities, as well as being given the opportunity to experience a quality of life which goes beyond an endless cycle of pregnancy, birth and poverty, they take steps to limit their families.

Organ transplantation

Organ transplants have become fairly common practice in many of our hospitals. Here we should, however, make clear what we mean by organ transplants. We first want to mention some aspects of this matter regarding similar medical procedures, but which are not usually considered as transplants. Today it is not unusual for people to receive artificially manufactured joints such as knees or hips. There have also been attempts to manufacture artificial hearts, remembering that the heart is a pump. These devices are then connected to the circulatory system of a person whose heart muscle has reached the stage that it can no longer adequately pump blood. So far this has not been very successful. People have also been given artificial heart valves, to replace their own valves which have started to malfunction by not closing properly, the so-called "leaking" valve. When people undergo heart surgery they are often connected to a heart-lung machine which oxygenates the blood and pumps it back into the circulatory system. Persons whose kidneys are failing can go for dialysis. This means that their blood is circulated through a machine that removes the impurities by letting it flow past a suitable membrane. They have to undergo dialysis several times a week to keep their blood in a reasonably "clean" condition. Because each treatment lasts several hours, it is time consuming and costly. But the issue is that here we have devices which have been manufactured to take over the duties of our organs. The purpose of these replacements or transplants is ethically justifiable. It is to increase both the quality and quantity of life of those who are being treated or receive transplanted organs.

Organ transplants usually refer to cases where a living organ is transplanted from one person's body to that of another. For some years, one of the most successful transplant programmes was that of transplanting corneas from the eyes of a donor, someone who has died, to another person to improve or restore their sight. The operation is fairly common and not prohibitively expensive. Here again, the moral justification for the procedure is that it improves the quality of life of the recipient by improving their vision.

Apart from the moral justification for this way of improving the quality of life of the recipients, the other ethically relevant aspects of this practice are the financial costs and the sources of the organs. The former has already raised a political storm in our country. When the Gauteng Provincial medical budget was being stretched, the authorities decided that there would be no more transplants, the money was needed to provide primary health care. This became a highly emotive issue where people who were waiting for transplants were portrayed as the victims of government policy. Further, the highly skilled doctors who were treating these people, were said to be considering emigrating. The cost of one such an operation and the expensive anti-rejection drugs required afterwards by the recipient on a permanent basis, if borne by the state, used money that could have been used to fund a primary health care clinic in a rural area where it would serve the needs of large numbers of people. One of the things which is sometimes said is that medical treatment is a human right. In fact, in the *Universal Declaration of Human Rights* we read that "Everyone has the right to ... medical care" (UN article 25). The question then arises as to who is responsible for seeing that the privileges to which this right entitles one are provided? One also has to ask whether the right to an organ transplant by one person, or even several people, is stronger than the right to primary health care in a community, if it is not possible to provide both.

Sources of organs

The sources of the organs is also an issue that has important ethical implications.

First, there are those organs which are obtained from cadavers (corpses). The organs have to be removed soon after death to prevent them from deteriorating. People may state that they wish this to happen when they die or their relatives may make the decision. The grounds for making such a decision is usually altruism (concern for others). One can perhaps help someone else to enjoy a reasonable quality of life by agreeing to donate one's own or a relative's organs. The first heart which was transplanted into another person, carried out in Cape Town by Prof Chris Barnard, was taken from someone who died in an accident. Second, organs are sometimes taken from living donors. Some of these are renewable tissues such as skin or bone marrow. One may even add blood to this category – and many people's lives have been saved by blood transfusions. In some cases people have given one of their kidneys to save the life of another person. The first such transplant was where a man gave one of his kidneys to be used in treating his identical twin brother because their organs were compatible. Both the blood and the tissues of the donor and recipient have to be compatible, but we will not go into this technical matter any further, it is purely a medical problem. From an ethical point of view, the situation can arise where pressure is applied to someone to donate an organ, which is ethically questionable. A third major issue is that a market could arise in organs. This raises a host of ethical questions such as the exploitation of other people's bodies which reflects values which ought not to be acceptable in society. In some countries it is apparently the practice to pay people for their blood. This matter is not an issue in South Africa and we will merely note it. The fourth source of organs could be animals. There is at present a program of trying to breed genetically manipulated pigs whose organs will be accepted as human organs by the immune systems of the people who receive them. Some would say that such a practice is an infringement of animal rights.

Human reproduction

Having children is one of the basic desires of human beings. In the Bible one of the important reasons for having children was to have an heir. We have such famous stories as Sarah giving birth to a son, Isaac, when she was past child-bearing age (Gn 21:1–7), and the birth of Samuel, whose mother prayed for a child at the temple at Shiloh (1 Sam 1:1–21). Although having children is not necessarily still regarded as a reward from God (Ps 127:3–4) and, conversely, being childless as a judgement from God, people still are anxious to have children and will go to great lengths to do so. In the Old Testament infertility was always attributed to the woman because of the understanding of procreation prevalent at that time. "The failure to have a child foreclosed the most important role available to women in Hebraic society, that of mother, and denied her a substantial component of a woman's worth" (McDowell 1985:57). This ongoing desire for offspring was the reason for the more recent development of human reproductive technologies. The problem of involuntary infertility is fairly prevalent. As many as one in ten couples are said to be affected (Uniacke 1987:243).

In vitro fertilisation

In 1978 Louise Brown was born in England as the result of a breakthrough in reproductive technique. Her mother's ova were fertilised with her father's sperm in a glass dish in a laboratory, the so-called *in vitro*[1] fertilisation (IVF) method, and the fertilised ovum was placed in her mother's reproductive canal. The rest of the pregnancy proceeded normally. Married couples who request this procedure do so to overcome involuntary infertility. After the initial excitement, matters quietened down and today most ethicists have little problem with this procedure. What is being done in using IVF is to help couples who long to have children of their own.

There is, however, a problem that arises concerning the fate of those fertilised ova, or embryos, which are not implanted in the woman. Are they discarded, or may experiments be carried out on them? These are significant ethical questions. Some people hold that as soon as an ovum is fertilised we already have to do with a human being and it should be accorded the respect due to human beings. Even among people who do not hold this view, the use of embryos for experimentation is not generally acceptable. If it is allowed at all, such experimentation should be severely restricted. On the question of what to do with "surplus" embryos, we should perhaps also take note of what happens in nature. "In natural human conception, 40 % of all fertilized ova never implant" (Nelson and Rohricht 1984:113). In other words, nature discards some fertilized ova. We do not regard the loss of these fertilised ova as deaths, so it would seem that we are illogical in regarding them to be so where surplus embryos are discarded.

The use of donor sperm or ova

A more controversial matter is using the sperm of a donor to impregnate a woman whose husband is infertile, usually referred to as AID, artificial insemination by donor.[2] Male infertility is the cause of 40 % of cases of marital infertility.

Another aspect of this matter which we must note is that, where both husband and wife are carriers of a recessive gene, causing their offspring to suffer from a genetically transmitted disease, use can be made of AID to obviate the problem. In the United States, the sperm is usually obtained from donors who are regarded as genetically "normal" – men who have fathered two normal children would typically be regarded as such. Individuals are chosen who belong to the same blood group as the husband and also those who generally resemble him. The practice is fairly common in infertility clinics. Some ethicists regard this as unacceptable practice because it brings a third party into the process. This is the reason for its condemnation by the Roman Catholic Church and some Protestant ethicists.[3] Some even go so far

---

1 In vitro means in glass, eg a dish or test tube.
2 To be distinguished from AIDS (Acquired Immune Deficiency Syndrome). AIH stands for Artificial Insemination Husband as opposed to AID which refers to Artificial Insemination Donor.
3 For a comprehensive discussion of these matters see the books by Schneider and Smith in the Bibliography.

as to call it adultery. Arguably, the latter position is an overstatement. Where the donor is not known to the couple one can hardly speak of adulterous introduction of a third party into the marital relationship. What is being said is that AID is an interference in, or even a breaking down of, the relationship between the spouses. Supporters of AID argue that they also hold to the exclusivity of the marriage relationship and disapprove of adultery, but that marital fidelity is not violated in this case. Where AID is the only means available for particular married couples to have a child, or to have healthy offspring, resorting to this method is often the expression of a deep love between the spouses. "Far from condemning AID as intrinsically adulterous, a more adequate Christian response will welcome its *possibilities* for expressing marital faithfulness and fulfilment in situations of involuntary sterility" (Nelson and Rohricht 1984:109). If this is so, the question that ought to be asked concerns the fitness of the couple for parenthood and of their acceptance of their infertility, essentially that of the husband. There have also been cases where a woman who does not ovulate receives donated ova which are then impregnated with the husband's sperm and placed in her uterus for a normal pregnancy. Here the role played by the third party is limited to the donation of ova. A further complication in this debate is the fact that in some countries there is a growing number of single women who wish to have children and resort to AID to fall pregnant. It is even more complex, and ethically dubious, where two lesbians who are living together use AID to "have a family" (Schneider 1985:19).

Genetic disorders

Earlier we mentioned the use of AID to overcome the probability of having children with genetic disorders where a couple both have a recessive gene. There are many genetic disorders, "scientists have now identified more than 3 000 genetic disorders" (Childs 1985:100). Many of these defects are not that serious or life-threatening, but "two to three percent ... show major genetic or congenital disease" (Childs 1985:100). There are four different types of inherited genetic disorders. We shall mention them without discussing them in detail. First, one of the parents possesses a dominant genetic trait which may be passed on to the offspring. There is usually a 50 % chance that the disease will be passed on to the next generation. They are generally mild in nature and only appear later in life. However, one of them, Huntingdon's chorea, is a progressive degeneration of the nervous system and is fatal. Because the symptoms appear late in life, people usually pass them on to their children before they become aware of them. The second type (mentioned above) is where there is a recessive gene in the genetic makeup of both parents, who themselves show no ill effects as a result of their condition. One in four of the children of these parents will develop the disease and, if they do not, they have a 50 % chance of being carriers of the defective gene. Cystic fibrosis is one of these disorders, and the life expectancy of sufferers is low, only half of them reach 20 years of age. A third type of disorder is linked to the sex of the person. Women with this defective gene have a 50–50 chance of passing it on to their children. Their daughters, who become carriers, do not suffer from the disease themselves but may pass it on to the next generation. Sons who inherit the gene will suffer from the disease. Males who carry the defective gene pass it on to all their daughters who become carriers, but not their sons. Two of the best-known diseases in this category are haemophilia, the tendency to severe bleeding, and muscular dystrophy. The fourth group apparently consists of all those genetic disorders which do not fall into the other categories. The best known among these are Down's syndrome, sometimes referred as mongolism, "characterized by mental retardation and a variety of physical abnormalities" (Childs 1985:103). In the face of these problems, genetic screening has developed to help people deal with the problems inherent in these diseases. Many of the carriers of genetic defects can be identified before people pass them on to the next generation. What do we do with that knowledge? Do we advise people not to have children if it is possible, or even probable, that their offspring may suffer from debilitating genetic diseases? Does one even advise some couples not to get married because it is not advisable that they have children, knowing that this is a deep desire in many people?

There is also an important negative side to the debate on genetic questions. Some people have advocated the use of genetic selection to breed superior human beings. Not only would parents be selected on the basis of their physical health but also on the basis of other features such as intellectual ability. In other words, people would be bred much in the same way as is done with animals. This is a frightening prospect and one that should be rejected out of hand. It would severely curtail human freedom. During the Nazi regime in Germany, Hitler's aim was to have a superior German race and proposed breeding what he regarded as a "master race". They did not have the theoretical knowledge about genetics available today but the prospect is alarming. Who would decide who would be allowed to breed and would the decision-makers manipulate the genetic make-up of people to fit their desired standards? Clearly this type of genetic engineering is fraught with ethical objections of the gravest kind and ought not to be countenanced.

Prenatal diagnosis

We now turn our attention to a next possible stage in the argument, that is, prenatal diagnosis. What this means is that using various medical procedures doctors can diagnose in utero several hundred abnormalities of pregnancy, although, in many cases doctors are not able to provide any sort of treatment until after birth. It is often possible, however, to establish whether the foetus is suffering from a genetic disorder which will result in the birth of a child who is suffering from some degree or form of mental or physical disorder. This is important, for example, in the case of Down's syndrome because, in women over the age of 35, the possibility of conceiving a child with Downs' syndrome is 1 in 400 pregnancies. "The chance that a woman at the age of 44 will conceive a child with Down's syndrome is 1 in 35, and at age 48, 1 in 12" (Santurri 1985:127). In order to identify genetic problems *in utero*, certain medical procedures are used. The problem is, however, that it is usually not possible to establish the severity of the condition during the prenatal diagnosis. One medical procedure which is used in prenatal diagnosis, amniocentesis, carries with it a small risk to the pregnant woman and a statistically slightly larger risk of injury to the foetus. This procedure entails inserting a needle through a woman's abdomen into her uterus and withdrawing some fluid from the amniotic sac.

As medical knowledge and skill increases, it is probable that more and more of the conditions that have been diagnosed will be treated *in utero*. The question then arises about the use of the knowledge gained from prenatal diagnosis. What do we do once we have established that the child will suffer from a mental and/or physical disability? At present this knowledge provides for two options only (except where the disability can be successfully treated *in utero*), that is, to carry the child to full term, and care for it afterwards, or to have an abortion on genetic grounds. The arguments in favour of the latter course of action are fairly strong. In the first place, bearing and rearing a handicapped child places emotional, financial and social burdens on the family. In the second place, such an abortion means that the resources of society do not have to be used for the special care and education of such children. It would also mean that where the symptoms of the disease appear only later in life, when such people have already passed on their genes to the next generation, abortion would improve the quality of life for future generations and save society's resources which would be needed to treat such people. Finally, where the quality of life of the child is very poor, and this is indeed the case with many genetic disorders, it may be argued that one is saving the child from pointless suffering. Many people find abortions completely unacceptable, others hold that it is acceptable only in very limited and specific circumstances, such as rape or incest. They see human life as being created in the divine image, which gives it a dignity and sanctity. For these people abortion is a denial of the sanctity of life, and therefore unacceptable. But, the decision to continue with the pregnancy to full term and bear the child can lead to problems mentioned above, particularly where the child is severely handicapped. We now turn to the question of what to do in these circumstances.

Severely handicapped new-born babies

In a mission hospital in Zululand a saintly old nun, who worked as a midwife for forty years, said that in such cases she made the child as comfortable as possible and gave it water, but no nutrition, allowing it to die. She believed that was the kindest and most loving thing to do. The poor rural families did not have the skills, facilities or resources to care for such children. They would therefore inevitably suffer and eventually die from neglect. In the United States, criteria have been laid down for action by medical and nursing personnel in such cases. Doctors will treat such new-borns, that includes appropriate nutrition, hydration and medication, if they believe that they can alleviate or correct life-threatening conditions.

> [But] there are three exceptions: (1) for infants who are irreversibly comatose;
> (2) for infants for whom such treatment would merely prolong dying, not cor-

rect all of the infant's life-threatening conditions, or be useless in ensuring the infant's survival; or (3) for infants for whom such treatment would be "virtually futile" and its provision would be inhumane (Nolan 1987:9).

Surrogate motherhood

The final matter in this discussion of human reproduction is the question of surrogate motherhood. In South Africa we had the singular case where a young woman was unable to carry her foetus to full term. She provided the ova which were impregnated with her husband's sperm, by the IVF method, and the ova was placed in her mother's uterus. Her mother then carried the foetuses, it was a multiple birth, to term and handed the children over to her daughter after birth. There have been cases where a woman's sister acted as surrogate mother. In these cases the motive was altruism, the surrogate mother was merely trying to help the childless woman, receiving nothing in return, except the gratitude of the childless woman and the satisfaction of having helped someone fulfil a deeply felt need. But in many cases the surrogate mother is a stranger:

> Most surrogate motherhood arrangements are similar in their basic structure. A woman, designated the surrogate, agrees to conceive a child via artificial insemination and to surrender the child at birth to the man who provided the semen (and to his wife, if he is married). It should be emphasized that the surrogate usually is severing all ties with the child, who is hers genetically. She allows the child's biological father to assume responsibility for the child's upbringing and permits the father's wife to adopt her husband's child. All this is agreed in advance, prior to conception, and may be formalized in a written contract. Ordinarily the surrogate will be compensated for at least her medical expenses (McDowell 1985:50ff).

There is a continuing debate about whether women should be paid a fee for acting as surrogate mothers. Some compare it to the selling of a baby. It has some similarities but it is not the same. It is much more like providing a service for a fee. The matter itself is very complicated. We have already mentioned a grandmother, a sister and an anonymous woman acting as surrogate. There is also the question of the relationship of the surrogate with the parents and the child after birth. In the case of the grandmother and an aunt there will surely be a continuing relationship. This may also be so in other cases of surrogacy.

Very often when this matter is discussed by theological ethicists they refer to the story of Abram, Sarai and Hagar. Sarai apparently could not bear children and told her husband to have a child with her servant Hagar (Gn 16:1–4). As noted in the introductory remarks to human reproduction, procreation was regarded as important to the women in the Bible, indeed it is regarded as important in its own right. According to the biblical witness, men and women were commanded to be fruitful and multiply. Children were to be regarded as gifts from God. Today, of course, we have to temper this with the concern for over-population and the depletion of the world's natural resources. The question of surrogacy must therefore be considered from a number of angles. One of them, mentioned in connection with AID, is the introduction of a third party into the relationship. Here it is more difficult than was the case with AID because another person is physically involved for the whole period of the pregnancy.

Where one regards the biological aspect of parenthood to be primary, the introduction of a third party for whatever reason will be regarded as unacceptable. However, where parenthood is seen as a voluntary choice made by people and the real ties that bind us together are regarded as emotional, mental and moral, various means of "having children", including surrogacy, can be justified. It would seem that biological parenthood fulfils a deep-seated urge in human beings. However, people can develop meaningful relationships with others who are not genetically related to them. Proof of this is the relationship that can develop between spouses, and between parents and adopted children. There are some ethicists who justify all these ways of having children but many ethicists have reservations about surrogacy and even AID.

What are some of the other ethical issues raised in medical ethics?

Freedom of Choice

To begin with, there is the issue of the freedom of choice for the individual. To what extent can Christians argue that all individuals have the right to make a choice concerning medical issues? Thus, for example, does a woman have the right to make the choice as to whether she wishes to give birth to a child or may she decide to have an abortion? If one argues that she does have the right to an abortion, the question arises whether there are certain ethical criteria according to which such a decision ought to be made. Further, what about the right to life of the foetus or unborn child?

Rights of the poor

This raises the issue of the rights of the poor, sick and vulnerable. If it is true, as argued by the Old Testament prophets, that the rich and powerful have a responsibility towards the poor and powerless (symbolised by the orphans, widows and aliens within Israelite society), how ought the poor, sick and vulnerable of today to be treated? Do they also have the right to nutrition and medicine and do they also have rights even though they may be considered to be the "least" in any given society? Thus, within our present context, can it be said that health care (broadly understood) is itself a right?

The right to life

What then about the right to life itself? The right to life is enshrined in the new South African Constitution. But it is easier to state that citizens ought to have a right to life than it is to ensure that such rights can actually be enjoyed by the citizens of a country. The issue of the right to life of a foetus has already been mentioned, but what about capital punishment? On the one hand, the new Constitution rejects capital punishment and yet it permits the termination of any pregnancy up to 12 weeks. Is this position ethically consistent?

With regard to euthanasia, it can be argued that advances in medical technology have now created a problem which medical personnel, terminally ill patients, and their family and friends have to face. The question of euthanasia is a question which has arisen in a First World, largely urban, situation. In rural areas, where the medical facilities are not as sophisticated as in the cities, people do not have easy access to this new technology. This means that those people would more probably die than be connected to a life-support system. Where the technology is available, persons who would have died "naturally" 50 years ago, can now be kept alive artificially for an indefinite period of time. This raises the question of whether it is right to switch off a life-support machine which is assisting a severely brain damaged person to breathe. Ought a person's right to life be protected – artificially – at great financial and emotional cost (see Hulley 1997:45–56).

The right to know

One of the matters that affects all of us who consult members of the medical profession is the right to know what the situation is in respect of our condition. Our first contact with the medical world is usually with the general practitioner whom we consult when we take ill. How much do the people whom we consult tell us about our illness or about the prognosis for recovery? Here we do not refer to minor illnesses such as influenza, commonly called the flu, but about more serious illnesses that could be life-threatening. It is important that we be properly informed about the dangers we face. So, for example, even with a relatively minor illness such as influenza, we should not undertake strenuous exercise because the virus could affect the heart muscle.

One of the instances where there is often concealment rather than honest revelation of the actual condition is when people suffer from terminal cancer. Neither the doctor nor the family of the patient mention the word in the person's presence, and they often speak as if recovery is probable. People talk about "what we are going to do when you come home", knowing full well that it is out of the question. Part of the problem is that one is not sure how the patient is going to take the news. At a recent oncology conference a psychiatrist said that the most dangerous time for people is when they have just heard that they have cancer. It is in this period, when they are still coming to terms with the news, that they are most likely to attempt suicide – if they contemplate it at all. After they have accepted the fact of their illness, they show a determination to fight back. It is the fear of the possible destructive reaction to the news that keeps people from divulging the truth to them. This, however, is to treat people as irresponsible infants who are unable to take decisions for themselves. It is a negation of their autonomy. This is perhaps the most important aspect of the right to know.

There is also a significant personal aspect to the matter. Not accepting the fact that an illness is terminal, and openly talking about it, also deprives people of the opportunity of sorting out their personal affairs. We do not mean personal financial matters, although those are also important, but matters relating to interpersonal relationships and even matters of faith. When one counsels the bereaved they view the opportunity, or lack of such opportunity, to sort out relationships before someone dies as being of primary importance. Where there has been a breakdown in a relationship which has not been resolved, it adds significantly to the experience of grief for those who are left behind. Conversely, when people have been able to set matters straight with regard to these relationships, it is a source of great comfort to all concerned.

Motives, goals and consequences

In the preceding sections, attention has been focused on the issue of rights and the ethical rights and wrongs of medical issues. Ethical theorists refer to this as a deontological approach. Important though this approach is, we must also consider other ethical criteria. Those employing a teleological approach would speak in terms of the motives, goals and consequences that are central to those complex medical ethical issues. Thus, with regard to abortion, is the motive to seek to avoid the consequences of unthinking promiscuity or is the motive to save the mental sanity of a 14 year old child who has been raped by her friend's father and who is now pregnant through no fault of her own? In the case of genetic manipulation, is the *goal* to produce a so-called "master race" which can be used to pursue evil nationalistic aims or is the goal to prevent the conception and birth of severely mentally or physically retarded infants? Finally, with respect to *consequences*, if a happily married couple are assisted by have children, can this be thought to be a morally bad result? Having said this, however, it must be borne in mind that not all methods of human reproduction are morally neutral.

Concluding Remarks

We have merely touched on some issues raised in connection with the ethics of medical care and medical practice. In our generation AIDS (Acquired Immune Deficiency Syndrome) is creating great social and ethical problems. We have not discussed it at length in this book. One of these problems which has caused a great controversy in South Africa is the attempt to develop a remedy to cure the condition. Under what conditions may experiments be carried out to test the drugs? Can such experiments be carried out on humans? What about testing on animals?

In recent years there has been a resurgence of malaria. Areas that were free of the disease-carrying mosquito, Anopheles, have once again been declared danger zones. But the problem is greater than that. The insecticide previously used to kill the mosquito, DDT (dichlorodiphenyltrichloroethane), has been shown to have a major negative impact on the environment, eg birds which ingested DDT laid eggs without shells. We are thus faced with the question: "Do we have a right to safeguard our health at the cost of the environment?"

Every aspect of life which impacts on mental and physical wellbeing potentially raises questions which have ethical dimensions. Health and medical ethics impact on a wide spectrum of human experience. We trust, though, that the issues raised in this brief discussion have highlighted some of the key medical issues of our time.

BIBLIOGRAPHY

Childs, JM. 1985. "Genetic screening and counselling", in Schneider, E (ed). *Questions about the beginning of life: Christian appraisals of seven bioethical issues.* Minneapolis: Augsburg.

Grenz, S. 1990. *Sexual Ethics: A Biblical Perspective.* London and Dallas: Word Publishing.

Hulley, L. 1997. "Genadedood", in Jones, C and Hulley, L. *Wonder jy ook oor: gedagtes oor omstrede kwessies van ons dag.* Kaapstad: Lux Verbi.

Hulley, L, Kretzschmar, L and Pato, L (eds). 1996. *Archbishop Tutu: Prophetic Witness in South Africa.* Cape Town: Human and Rousseau.

Lammers, Stephen E and Verhey, Allen. 1987. *On Moral Medicine: Theological Perspectives in medical ethics.* Grand Rapids: Eerdmans.

Lawrence, Gilbert. 1994. "Medical ethics", in C Villa-Vicencio and J de Gruchy (eds). *Ethics in Context.* Cape Town: David Philip.

MaCquarrie, J and Childress, J (eds). 1986. *A new dictionary of Christian ethics.* London: SCM.

McDowell, J. 1985. "Surrogate Motherhood", in Schneider, E (ed). *Questions about the beginning of life: Christian appraisals of seven bioethical issues.* Minneapolis: Augsburg.

Nelson, JB and Rohricht, JS. 1984. *Human Medicine. Ethical perspectives on today's medical issues.* Minneapolis: Augsburg.

Nolan, K. 1987. "Imperiled newborns", in *Hastings Center Report*, Vol 17:6: 5–32.

Santurri, EN. 1985. "Prenatal diagnosis: Some moral considerations", in Schneider, E (ed). *Questions about the beginning of life: Christian appraisals of seven bioethical issues.* Minneapolis: Augsburg.

Schneider, E. 1985. "Artificial insemination", in Schneider, E (ed). *Questions about the beginning of life: Christian appraisals of seven bioethical issues.* Minneapolis: Augsburg.

Schotman, P. 1989. "Bioethics and human reproduction", in *Tijdschrift voor filosofie en theologie* Vol 50:4: 414–429.

Smith, HL. 1970. *Ethics and the new medicine.* Nashville: Abingdon.

Uniacke, S. 1987. "In vitro fertilization and the right to reproduce", in *Bioethics* Vol 1:3: 241–254.

United Nations 1948. *Universal Declaration of Human Rights.*

PART 3

Social problems we face in society

8

What is social ethics?

Mokgethi Motlhabi

Several approaches may be taken in attempting to find an answer to the question, "What is social ethics"? One approach may be to determine what a student of social ethics studies to qualify as a practitioner. The other may be to find out what a qualified social ethicist does in practising or implementing his/her discipline. We may go further and ask what kind of literature is available in the field of social ethics and what it teaches us about the discipline. As an introduction to the study of social ethics, this chapter will not restrict itself to any one of these approaches, but will try to answer the questions posed by all of them. It will be divided into six sections under the following headings: the study of social ethics; ethics, morality and social ethics; the task of social ethics; approaches to social ethics: selected "case studies"; social ethics and the Bible; and the subject matter of social ethics. A brief summary of the discussion will be given in the conclusion.

The study of social ethics

Students of social ethics – Christian social ethics, to be precise – normally come to this discipline with a background in theological studies. The majority of them are ordained ministers of religion who, eo facto, have studied most theological disciplines such as the Old Testament, the New Testament, church history, practical theology, systematic theology or dogmatics and Christian ethics. Some of these disciplines are, naturally, studied in greater depth than others, with one or two as major subjects. All these disciplines may be considered to form the base for the study of social ethics. As such, however, some of them have a greater contribution to make than others and are similarly more relied upon. In this regard, Christian ethics comes to the fore. It draws its insights particularly and to varying degrees from systematic theology and the two biblical Testaments. While the different disciplines of theology do shed some light on the study of social ethics, it is chiefly the hermeneutic task of systematic theology which is useful for social ethics as a part of Christian ethics.

As Christian ethics is part of the general discipline of ethics, philosophically understood, it is also important for a student of social ethics to study philosophical ethics in order to determine what light the latter can or does shed on the field of social ethics. In addition to Christian and philosophical ethics, social ethics requires the assistance of social sciences such as sociology, anthropology, economics, political studies, and history for the efficient performance of its task. As in the case of the theological disciplines, however, not all these areas need to be studied in depth. Some theologians have spoken of the need to have at least a working knowledge of them, especially those with direct relevance to the task of social ethics. Gibson Winter, among others, is aware of the possible implications of a broad study focus for social ethics. Hence he suggests with some caution that a social ethicist, in effect, is "first and foremost an ethicist but inseparably a social scientist or consumer of social science" (Winter 1968:12).

As the role of the social sciences in social ethics is chiefly analytical and interpretive of social matters, some of them acquire more prominence than others in social ethics, depending on the needs of a particular social setting. Social ethics, therefore, is an "interdisciplinary discipline." What this means is that none of its constituent disciplines are considered in isolation from the others. All of them contribute to its existence as a discipline. Further, being interdisciplinary means that social ethics seeks to "furnish an interdisciplinary approach to problems of social order, integrating science, ethics, and theology" (Winter 1968:5).

One of the leading figures in exploring the method of social ethics in America, Walter Muelder, emphasises precisely its interdisciplinary nature. According to him, Christian social ethics is

> not theological ethics with applications to current social questions made apart from philosophical and scientific analysis. It is not even when the problems discussed are a social presentation of general theoretical ethics with biblical sanctions. It is not sociology of religion or any other behavioural science. It is interdisciplinary (1966:20).

This means that students of social ethics are committed to undertake "joint, supplementary, or complementary theoretical and empirical studies in theology, philosophical ethics, behavioural and historical sciences." In this way, Christian social ethics seeks "emergent coherence" (Muelder 1966:20). What Muelder says here corresponds to Winter's view: the emergent coherence that he speaks of is the result of "integrating science, ethics, and theology," in the words of Winter.

Moral judgements, especially social ones, cannot be made in a vacuum. We cannot, for instance, respond to each moral situation by merely asking, "What does the Bible say?" As Muelder puts it,

> We cannot solve hunger's moral crises by saying "Give ye them to eat" or "When saw we thee ahungered?" Population control problems are not solved by citing "Increase and multiply" or "Be not anxious about the morrow." Poverty does not abate with recalling that "The poor ye have always with you" (1983:288–89).

We need to be clear about the tangible facts of the situation, and for this we need social analysis. This is mediated through the social sciences. The "descriptive generalizations of science are needed by the ethicist in discerning the problems of moral order" (Winter 1968:12). We also need to be clear about the criteria we employ in our judgments and decisions. It is the task of theological and philosophical ethics to provide these criteria. Hence the contribution of theology and philosophy to social ethics can be said to be that of illumination. According to Deats (1972:33), it is "illumination through historically derived loyalties, traditions, insights and categories of interpretation." Philosophy and theology also contribute "categories and procedures of logical consistency and rational coherence."

It has been implied – implicitly – that the scope of study suggested here for social ethics might be too broad. This approach has not gone unchallenged by other social ethicists in the early 1970s. A Harvard professor of social ethics, Ralph Potter, launched a stinging attack against Walter Muelder and his idea of an interdisciplinary approach. He charged that such an approach reduced its adherents to the status of "ridiculous dabblers and dilettantes, eager for interdisciplinary work but unable to define their own discipline" (1972:98). While it may be difficult to imagine how a person can be "fully steeped" in all the suggested relevant disciplines, as Potter suggests, it is equally difficult to imagine how social ethics can be done without some amount of exposure to some of them. Winter's view of the social ethicist as a consumer of social science is, at least, the minimum requirement. It must be remembered that some of these disciplines, being preparatory for ethical evaluation, often function in the background or implicitly in our ethical reflection. Besides, exposure to most of them is sometimes obtained as part of the undergraduate programme (depending on the syllabuses of various institutions), some of them being possible majors.

Potter's concern is that the interdisciplinary approach suggested by Muelder and others leads to lack of sufficient focus as well as depth. As far as focus is concerned, according to Potter (1972:93), "Some [social ethicists] accentuate the qualifier, 'Christian'; others place stress upon the second modifier, 'social.' There are those who emphasize that Christian social ethics is a subfield of the general philosophical discipline of ethics." Each of these emphases, taken on its own, understandably has certain implications for the practice of social ethics. It has already been seen how Muelder reacts to such tendencies. As far as depth goes, it is Potter's opinion that an interdisciplinary approach to social ethics can offer no meaningful contribution to the field through half-witted employment of each constituent discipline. Left to themselves, each of these disciplines obviously makes a far greater contribution in its own area. Why not, he suggests, similarly confine social ethics to ethics. With only a little knowledge of each constituent discipline it may be possible for the ethicist to become a kind of "jack of all" disciplines, but certainly master of none. The point Potter seems to miss, however, is that these disciplines are not studied for their own sakes, but rather for the contribution that they can make jointly to a different discipline of social ethics.

In spite of his criticism, Potter does not seem able entirely to escape the need for an interdisciplinary approach. What he proposes as an alternative consequently amounts to a less noble, but nevertheless interdisciplinary, approach. According to

Potter, social ethicists must, as already seen, remain confined to the discipline of ethics. Their main role would thus be to concern themselves with the logic of the moral argument (Potter 1972:105). However, they can find greater benefit for their work by staying in dialogue with experts from the other disciplines which may contribute to the successful implementation of own discipline (Potter 1972:111, 113). Thus Potter seems to take a round-about way – filled with controversy – to arrive at much the same, though seemingly less appealing, conclusion that Muelder and his supporters are advocating.

Notwithstanding this tacit acknowledgement of the need somehow to involve other disciplines, it is not quite true to say that an interdisciplinary approach to social ethics cannot make an effective contribution to the discipline. Failure to use an interdisciplinary approach will result in undermining the relevance or significance of insights that can be derived from the constituent disciplines of a multidisciplinary discipline. Secondly, the contribution of social ethics as a discipline inheres precisely in its interdisciplinary nature. It is its constituent disciplines taken together which make social ethics what it is; and it is the light which they together shed on the task of social ethics which contributes to its effectiveness. Without this joint effort, there can be no social ethics as a discipline. Consequently, it may be said that the chief contribution of social ethics as a discipline is in its blending together of these various disciplines to facilitate arrival at more meaningful decisions and resolutions of the social moral predicament.

Ethics, morality and social ethics

While thus, by implication, insisting on the relative distinctiveness of social ethics from the traditional discipline of ethics – be it philosophical or theological – it is perhaps proper to go a step further and examine another distinction which will become relevant in this discussion as we proceed. It is the distinction between ethics and morality. Although the terms "ethics" and "morals" are often used interchangeably, it is important to note that their import is not the same. We may discuss their significance here without going into their etymological definitions and evolutions to their present meanings.

Strictly speaking, morality pertains to the conduct of life, while ethics pertains to the principles behind such conduct. Morality relates to actual behaviour on the basis of ethical principles; ethics relates to the theory of the principles governing moral behaviour. In other words, ethics deals with what it takes for behaviour to be regarded as good or bad, right or wrong, just or unjust, obligatory or optional, etc. Morality is actual behaviour based on our knowledge of these principles – which are principles of acceptable and unacceptable behaviour. Consequently, ethics – as a theory – is in the service of morality, but is not morality. Morality, in turn, receives guidance from ethics and at the same time provides it with material for reflection; but morality is not ethics.

There is an inextricable bond between ethics and morality without necessarily being the same or one. The result is that true morality can take place only within the context of some ethic, however basic the theory of behaviour – that is, however elementary the "knowledge of good and evil." The mere knowledge and ability to act on the basis of our knowledge of right and wrong means that morality presupposes ethics. Hence Winter, applying a similar argument to social ethics, states: "Reflections on the rightness [or wrongness] of ... communal arrangements, however rudimentary, are social ethics in embryo" (1968:3–4). By the same token, ethics can exist meaningfully only with a view to moral practice: "Ethics becomes practical in the choice situation. It is when an individual must choose between the acts possible in a given situation that he can and must put his ethical theory into practice" (Wellman 1975:285). Its goal is to inform moral behaviour and so ensure that it is the best type of behaviour possible. It follows that without ethics – without the knowledge of or reflection on "good and evil," right and wrong behaviour cannot be considered to be either moral or immoral. Rather, it is amoral, which means that it is of no moral significance.

As an academic discipline, ethics is a little removed from the ethical demands of everyday life. It is a systematic reflection on the theory or theories of good conduct. Such reflection generally leads to the establishment of an ethical system. This means that at an academic level ethics is beyond the simple "knowledge of good and evil" and has a much deeper meaning. For instance, theoretically the very fact of moral knowledge may be put into question: How do I know that a particular act is right and another one wrong? In other words, what makes right **right** and wrong **wrong**? I may answer that an act is right because it conforms to God's commandment, and vice versa. Since this answer presupposes the existence of God, the question may proceed further to try to establish my basis for believing in the existence of God and what God has to do with morality. Hence it becomes clear that there is more than one presupposition in the theory that an act is right or wrong because God either approves or disapproves of it. In considering these presuppositions, we are moving into an area of ethics known as *metaethics*. Thus to argue that it is wrong to kill a human being because this violates God's commandment presupposes, according to Wellman (1975:316), three facts: (1) that there is a God, (2) that he promulgates moral laws, (3) that human beings ought to obey his laws. The theoretical questions leading to these presuppositions are: Is there any Divine Lawgiver? Do we have a moral obligation to obey the commands of God? What is the ground of obligation? It is obvious from these considerations that there is more in the academic discipline of ethics than the mere "knowledge" of right and wrong.

The academic discipline of ethics also deals with more than one theory of ethics. A collection of such theories forms an ethical system. Thus an ethical theory would consist of theories such as those of obligation, value, the end of the law, rights, moral knowledge, etc (Wellman 1975:317). Some of the well-known philosophical theories of ethics are teleology, deontology, utilitarianism, egoism, intuitionism, among others. These theories are studied historically, systematically, and comparatively in the academic discipline of ethics. The emphasis is always on theory rather than on practice, though the former necessarily implies the latter. It follows that a practitioner of ethics is largely a theorist rather than an activist. As a private individual, however, s/he is occasionally called upon to put his/her theory into practice. More often than not it is the activist, as opposed to the ethicist, who is the consumer of the latter's theory and the one who gives it form by putting it into practice (see Wellman 1975:323).

Like ethics in general, social ethics is a theoretical discipline. Therefore, it focuses on the systematic study of moral order in social organization, in institutions, and in communities. The systematic study of social ethics means determining how the different disciplines constituting social ethics can be made to cohere in working toward the resolution of social problems and also directing this process of reflection. The results of such theoretical and systematic study, as in the case of general ethics, are adopted and used by various social actors – individual activists, churches, social organizations, policy makers, and others in the determination of social policy. In Winter's words, "Systematic social ethics should be a resource for an informed citizenry and its public representatives, although a market for their products has yet to be developed" (1968:9). Social policy, therefore, is to social ethics what moral practice is to ethics in general. What the social ethicist is doing is "considering problems of practice and organization from an ethical perspective, but he has a commitment to clarity of concepts, to testing the logical consistency of evaluative statements, and to developing the systematic unity of the discipline" (Winter 1968:9). This anticipates the next section of this discussion on the task of social ethics.

The task of social ethics

By now it is obvious that the task of social ethics focuses more on the theory of behaviour than on its actual practice. Paul Deats has described this task as being "to work to improve the quality and clarity of public dialogue and debate over ethical decisions" (1972:36). For Potter, in similar vein, the social ethicist must "direct his energy and skill to the resolution of actual confusions and controversies as they occur in the lives of individuals and groups engaged in deliberation and justification of behaviour" (1972:94). Gibson Winter (1968:15) goes a step further, emphasizing the practical implications of social ethics. The social ethicist, he writes,

> cultivates the practical integrity of the society by challenging its inequities and bringing moral considerations to bear on its policies. Practice in the society is the material of his reflections, even as practice is the aim of his work. Social ethics is a practical discipline.

These views on the task of social ethics may be inferred directly or indirectly from the preceding pages. The following key words are noteworthy: improving the *clarity of ethical decisions; resolution of confusions and controversies* in ethical deliberation; bringing *moral considerations* to bear on *policies*. This focus clearly corresponds with the distinction made above between ethics and morals: it identifies social ethics primarily with theoretical reflection.

In simple terms, we may see the task of social ethics as being at least four-fold:

1   to reflect on ideal types of human conduct and social organization, as well as on the norms and values required to attain these ideals;
2   to deliberate on those aspects of social life which impact negatively on accepted social, moral and religious norms and values, thus causing harm and conflict in the community;
3   to seek to arrive – through philosophical, theological and scientific analysis, on the one hand, and ethical deliberation, on the other – at social solutions consonant with acceptable moral standards and so conducive to harmonious and happy social life for all;
4   to work, through providing society with moral ideals and principles of decision-making, toward the establishment of a truly responsible society.

According to this description, social ethics has to do with reflection on the ideal state of living in society. For life to be ideal it must conform to certain moral and social norms and values. If such conformity is disturbed, there is disharmony and conflict, leading to unhappiness. It is the task of social ethics to work, reflectively, toward the preservation of conformity and harmony in society. Such reflection encompasses suitable norms and values that guide society in its quest. When such conformity and harmony are disturbed, social ethics is to work toward their restoration through reflection which reaffirms and relegitimates the norms and values which have been violated.

Social ethics also appeals to certain principles of moral decision-making. These principles may be in the form of laws or maxims and rules that regulate action. To relegitimate norms and values is to clarify once more why they are important for society and why it is necessary to conform to them. Moral principles, on the other hand, outline the steps that have to be followed for the achievement or restoration of set values. They are universal ethical principles which social ethics translates, through reflection, into "concretely specified situational duties" (see Stamey, quoted by Deats 1972:39). Being principles of decision-making, they are more concerned with how to think in order to bring about action than with moral action itself.

Social ethics, therefore, operates at four basic levels: (1) the level of analysis (scientific, philosophical, and theological); (2) the level of norms and values; (3) the level of moral principles/moral laws; and (4) the level of decision-making. Scientific analysis, as already seen, reveals the facts of the situation while philosophical and theological analysis is for both the clarification and interpretation of concepts; norms and values are to be discovered or established for the maintenance or restoration of social equilibrium; moral principles are necessary for aiding in the decision-making process, while decision-making is the penultimate step toward effecting desirable social action for the attainment of sought values. Actual social action, however, is beyond the scope of social ethics and falls under the sphere of social policy. Social ethics, as already stated, is concerned more with how to decide rather than with decision-making itself.

These levels of social ethics, as of ethics in general, presuppose certain social, moral, and religious beliefs which inform them implicitly. Such beliefs are referred to as world-views and loyalties by Charles Kammer III (1988) and as moral presumptions by J Philip Wogaman (1976). While implicitly underlying the ethical process, it often becomes necessary to bring these beliefs also to the level of analysis, along with what Kammer calls the "experiential and empirical elements" (1988:28). This is for the purpose of completely laying bare the facts of the situation. It is probably what Pickering (1978:218) is referring to when he says that the first task of social ethics is "uncovering those socially embodied and culturally articulated structures of faith and reason." According to him, such structures of faith and reason

> will be found wherever there are real social relations which embody, imply, and evoke principles, values, beliefs, symbols, rituals and associations which represent a claim as to the referred and pre-eminent modes of being by which a community either is or should be characterized (Pickering 1978:221).

The main feature of these structures is that they are taken for granted and, therefore, tend to be seen as a way of life – however evil or misguided they may be. It is only by being brought up to the surface through proper scientific analysis that they can be adequately morally assessed.

The task of social ethics, in the final analysis, is not to dictate social policy but to guide it. Nor does it compel action by virtue of its objective aim. As Wellman (1975:322) puts it: "An ethical theory does not tell a person what to do in any given situation, but neither is it completely silent [as already shown]. It tells him what to consider in making up his mind what to do", should an occasion present itself. It is the task of ethics in general and social ethics in particular to provide guidance for the solution of practical moral problems that arise for any human being or social group (see Wellman 1975:16).

Approaches to social ethics: Selected "case studies"

There are various categories of works on social ethics reflecting differences in approach. We may distinguish among works by professional social ethicists and theologians, those reflecting the actions of religious social activists, and those by institutions such as churches and their organizations, among others. As seen in the preceding argument by Potter, uniformity of approach in each of the categories cannot be taken for granted. It also needs to be pointed out that many other works and activities which go by the name of social ethics fall far short of the requirements of social ethics – at least if we accept the recommendations of Muelder and his followers.

According to Gibson Winter, in what appears to be a restatement of Muelder's perspective, social ethics is characterized by three elements. These are already implicit in the foregoing discussion. They are factual descriptions, evaluative norms, and religious perspectives (Winter 1968:4). The first involves descriptions of social conditions; the second, norms for evaluating their moral worth; and the third, interpretations of human fulfilment. According to the discussion above, it is obvious that the first element may be termed the scientific or analytical level; the second, the ethical or normative level; and the third, the philosophico-theological or interpretive level. Winter proceeds: "[d]ifferent perspectives on social ethics are ways of organizing these three elements – social conditions, evaluative norms, and religious vision. Each perspective makes one of these elements decisive in its view of man" (Winter 1968:15).

It is to be assumed that works by professional social ethicists or theologians contain all these elements, to whatever varying extents and emphases. Many of them, however, tend to take social conditions for granted and place their emphases more on ethics (evaluative norms) and theology (religious vision). Hence they do not employ the social sciences – nor consider them necessary – for social analysis and fuller exposure of social conditions before interpreting and evaluating them theologically and ethically. Their ethical evaluation is based largely on personal experience and observation of the social conditions. Besides, the ethical approach employed also tends to be largely biblically derived, with no room being left for philosophical moral principles and general philosophical analysis. Such an approach is typical of writings on social ethics by many theologians in the history of the church, with a few notable exceptions with regard to the use of philosophical along with theological analysis.

For many of these theologians, social ethics was largely academic and cerebral. It came from people who, from their personal witness of social problems, were concerned to testify to what the word of God had to say about these problems. Hence they wrote works on private property, slavery, sexual ethics, love of neighbour(s), duties to the state, etc. They assumed generally that quotations from the Bible were sufficient authority to rule on the acceptability or non-acceptability of a particular practice. Their approach to social ethics, therefore, was that of an "ethic of biblical application" – that is, an ethics based on the application of relevant biblical commands to the social situation. Many more works on social ethics today continue to follow this approach. Hence much of social ethics today continues to be largely superficial in its social appraisal and more like sermonizing than social ethics in its approach to moral issues.

Tutu and Boesak

It may be pointed out that most of the social ethics of religious activists is of this nature. Paradoxically, some of it has had more impact than that of academic theologians. We may cite in this regard the relatively successful campaigns – *other factors considered* – of theologians like Martin Luther King, Jr. in the United States and Archbishop Tutu and Allan Boesak in South Africa. When Archbishop Tutu lamented that "Apartheid is evil, totally, without remainder!" (Tutu 1983:125) he was speaking mainly from both personal experience and observation of the effects of apartheid on black people in South Africa. He was not concerned about the strict scientific analysis of the social conditions and whatever psychological or other underlying effects these might possibly have on the victims of apartheid. The physical consequences, on the other hand, were there for everyone to witness:

> ... [T]he children starve in resettlement camps, the somewhat respectable name for apartheid's dumping grounds for the pathetic casualties of this vicious and evil system ... [P]eople die mysteriously in detention. ... [They] are condemned to a twilight existence as non-persons by an arbitrary bureaucratic act of banning them ... (Tutu 1983:125).

However, the total human consequences – including the psychological ones – could not be explained simply in this way. This could only happen through analysis by the socio-behavioural sciences.

To say that apartheid is evil is to pass a moral judgement on it. The standard or criterion used by Tutu for doing so is biblical and based on God's love for his people, and not a philosophical principle or determined by the human condition itself. Hence he writes: "Apartheid is evil for at least three reasons ...", of which we need only mention one here:

> The Bible declares right at the beginning that human beings are created in the image and likeness of God ... And what makes any human being valuable therefore is not any biological characteristic ... Apartheid exalts a biological quality which is a total irrelevancy, to the status of what determines the value, the worth of a human being (Tutu 1983:133–34).

It is immediately obvious that the source of knowledge about this God and God's plan for humanity is the Bible. The Bible further, according to Tutu, provides a religious vision based on the interpretation of the "divine intention":

> I will show that the Bible describes God as creating the universe to be a cosmos and not a chaos, a cosmos in which harmony, order, fellowship, communion, peace and justice would reign and that this divine intention was disturbed by sin ... God then sent His Son to restore that primordial harmony to effect reconciliation (Tutu 1983:125).

Hence we detect in these two quotations an emphasis on, in Winter's words, both the evaluative norm and the religious vision. In the absence of a much fuller analysis and exposure of the social conditions, however, the solution to be expected from Tutu's approach could depend only on moral suasion rather than on a step-by-step practical recommendation backed by philosophical, theological, and moral principles. Without other appeals – such as those of economic sanctions, etc – and social alliances, therefore, such a social ethic could not have achieved its purpose.

Boesak's approach to social ethics is more rounded than that of Tutu and reflects more clearly Winter's elements of social ethics. Prefacing his call for apartheid (as a form of racism) to be declared a heresy at the 1982 meeting of the World Alliance of Reformed Churches (WARC) in Ottawa, Canada, he gives this social analysis of racism:

Yet we must have some idea of what we are talking about, if only to give our discussion some direction. First of all, racism is an ideology of racial domination that incorporates beliefs in cultural or inherent biological inferiority of a particular ethos. It uses such beliefs to justify and prescribe unequal treatment of that group. In other words, racism is not merely attitudinal, but structural. It is not merely a vague feeling of racial superiority, but a system of *domination*, furnished with social, political, and economic structures of domination. To put it another way, racism excludes groups on the basis of race or colour. It is, first, exclusion on the basis of skin colour or ethnicity, but exclusion is then cemented into place for the purpose of assuring subjugation ... It is clear that racism cannot be understood in individual, personal terms only. It must [also] be understood in its historical perspective and in its structural manifestations (Boesak 1984:110–111).

The evaluative norm is expressed as follows:

Racism is sin. It denies the creatureliness of others. It denies the truth that all human beings are made in the image of the God and Father of Jesus Christ. As a result, racism not only denies the unity of all humankind; it also refuses to acknowledge that being in the image of God means having 'dominion over the earth.' ... (Boesak 1984:112).

Finally, Boesak's (1984:113) religious vision is reflected in the words:

Through his life, death and resurrection Christ has reconciled human beings to God and to themselves; he has broken down the wall of partition and enmity, and so has come our peace (Eph 2:14). He has brought us together in the one Lord, one faith, one baptism, one God who is the Father of us all (Eph 4:5–6).

Consequently, according to Boesak, the action that his *social ethical analysis* calls for – to facilitate compliance with the given *norm* and so lead to the *religious vision* expressed – is that apartheid should be declared a heresy. The underlying assumption is that such declaration will hurt the supporters of apartheid, who regard their country as a Christian state. In doing so, it will prompt them to prevail upon their leaders to change their evil policies. Further, it is assumed that being regarded as a pariah nation by other nations of the world will shame them into mending their ways and abandoning their evil social practices and policies.

The Catholic Church and the World Council of Churches

The third category of works on social ethics is that of the social teachings of the churches and their organizations. Among these may be counted the papal encyclicals of the Catholic Church, the ecumenical social teachings of the World Council of Churches (WCC) as well as those of various national church councils – eg, the South African Council of Churches and the South African Catholic Bishops' Conference. Although not a church organization, but a Christian social movement, the Social Gospel movement of the late 19th century and early 20th century in America and Europe also reflected a Christian social ethic. The works of all these groups reflect to varying extents and emphases the elements of social ethics suggested by Winter.

In Catholic social teachings, represented chiefly by the papal social encyclicals, these elements have often been expressed by the words "See, Judge, Act." Here "judge" seems to represent both the norm and the religious vision. In Winter the "act" aspect, which is missing, is probably assumed in the religious vision, because the vision functions as the motivating force. Since the first social encyclical of Pope Leo XIII, *Rerum Novarum*, in the late 1800s, the papal encyclicals have included a social analysis of some sort. "Seeing" thus meant more than just witnessing through the eyes. It meant analysing the causes, effects, and implications of social conditions as resulting from national social policies.

Initially the social sciences were not used to any great extent, if used at all. The social conditions were seemingly largely experienced and observed, directly or indirectly, by the writer and/or his assistants. Gradually, however, and especially since the early 1960s, following the Second Vatican Council (Vatican II), the social sciences began to be regarded as indispensable, analytical tools. Their role was to reveal more fully the facts of the social situation requiring moral evaluation. This was in accordance with Pope John XXIII's exhortation for the church to "read the signs of the times." Lately, in the papacy of John-Paul II, the Pope has reaffirmed the key role of the social sciences as follows: The church "reads events as they unfold in the course of history. She thus seeks to lead people to respond, with the support also of rational reflection and of the human sciences, to their vocation as responsible builders of earthly society" (1990:2, 1). Ricardo Antoncich (1980:59), a Latin American moral theologian, affirms this use of the social sciences in Catholic social teaching as follows:

> Insofar as the church's social teaching is concerned with specific areas of ethics (the social and political), it also has links with other non-theological forms of knowledge, namely, the social sciences which explain and render an account of social phenomena.

"Judging," or the evaluative norm of papal encyclicals, was (based on) natural law and scripture. The interpretation of natural law was based chiefly on the writings of St Thomas Aquinas, which had a long history behind them (see Crowe 1974:261, 271–2). According to Aquinas, there are four types of law: the eternal law, the natural law, the divine law, and the human law. The eternal law is self-explanatory. It is seen as general and diffuse, and having been with God since the beginning of time. As such it cannot be known by human beings. The eternal law, however, may be said to be reflected to some degree in nature in the form of natural law. Natural law itself is explained as the general course of nature as reflected in the world of natural phenomena and events. In this way it can be known by human beings through the use of reason. From this knowledge they are able to formulate human law, which may be both moral and legislative. Although, according to Aquinas, human law is a derivation of natural law, and ultimately of eternal law, it cannot be a definitive expression of eternal law because human knowledge is limited and affected by sin. For eternal law to be known by human beings it has to be made more specific. This happens through the divine law. Scripture is the source of such divine law, which is nothing but "particular determinations" or specifications of eternal law. In the same way, human law is nothing but particular determinations of natural law.

Scripture, therefore, is seen as containing the primary evaluative norm of Catholic social ethics. It also provides the religious vision, which may be expressed in the words adopted by John XXIII as the title of his second encyclical, *Pacem in Terris*. The culmination of this vision may be said to be the post-worldly *visio beata* or beatific vision. Natural law was a secondary, but nevertheless also important, norm. The impact of natural law in the church's social teaching has, however, receded since Vatican II, at the same time as the influence of the social sciences was gaining prominence. Prior to this recession, both scripture and natural law were used jointly to evaluate the social condition after it had been described and analysed – not necessarily scientifically. In doing so, they urged compliance with moral principles that were aimed at the ideal state of life for human beings both now and in the hereafter.

While the main social teaching of the Catholic Church is contained in the papal encyclicals, Catholic bishops' conferences in various countries also produce documents on social teaching specific to their own areas. The Protestant counterpart to Catholic social doctrine is normally taken to be the ecumenical social thought of the WCC. From this it becomes immediately clear that ecumenical social teaching is more representative of the teachings of the churches as it involves the collaborative effort of more than one denomination. Catholic social teaching, on the other hand, reflects the views of only one church, and at its highest authority.

Like the papal encyclicals, ecumenical social thought also reflects the three elements of social ethics we have been considering. Most of the papal encyclicals are written to coincide with the anniversary of the first social encyclical, Leo XIII's *Rerum Novarum* (published 1891). Ecumenical social thought begins as preparations, study, and consultations for WCC assemblies, culminating in the latter's proclamations to world Christians. Preparations involve the scientific study and analysis of specific social problems, eg, the world economy. This happens through study committees, following which drafts are circulated to member churches around the world for comments and suggestions. After this, improvements are made before the drafts are presented to the assembly for further study and consideration.

In addition to scientific study during the preparatory stage, theological and ethical criteria are brought forward – especially from scripture – examined and interpreted in order to be made more meaningful in evaluating the social matters under consideration. Bock (1974:35) refers to the earliest phase of the search for an ecumenical social ethic as an international social gospel phase. It was characterized by the "applications of the principles of love, brotherhood, and justice to the social order ... The church was to convert men to social responsibility and thus imbue a

Christian spirit into all of society, thereby humanizing society." Subsequently, however, a more "realistic" approach was adopted. As in the case of the early papal encyclicals, social analysis through the use of the social sciences evolved gradually until it became central to the process of social evaluation.

Some of the well-known historical developments in the consideration of evaluative norms in the WCC include earlier distinctions made between an ethic of ends and an ethic of inspiration; the development of standards known as middle axioms; and the standard of the idea of the responsible society, *inter alia*. The development of these standards was naturally an attempt to find the best ways of fulfilling the Christian principle of love in social matters. This concern led to the questioning of universal philosophical principles in ethics and of the focus on the consequences of actions. The emphasis on the ethics of inspiration was seen as being in accordance with the scriptural assurance that "the Spirit moves where it will." Middle axioms, for their part, developed as an attempt to find a mid-way between a general (theoretical) ethical principle and a specific (practical) moral rule. The hope was to provide more clarity with regard to the demands of the love commandment, and less rigidity in moral decision-making. They sought, in Bock's view, "to remain within a Biblically centred approach stressing response to God's actions in history and yet to provide some guidelines as to what the response might be" (1974:38). Finally, the idea of the responsible society was described as that of a society "where freedom is the freedom of men who acknowledge responsibility to justice and public order, and where those who hold political authority or economic power are responsible for its exercise to God and the people whose welfare is affected by it" (Bock 1974: 69).

In both the papal encyclicals and ecumenical social teachings – indeed, in all Christian social teaching – the evaluative norm is linked to the religious vision and is motivated by and directed to it. The latter serves as a meta-ethic, providing the reason for morality and its norms: "The Christian, responding in gratitude to the undeserved love of God expressed most fully in Jesus Christ, manifests love toward his neighbor" (Bock 1974:17). Hence social ethics, like all Christian ethics, is said to be relational. It is because God has first loved us that we should love others. The religious vision directs us to improve our relations with one another as human beings for the sake of God. In social ethics, the norm of love is translated into the principle of justice, which may seemingly serve both as a middle axiom and a "vehicle" or expression of a responsible society.

Social ethics and the Bible

It has been made clear throughout this chapter that Christian social ethics is part of the general discipline of Christian ethics. The assumption behind the existence of a specific Christian social ethic is that Christian ethics in its traditional form does not sufficiently address ethical matters affecting communities or societies at large. Rather, it focuses primarily on individual moral life and the individual's relationship with God. This view will become clearer in some of the works discussed below. As a part of Christian ethics, Christian social ethics naturally derives inspiration from the person of Jesus Christ and the whole New Testament tradition, through which he is made known. Jesus and the New Testament, however, can only be understood properly in light of the background provided in the Old Testament. Hence Christian social ethics, like general Christian ethics, finds its source not only in the New Testament but also in the Old Testament – that is, in the Bible as a whole.

As in the case of general Christian ethics, however, some theologians have argued that it is not quite true to say that both Testaments of the Bible are a source for Christian social ethics. While some of them argue merely that the contribution of the two Testaments is not equal, others go to the extent of saying that the New Testament, in particular, focuses purely on an individual ethic. "It is vain," they say, "to search the New Testament for precise norms of, or even directives for, a social ethic" (Mehl 1966:47). Referring to the New Testament in particular, Mehl (1966:45) emphasizes that the "biblical message is addressed fundamentally to the individual: Whether it is a question of faith ... or of repentance ... or of regeneration ... it is always the individual who is addressed." Others acknowledge that at least small groups, though not society as such, were part of the focus of Jesus' message. The "focus on the individual and small groups, rather than social structures, was [seen as] a necessary consequence of the structure of Jesus' thought" (Bultmann and Cadbury, quoted by Mott 1987:226). Yet others like Troeltsch (quoted by Mott 1987:226) argue that inasmuch as Jesus dealt only casually with matters of equity and justice, he had no programme of social reform.

Mott

These arguments against the social nature of New Testament ethics have not gone unchallenged. Many other theologians, social ethicists, as well as some ordinary Christians, have strongly rejected them. According to Mott (1987:227), such arguments do not provide sufficient framework for the individual and the small group, which they emphasize: "Three crucial elements of New Testament thought, which provide a social framework for its teachings, are missing". These are: (1) the relationship of the New Testament to the Old Testament, (2) the importance that status has in the New Testament as well as in social structures, and (3) the concept of the cosmic "principalities and powers." On the first element, Mott argues that the New Testament can be seen in its proper perspective only when its heritage from the Old Testament is taken into account. This heritage demonstrates "deep concern for the social order, for justice, for the economic and social relationships of the powerful and the weak" (Mott 1987:227–228). Structural components for a social ethic to which the Bible as a whole contributes include justice, the nature of humanity, the concept of history, the nature of society and groups, the understanding of power and property, and the purpose of government. To some of these components, the New Testament contributes more than to others (Mott 1987:241).

Regarding status in the New Testament, Mott points out that it is as much the key to New Testament social ethics as economic deprivation is to Old Testament social ethics (Mott 1987:234). Status represents a social position, where one is rewarded or undermined according to the position one occupies in society. On the other hand, economic position is reflected by class structure, which has the same implications for its members as status has for those in their respective social positions. Both status and class are "power resources," rendering one weak or powerful according to one's social or economic rank. Further, they are crucial for maintaining the status quo in society. Hence, "When Jesus by his actions and words challenged the existing status system, he defied a major requirement for operating a social system" (Mott 1987:236). For this reason he provoked hostility. The way Jesus dealt with the inequalities of status as well as his attempts to restore the community of his time would, according to Mott, constitute a ministry of justice. It was the purpose of justice, in biblical terms, to restore community.

The third New Testament element overlooked by those who reject the idea of a New Testament social ethic, as suggested by Mott, is that of the "cosmic 'principalities and powers'." The Old Testament background to this reflects God's saving concern as including the whole creation. Thus "God is concerned with the morality of the social order and not merely with the salvation of individuals or small groups of individuals" (Mott 1987:230). This concern is summed up in the concept of the reign of God, in which "God's creation [will be] renewed in such a way that creation and redemption [will] become merged" (Mott 1987:231). In the New Testament, in what Mott calls Jesus' "inaugural address," Jesus gives a comprehensive summary of his mission in the words of Isaiah 61:1–2 (Lk 4:18–20). This mission, which culminates in the charge to proclaim the Lord's year of favour, includes preaching good news to the poor, proclaiming liberty to captives and to the blind new sight, and setting at liberty the oppressed. Who can deny the social nature of this message, which appears in both the Old Testament and the New Testament as a form of link between the two.

Longenecker

Another theologian who denies the absence of a social ethic in the New Testament is Longenecker. Like Mott, he also makes reference to Lk 4:18 (1984:52), stressing that the New Testament "has much to teach us regarding social thought and practice today" (Longenecker: Introduction). Referring to the Old Testament, he states,

> The early Christians, like the Jews, knew their God to be the God of freedom. In their Old Testament Scriptures they read how he released his people from bondage in Egypt ...; how he removed foreign subjugations when they turned to him ...; how he delivered [them] from Babylonian captivity ...; how he instituted the Year of Jubilee ...; and how he promised a day when his servant would 'proclaim freedom for the captives and release for the prisoners' ... (Longenecker 1984:67).

Longenecker concludes that the pattern of social ethics throughout the Bible is what

God has done for his people and how they, in turn, should have a similar concern for their fellow human beings (1984:10).

The main focus of New Testament ethics, however, is placed by Longenecker on what he refers to as the three mandates, summed up in Galatians 3:28. For him this is the "most forthright statement on social ethics in all the New Testament" (1984:30). The three mandates, based on the oneness of all humanity in Christ, are presented as: (1) the cultural mandate: "There is neither Jew nor Greek"; (2) the social mandate: "[neither] slave nor free"; and (3) the sexual mandate: "[neither] male nor female." These three "pairings," for Longenecker, "cover in embryonic fashion all the essential relationships of humanity" which are "implied in the gospel proclamation that resounds throughout the New Testament" (Longenecker 1984: 34).

The cultural mandate, which may be more appropriately called the political mandate, warns against discrimination on the grounds of race, culture, or merit of whatever kind. Christians are to measure all their attitudes and actions in terms of impartial love and by so doing "break down barriers of prejudice and walls of inequality." The social mandate, perhaps also better called the socio-economic mandate – for slavery includes economic gain and exploitation by the slave-owner – is based on two principles. The first is that God is the liberator of the oppressed, who also commanded his people not to mistreat aliens. Hence he did not tolerate the bondage of slavery. The second principle is that of Israel's own experience of oppression and of being aliens: "'you yourselves know how it feels to be aliens, because you were aliens in Egypt'" (Longenecker 1984:51). It is to be noted, though, that Paul never spoke out against slavery to the same extent as he did against "race discrimination." Rather, his general attitude toward slavery was that of condonement. He "sought to elevate the quality of personal relationships within the existing structures of society" (Longenecker 1984:59, 53). Finally, on the sexual mandate, Longenecker notes that there are both positive and negative attitudes toward women in Paul's Epistles. There has been a general tendency by Christians, however, to emphasize either to the exclusion of the other. Yet both need to be taken into consideration in evaluating Paul (Longenecker 1984:83). The sexual mandate, taken on its own, is in accordance with the requirements of social ethics in advocating non-discrimination and equality of the sexes among all people as human beings.

Notwithstanding the above considerations, the main purpose of exploring the relationship between social ethics and the Bible is not merely to show that the Bible has something to say about social matters, even though this is also important. The question is how the Bible serves as a motivating source – as an inspiration – for social ethics. Is it a matter of searching for biblical commands, prescriptions, or moral rules and then applying them as they are to the present life situation? Is it a matter of searching for general moral principles and values that can be translated into concrete practice in our own time and place? Is it a matter of digging through biblical texts in the hope of deriving inspiration that will stimulate our ethical thinking and moral practice? Or is it a matter of determining how believers, and above all Jesus, responded to moral situations in apostolic times in order to imitate those actions – as in *The Imitation of Christ* – in our own moral quests?

These four questions seem to sum up the general ways in which Christians have sought the help of the Bible in approaching moral questions. Since they are treated in more detail in the chapter on biblical ethics in this volume, no consideration will be given to them in the present chapter. We will, therefore, proceed to the next section, while referring the reader to the chapter in question.

Subject matter of social ethics

Before concluding this chapter it is appropriate to refer, however briefly, to some of the issues which constitute the subject matter of social ethics. Although some social ethicists do not distinguish between the subject matter and the task of social ethics, the two are viewed as distinct in this chapter. The subject matter refers to moral issues to the solution of which social ethics contributes. The task, on the other hand, refers to how this is done. It seems more appropriate to speak of the "point of reference" rather than "subject matter." However, I will follow current practice in social ethical writings and use the latter term.

Issues to which social ethics relate are inexhaustible. It is important to stress that social ethics relates to issues not in the sense of providing solutions to them but rather in the sense of providing means (tools) toward their solution. Such issues include those falling under the scope of political ethics, economic ethics, sexual ethics, and similar socially related moral issues. Thus social ethics is all-embracing in its fashioning of tools for moral deliberation in social matters, while these other types of ethics are more specific to their limited subject.

Matters which the Reconstruction and Development Programme (RDP) presently seeks to address in this country, particularly their motivations, goals, implementation, and consequences, form part of the subject matter of social ethics. As recorded in the RDP document, these include the satisfaction of basic human needs such as housing, nutrition, health, jobs, education, land for both production and habitation, and affirmative action for the accommodation of those previously disadvantaged in society. However, the scope of social ethics goes beyond considering grounds for the fulfilment of such basic human needs. It includes examination of the ethical worth and implications of causal issues such as racism/apartheid, political oppression including injustice, inequality, and the status of human rights, economic exploitation and class differentiation, sexist oppression, government corruption, the current scandal of the "gravy train" factor alongside dire poverty, and related forms of human suffering, among others.

In an interesting and quite informative discussion of ethics and community in a book of that title, Enrique Dussel (1988) divides the book into two parts. The first part deals with what he calls fundamental (ethical) themes. In the second part, which deals with "disputed [moral] questions," he examines moral issues relating to work, capitalism, economic dependency, multinational corporations, international loans and weaponry, violence and revolution, socialism, and ecology. In a related approach, Carl Wellman deals alternately with ethical and moral issues in his book, *Ethics and Morals* (1975). Chapters on ethics include considerations of right and wrong, the good, moral value, the end of the law, a right, and moral knowledge. Moral issues are considered in chapters on civil disobedience, the use of drugs, premarital sex, abortion, open housing, and capital punishment. As I have stated, social problems which provide the subject matter of social ethics are inexhaustible. It is important to stress that these are not, strictly speaking, ethical but moral problems, as their treatments by Dussel and Wellman show. It is in their solution that appeal is made to ethics or social ethics, since it is ethics which provides the relevant tools of analysis and deliberation for their solution.

McNaughton

What Wellman and Dussel distinguish as morals or moral problems rather than ethics, however, is termed "practical ethics" by other ethicists. Thus McNaughton (1988) distinguishes between practical ethics, moral theory, and meta-ethics. What I refer to as ethics in this chapter is what he calls moral theory. For him, ethics proper falls under meta-ethics rather than moral theory. Nevertheless, there is an interaction between these three sections of moral philosophy, so that they cannot be viewed entirely apart from one another: "Any satisfactory ethical theory must have things to say in all these areas and so form an integrated picture of the world and of our place in it which is much wider than the field of ethics" (McNaughton 1988:16).

McNaughton defines practical ethics (morals) as "the study of *specific moral problems.*" The examples he gives of these are questions such as: Is abortion ever morally acceptable? What structures would we find in a perfectly just society? Moral theory he describes as "a theory of morality that will give us a *general method* for answering all the specific moral questions that are raised in practical ethics." This, as we have seen, is what I have chosen to call "ethics" in the rest of this chapter, following Wellman. Meta-ethics, which for McNaughton constitutes the core of ethics, is generally understood to be concerned with the *"nature and status of our moral thought*:[1] Are there any moral truths? Is it possible to show that one moral view is better than another?" He draws the following conclusion regarding meta-ethics:

> [Meta]Ethical questions are basic; the conclusions we come to about the nature and status of our moral thought are bound to have an effect on our views about how we may set about determining the correct solution to some moral problem, or even whether there is such a thing as a correct answer (McNaughton 1988:16).

In determining ways to solve these problems, practical (social) ethics – to adopt

---

1   All italics mine.

some of McNaughton's terminology – will seek to reveal why they are considered right or wrong (a problem of meta-ethics), what values and norms they uphold or violate (eg, the value and standard of love), what principles and method of decision-making to use in searching for solutions (eg, considering the general good or the consequences of possible actions), and how to review the adequacy of analysis made and decisions taken for future dealings with similar ethico-moral problems (what more could have been done, what should have been avoided?). These levels of ethical deliberation must be present in the evaluation of each of the moral problems listed above. Each level is analytical and it is through such deliberative analysis that an advance is made toward reaching the solution to a moral problem.

Analysis in social ethics

Many ethicists normally restrict the task of analysis to social analysis. Analysis in social ethics, however, certainly goes beyond this, as the preceding paragraph shows. We may identify at least four types of analysis, implying some degree of adjustment to Winter's three elements of social ethics. The first is social, determining the social issues involved, their nature, the structures responsible for them, and the consequences of these issues on society in general. The second type of analysis is moral. This is both pre-ethical and post-ethical. First, it determines the worth of these social issues on the basis of accepted human values and norms, presumptions (Wogaman), loyalties and worldviews (Kammer), be they moral, religious, social, or cultural. This stage does not proceed beyond exposing and identifying the moral problem as well as its source. It is based on the fact that "[b]ecause we are creatures with certain feelings, needs and desires, we react favourably to some actions and unfavourably to others" (McNaughton 1988:1). The post-ethical stage is more deliberative, employing ethical tools derived from ethical analysis (see below) to moral problems for their solution. As already seen, the solution of practical moral problems is more the task of morals or practical ethics than that of ethics proper, including social ethics. The third type of analysis is ethical (in the theoretical sense). Ethical analysis takes into account both social and moral (especially pre-ethical) analysis. On this basis, it proceeds to determine and formulate ethical principles, rules, and method of approach that can be employed in seeking solutions to social moral problems. Ethical analysis cannot, therefore, proceed without social and moral analysis. Further, while social analysis can be undertaken for purposes other than moral or ethical, moral analysis without ethical analysis is incomplete. In formulating its analytical tools, ethics further takes into consideration philosophical and theological analysis of the whole moral situation. In this way it not only develops as a theory, but also improves meta-ethically.

To summarize this section: Social ethics does not address moral or practical ethical problems directly. Its role is chiefly to provide ethical grounds (meta-ethics), principles and methods of deliberation (normative ethics) for moral engagement or for use in seeking moral solutions to social problems (morality or practical ethics).

Summary and conclusions

By now it has become crystal clear that much controversy still surrounds the idea and structure of a social ethic. However, a distinction needs to be made between social ethics as a form of theory of social control and social ethics as a method toward the realization of such control – that is, as a discipline.

There is no doubt about the fact that social ethics in the former sense has been practised throughout biblical and Christian history. The "case studies" discussed earlier in this chapter are testimony to this. What has been in dispute as social ethics attempted to establish itself as an academic discipline has been the question of its method. The problem of method ranges from: (1) whether social ethics is the application of biblical commands to the present social situation without taking into account the huge gulf of space and time *(Sitz im Leben)* that separates the present from biblical times; to (2) seeing social ethics as an "interdisciplinary discipline" that is not only limited to Christian ethics and other theological disciplines, but also extends to philosophy and the social sciences; and one that must work toward a solution of social moral problems through analysis and interpretation resulting from an integrated approach of all these disciplines. Our conclusion on this question favours the latter approach.

The question of method extends to the theory and practice of social ethics. Here the question is, "Is social ethics concerned only with the theory of morals or only with its practice – or both?" As social ethics is part of the general discipline of ethics, it seems that the distinction normally made between ethics and morals applies equally to social ethics. Hence it has been argued that, like ethics in general, social ethics involves the theoretical study of the principles of acceptable types of human conduct. Such conduct in the case of social ethics depends on the facilitation provided by certain social structures through social policy. Consequently, the place of moral practice in general ethics is occupied by social policy in social ethics. In other words, social policy is to social ethics what moral practice is to ethics in general.

This comparison between ethics and morality makes it possible for us to review the task of social ethics. Its major task has been seen to lie precisely in its implications for social policy. These implications follow from the prior analytical, interpretive, and clarifying role of social ethics on the moral requirements of society and social structures.

A few selected cases of social ethics in practice show that they all comply – to varying extents – with Gibson Winter's suggested three elements of social ethics. These are the description of social conditions, evaluative norms, and religious vision. These elements were found to correspond to Walter Muelder's requirements for an interdisciplinary approach to social ethics. Such an approach, according to Muelder, requires the socio-behavioural sciences for social analysis; philosophical and Christian ethics for ethical deliberation; philosophy and theology for interpretation and evaluation of moral concepts. Potter's objections to this type of approach were found to be somehow defective. He, too, does seem to subscribe to his own type of interdisciplinary approach, which may be called a "dialogical interdisciplinary approach."

Finally, in considering the relationship between social ethics and the Bible, it seems conclusive that inasmuch as social ethics is part of Christian ethics, and inasmuch as Christian ethics has the Bible as its primary source, so also is the Bible a primary source for social ethics. Not only one of the Testaments of the Bible is a source for Christian social ethics, as some theologians have argued, but both the Old Testament and the New Testament are joint sources. While the Old Testament generally has more of a social emphasis than the New Testament, the latter is to be understood in light of the background provided in the former. Nevertheless, it also has its own social focus. This is found in Jesus' liberating mission expressed in the words of Isaiah in Lk 4:18; in the Beatitudes; in the Sermon on the Mount; in Paul's Letter to the Galatians, among other texts.

Notwithstanding the social messages found in these texts, however, what is more important about the contribution of the Bible to social ethics is the norms it provides for social living rather than the instances given of its social practices. The primary norm that the Bible provides is believed to form the basis for a relational ethic, namely, that it is because of what God has done for humankind that human beings are, in turn, to conduct themselves with love and justice toward one another. Thus what God has done serves as a standard for what we are to do. James Cone has interpreted this as expressing the central relationship between theology and Christian ethics. According to him, theology asks, "Who is God?" Christian ethics asks, "What are we … to do?" (Cone 1975:197). This means that who God is is known through what God has done, and what we are to do should be based precisely on what God has done. Social ethics, however, has to go beyond this theological enquiry to provide practical guidelines, in the form of moral laws or principles, toward determining more exactly what we are to do. That is why philosophy and the social sciences have to be brought to the aid of ethics and theology. That is why, in effect, social ethics is an "interdisciplinary discipline."

BIBLIOGRAPHY

Antoncich, Ricardo. 1980. *Christians in the face of injustice: a Latin American reading of Catholic social teaching*. Trans. Matthew J O'Connell. Maryknoll, NY: Orbis Books.

Bennet, John C (ed). 1966. *Christian social ethics in a changing world: an ecumenical theological enquiry*. New York: Association Press.

Birch, Bruce C and Rasmussen, Larry L. 1976. *Bible and ethics in the Christian life*. Minneapolis, Minn.: Augsburg Publishing House.

Bock, Paul. 1974. *In search of a responsible world society: the social teaching of the World Council of Churches*. Philadelphia: Westminster Press.

Boesak, Allan A. 1984. *Black and reformed: apartheid, liberation and the Calvinist tradition*. Johannesburg: Skotaville Publishers.

Deats, Paul K. 1972. "The Quest for a Social Ethic," in Paul Deats, Jr. (ed). *Toward a Discipline of social ethics: essays in honor of Walter G Muelder*. Ed. Boston: Boston University Press.

Forrell, George W. Ed. 1966. *Christian social teachings: A reader in Christian social ethics from the Bible to the present*. Mineapolis, Minn.: Augsburg Publishing House.

John-Paul II. 1990. Encyclical Letter, *Solicitudo rei socialis: On social concern*. Bombay: St Paul's Publications.

Kammer III, Charles L. 1988. *Ethics and liberation: an Introduction*. Maryknoll, N.Y.: Orbis Books.

Longenecker, Richard N. 1984. *New Testament social ethics for today.* Grand Rapids, Mich.: Eerdmans Publishing Co.

Mehl, Roger. 1966. "The Basis of Christian Social Ethics", in John C. Bennett. (ed). *Christian social ethics in a changing world: an ecumenical theological inquiry*. New York: Association Press.

Mott, Stephen C. 1987. "The Use of the New Testament for Social Ethics". *The Journal of Religious Ethics* 15: 225–256.

Muelder, Walter G. 1966. *Moral law in Christian social ethics*. New York and Toronto: The Edwin Mellen Press.

Muelder, Walter G. 1983. *The ethical edge of Christian theology: forty years of communitarian personalism*. Toronto Studies in Theology 13. New York and Toronto: The Edwin Mellen Press.

Pickering, George W. 1978. "The Task of Social Ethics", in W Widick Schroeder and Gibson Winter (eds). *Belief and ethics: essays in ethics, the human sciences, and ministry in honour of W Alvin Pitcher*. Chicago, Il.: Centre for the Scientific Study of Religion.

Potter, Ralph. 1972. "The Logic of Moral Argument", in Paul Deats (ed). *Toward a Discipline of social ethics: essays in honor of Walter G Muelder.* Jr. Boston: Boston University Press.

Tutu, Desmond M. 1983. Hope and suffering: sermons and speeches. Johannesburg: Skotaville Publishers.

Wellman, Carl. 1975. *Morals and ethics*. Glenview, Il.: Scott, Foresman and Company.

Winter, Gibson. 1968. Introduction to *Social ethics: issues in Ethics and society.* Gibson Winter (ed). London: SCM Press.

Aluta continua – toward an ethic for socio-political transformation

Des van der Water

Apartheid's legacy – a society in moral crisis

It is often said these days that we should stop "blaming apartheid for our present ills".[1] It all depends, of course, what a person means when making such a statement. If it is to convey the sentiment that our new-born democracy and not the past dispensation should be the focus of our attention and commitment as South Africans, then the intention is to be commended. I suspect however that those making the above-quoted statement, in the majority of cases, do so either out of an extreme naivete, or because they are in a state of perpetual denial about the harsh present and future legacies of an apartheid past. This past, according to Charles Villa-Vicencio, will "continue to haunt South Africa for years to come" (Villa Vicencio, in Du Toit 1994:101). It is my contention that this past does not have to "haunt South Africa for years to come".

However, it is going to require the whole-hearted commitment and collective engagement of individuals and communities if we are going to minimise the damage done, and to maximise the enormous latent potential for goodwill in South African society. What is clearly evident is that the legacies of apartheid are making their disturbing presences felt daily in ever new and destructive ways, both in the form of actions and attitudes that seriously undermine the processes of re-construction towards an integrated social fabric across the country. Bonganjalo Goba identifies some of the more prevalent signs of these legacies as "racism, sexism, ethnic chauvinism, economic exploitation, breakdown of family values and disregard for the sanctity of human life" (Goba, in Pityana and Villa-Vicencio 1995:74). These socially destructive tendencies are of course not unique to South Africa, but they have a specific socio-historic origin in the apartheid philosophy which, in the final analysis, has left us as a nation bereft of due respect and regard for each other as human beings, *especially across the racial divide.*

---

1 One only has to listen to the debates on the talk-show programmes on the Gauteng-based Radio 702, on any one of the number of the concerns raised (eg. escalating crime, corruption, etc.) to hear how many people hold this view. Refer also to the regular column by Barry Ronge, 'Inside Spit 'n Polish', in the *Sunday Times News Magazine*. (Note especially the December 15, 1996 column).

Villa-Vicencio is surely right when he observes that the dehumanisation of both blacks and whites is the most "inexorable heritage" of apartheid still to be faced, a heritage which emerges from our history of "black rebellion and white repression" (Villa-Vicencio, in Du Toit 1994:100).

> Designed to promote the 'good life' for whites, apartheid sought to reduce black people to a status within which they would be content with an existence devoid of human rights, without social and material wellbeing. Many blacks could do no other than conclude that their existence was located beyond the bounds of white compassion or reason. Whites, in turn, saw it as their right to enjoy social privilege at the cost of black suffering. They demanded this privilege. They fought for it. As black rebellion and white repression intensified, ethical ideals and human values were thrust aside in pursuit of political and material gain. The will to win was pursued at almost any cost (Villa-Vicencio, 1994:100).

The outcome of what Villa-Vicencio outlines above is a society largely without significant collective ethical ideals. We are now, most unfortunately, harvesting the bitter fruits of a socio-political and economic dispensation which systematically destroyed basic human values. These basic human values, of which I shall be saying more below, lie at the heart of a quest towards a viable ethic for socio-political reconstruction in South Africa. But, firstly, all those engaged in the task of building a more humane society have to look squarely and honestly at the way things are. Barney Pityana helps us to see what we are really confronted with, when he characterises the existing situation in South Africa as follows:

> We live with the human and physical devastation caused by apartheid. All around us are the symbols of the fierce struggle. We can see it in the victims: the widows, the crippled and those mentally and physically affected by torture. We see it in the breakdown of discipline in schools and in the breakdown of family life. We see it in the prevalence of crime as a way of life in many of our communities. We see the moral breakdown so much that we can no longer recognise it as such. It has become a way of life[2] (Villa-Vicencio 1994:100).

It is not a pretty sight. And the bottom line is that we are a nation and a society in serious moral crisis which, to a large extent, is the legacy of apartheid.[3] Therefore, a failure to deal with this legacy in an adequate way could have the effect of significantly undermining even the most sincere initiatives towards nation building. But, the question emerges, where do we go from here? Wherein do we, as a country, find a moral centre and a rallying point? This inquiry is an attempt to address this question, albeit in a very tentative way, but with the conviction that South Africans do have an essential basis for constructive communal and societal life.

---

2   Pityana B, quoted in C Villa-Vicencio, *op cit.*, p 100.
3   In this regard I am not in the first instance talking about prostitution and pornography, but referring to a moral decay which goes much deeper than that which meets the eye.

The moral influence of religious communities in South Africa

If we accept the submission that South African society at large is going through a moral crisis of one degree or another, then we are merely one step away from acknowledging that religion and religious affiliation does not appear to be stemming the tide of such moral decay. This anomaly becomes even more stark when we consider that, according to the 1991 State census figures of the estimated population of 26,3 million, only about 23 % profess an absence of religious affiliation (Froise 1996: 58). How, then, does one account for the fact that the sum total of ethical principles and moral teachings of Christianity, Judaism, Buddism, Islam, Hinduism and Confucianism, certainly on the face of things, make no significant impact on the moral fabric of South African society?

An authoritative answer to the above question would require fairly detailed research and some in-depth analyses, which are beyond the scope of this enquiry. However, it seems that a credible short answer can be found in the historically fragmented nature of South African society. Given that the potential for division and fragmentation is inherent in any given society or nation, the breaking up of a social fabric is not a natural and inevitable consequence of the human forces in history; it is the result of a specific policy and practice. In the South African context, the growing polarisation of ethnic groups and the current fragmented nature of society has, in no small measure, resulted from the role of missionary societies who were active in the 19th century in this country[4] (Pityana and Villa-Vicencio 1995:44).

The twin impact of a multiplicity of Christian denominations planted into African soil and the aggressively implemented colonial policy of "divide and rule" inflicted on us a legacy of division and fragmentation. This dubious inheritance has etched itself very deeply into the collective psyche of the nation. The seeds for an apartheid mentality were sown well before the Afrikaner Nationalists came to power in 1948 and it is a sad commentary on the history of Christianity in South Africa that the missionary movement was not able (or willing) to lay the kind of foundation which would work against, rather than buttress, the grand schemes of religious and social apartheid that ensued.[5]

One needs to acknowledge, however, that during the darker days of the apartheid era, a significant number of ecumenically-oriented churches and Christians[6]

---

4   When we consider, as Brigalia Bam observes, that South Africa once had the 'dubious distinction of having more missionary agencies at work in our country than in any other in the world', then we begin to have a clue as the causes of the state of fragmentation within Christendom and within the society at large.

5   Like the South African Airways television advert which goes, "We did not invent flying, we only perfected it", the Afrikaner Nationalists may also acknowledge that they did 'not invent apartheid'. However, they certainly "perfected it".

6   Although many other churches and Christians were not prepared to acknowledge it then, the ethical issues were much clearer to discern within the context of a doctrinaire apartheid dispensation. It is interesting, to say the least, that these days one has to look around very hard in order to find Christians and churches who acknowledge their previous support for apartheid. The fact that apartheid was founded and perpetuated by successive governments claiming to be acting on the basis of Christian principles only compounds the irony.

found a semblance of unity in a common struggle against the policies and practices of apartheid.[7] But, with apartheid now consigned to the scrapheap of history, a new ecumenical vision has yet to be articulated which is able to re-mould these erstwhile ecumenical allies in this new era of democracy.[8]

Our present enquiry, however, is more specifically focussed on articulating a vision and finding a source of inspiration for ethical norms that transcend both the ecumenical churches and the Christian denominations at large. We clearly have little hope of constructing a value system using only Christian socio-ethical norms. They represent the religious convictions of only a sector of the country's constituencies (albeit the dominant one) for the country at large. Moreover, it is abundantly evident that the state-sponsored brand of the Christianity of the past is fast losing its former privileged status within the new socio-political dispensation. We have to look elsewhere for a new kind of moral basis. One which is able to adequately address: the widespread moral crisis; the rising phenomenon of secularism; and the growing trend of religious pluralism in South Africa.

It is my contention that the New Constitution of the Republic of South Africa[9] as a whole, and the Bill of Rights in particular, provide us with an essential basis for the formulation of inclusive ethical norms and guidelines for acceptable moral behaviour. In other words the Bill of Rights is, amongst other things, geared towards the weaving together (rather than the rending) of the very delicate social fabric of our fledging democracy. It is, therefore, in the context of the principles enshrined in the New Constitution and, in particular, with regard to the chapter on fundamental human rights 10 that I will be discussing a few of the major factors impacting on what we have identified as a nation and society in moral crisis.

The *Bill of Rights* in the New Constitution – A foundation for basic human values

It is commonly accepted that a constitutional charter of any country is drafted against the background of a specific historical past. In the case of South Africa, the New Constitution reveals a clear intention not only to avoid the errors and evils of the apartheid past but also to reverse the former trends of division and alienation

---

7   I am here referring to those ecumenical churches and Christians who have historically sought to foster Christian unity in belief and action (orthodoxy and orthopraxis), in response to the ecumenical mandate of the Gospel and the needs of the world, both locally and globally.

8   See J de Gruchy, 'Becoming an Ecumenical Church', in *Being the Church in South Africa Today*, pp 12–24.

9   The Constitution of the Republic of South Africa, 1996, Act No. 108, 1996 (Published in the Government Gazette, 18 December 1996). The New Constitution was recently signed into law by the head of state, president Nelson Mandela, replacing the interim Constitution. This signing took place on Tuesday, December 11, 1996 (Human Rights Day) in the historically significant setting of Sharpville. It is worth noting that, with reference to the sections on the Bill of Rights, differences between the interim Constitution and the new Constitution are minimal and certainly not of substance.

amongst its citizens. This principle is clearly outlined in the *Preamble* to the New Constitution:

> We therefore, through our freely elected representatives, adopt this Constitution as the supreme law of the Republic so as to –

> Heal the divisions of the past and establish a society based on democratic values, social justice and fundamental human rights;

> Lay the foundations for a democratic and open society in which government is based on the will of the people and every citizen is equally protected by law;

> Improve the quality of life of all citizens and free the potential of each citizen; and

> Build a united and democratic South Africa able to take its rightful place as a sovereign state in the family of nations.[10]

My use of the Bill of Rights in the Constitution as a basis rather than the religious texts of either Christianity, Judaism, Islam or any other faith, in no way implies that religion and religious principles are of secondary importance in this process. On the contrary, I believe that the New Constitution affirms, rather than contradicts or detracts from, the best intentions of any of the religions in the country with regard to fundamental human rights and acceptable moral practice in the public arena.

I am, therefore, operating on the premise that none of the religious communities in South Africa have expressed any substantial objection to the principles and practices outlined in the New Constitution, as it pertains to basic human rights, and would be inclined to undergird the ethical norms implicit herein.

Some elaboration is needed at this point, and I propose now to discuss my hypothesis firstly, with reference to the political scene and secondly, in relation to the issues of social justice and, thirdly, in terms of the notion of human mutuality.

Ethics of political integrity

The Constitution sets out the following clear foundational principle in regard to the right of every citizen to freely take part in legitimate political activity expressive of his/her persuasion:

1. Every citizen is free to make political choices, which includes the right –

    (a) to form a political party;

    (b) to participate in the activities of, or recruit members for, a political party; and

    (c) to campaign for a political party or cause.

---

10 The question as to whether human rights have a legitimate theological basis is dealt with by, amongst others, Charles Villa-Vicencio who analyses the different theological traditions and concludes that 'the different theological approaches suggest sufficient common ground to project an ecumenical consensual statement on human rights'. *A Theology of Reconstruction: Nation-Building and Human Rights*, David Philip, Cape Town, 1992, p 153.

2. Every citizen has the right to free, fair and regular elections for any legislative body established in terms of the Constitution.
3. Every adult citizen has the right –
   (a) to vote in elections for any legislative body established in terms of the Constitution, and to do so in secret; and
   (b) to stand for public office and, if elected, to hold office.[11]

The fundamental political rights outlined above, if regarded and respected by all South Africans, would go a long way to reducing the tendency toward conflict and confrontation which has its origin in the repressive stance of the apartheid regime. One of the unmistakable consequences of the apartheid era is the so-called culture of political intolerance amongst followers of adversarial political parties. This unfortunate pattern has abated somewhat in recent times. However, the potential for conflict is still alarmingly high, especially in certain parts of the country.[12]

The right to freely express one's political convictions is closely related to another cluster of fundamental rights and principles contained in the Bill of Rights. These include the Right to Freedom of Expression (cf Section 16); the Right to Freedom of Assembly, Demonstration and Petition (cf Section 17); and the Right to Freedom of Association (cf Section 18). Provided, of course, that the exercise of such rights do not encroach on or violate the rights of other citizens, we have in the Bill of Rights an adequate basis for a commonly accepted code and ethical principle. One which is designed to foster a culture of tolerance and the unfettered practice of legitimate political activity by all citizens.

The recognition of and respect for the expression of different political persuasions is a major ingredient in the process of establishing, or re-establishing, an attitude of mutual respect amongst adversaries. Goba suggests that implicit in this process of establishing new human values is also the need for "redefining ourselves" as South Africans:

> One of the main challenges in this historical moment is the quest for a new identity – something that recreates the negative past and brings forth a more inclusive dimension of our humanity. What is new about the New South Africa is the imperative to reconstitute, to redefine, who we are as a people. It is in redefining ourselves that we are challenged to talk about human values – human values radically different from anything we have known, or indeed is known by those continuing to idealize the old South African way of life in the Volkstaat idea (in Pityana and Villa-Vicencio 1995:73).

With the New Constitution in place, therefore, the stage is set to reverse the politically corrosive ethical trends of the previous era emerging out of state repression

11 *Preamble* to The Constitution of the Republic of South Africa, p 3.
12 Bill of Rights – Section 19.
13 Although tensions have eased somewhat in recent months the extent of political intolerance between supporters of the Inkatha Freedom Party (IFP) and the African National Congress (ANC) in KwaZulu-Natal are still a matter of serious concern.

146

and the unfortunate consequence of political intolerance amongst opposing groups. It goes without saying, of course, that a mere piece of paper cannot effect such significant change of heart and of direction in society. This is precisely where the collective efforts of the religious communities, the electronic and print media, the educational sectors, the state, NGO's and businesses have such a major role to play to bridge the gap between the New Constitutional principles and the actual practice "on the ground". It goes without saying, of course, that political parties themselves have a major role to play in fostering an ethos of tolerance amongst political adversaries. The run – up to the 1994 democratic elections clearly showed to what extent political parties have the potential to either promote and safeguard free political activity, or contribute to an atmosphere of repression and violent resistance.

A question has to be raised, therefore, about certain political parties' recent refusal to allow their Members of Parliament to vote on the basis of conscience on the Abortion Bill.[14] The question is whether such a stance by a political party is not, in fact, tantamount to political intolerance by the majority party against those within its own ranks who want to express a different opinion. Is the danger not precisely that in the exercise of political expediency by parties such as the ANC, the cost to be paid is the stifling of legitimate public expressions of moral conscience?

The *Sarafina II* controversy is another recent incident which highlights the importance of democratic accountability and transparency. The controversy arose following a press disclosure that the producer of *Sarafina II*, Mbongeni Ngema, was being paid a fee of R14 million for a play which purports to create awareness about AIDS. This action, on the part of the Minister of Health, Dr N Zuma, has been widely criticised and the controversy was compounded when it came to light that the state funds which were to have been used for this purpose were never earmarked for that purpose by the overseas donors. Despite the obvious questionable actions of the minister, the ANC and the president, Mr Nelson Mandela, instead of embarking on an appropriate response designed to promote good government and commendable financial administration, closed ranks on the issue and effectively swept the matter under the carpet. The exercise of such accountability and transparency is surely the substance of political integrity on the part of those in public office.[15] If the voting public allows politicians and parliamentarians to have free reign, how can we expect integrity in the type of politics practised in the market places of everyday

---

14 When interviewed on radio some days before the vote was taken in parliament on the Abortion Bill, spokespersons for the African National Congress and the Democratic Party declared that their MP's were required to vote along party lines, and not allowed a conscience vote. (Radio SAfm – October 1996). In my opinion the reasons given for these rulings were as vague as they were unconvincing.

15 The question of *delivery* is another crucial test of political integrity on the part of the ruling party. One has to begin asking the question, some 30 months after the ANC has come to power as to whether the ANC-led government is able and willing to deliver on the election-campaign promises of a better standard of living condition for the deprived black masses.

life?[16] It is precisely in the face of political malpractice by those in power that the prophetic voices of the religious communities should be heard loudly and clearly. First, in terms of the ethical demands of the respective religions themselves, and secondly, on the basis of values espoused by the Bill of Rights in the New Constitution. Thus, with regard to the prophetic ministry of the church, Albert Nolan makes the important point that such prophetic ministry should not limit itself to criticism of the state:

> Because of our experience in an apartheid state, we in South Africa tend to think of prophetic witness as something that must always be directed against the state ... In fact the basis of all prophetic criticism is self-criticism – criticism of my people, my nation, my church, my institutions and my government (Pityana and Villa-Vicencio 1995:152).

Ethics of social justice and fair-dealing

The need for transparency and accountability in public life, of course, extends beyond the political realm. Again the Bill of Rights lays down some clear guidelines with regard to social justice and fair-play in public life, notably as articulated in the following cluster of democratic rights, namely the Right of Access to Information (cf Section 32), the Right to Just Administration (cf Section 33), and the Right of Access to Courts (cf Section 34). These rights are supported and supplemented by other related rights such as that of Citizenship (cf Section 20), Freedom of Movement and Residence (cf Section 21), Freedom of Trade, Occupation and Profession (cf Section 22), and the rights governing fair Labour Practices (cf Section 23).

The denial of social justice and fair-dealing to the majority of black South African citizens for such a long time under apartheid has, not surprisingly, undermined their faith in being given a fair deal through the courts and other due processes. Likewise, the fact that scores of the younger generation of black South Africans have nothing but scorn for the law should not surprise us. The experience of many young black people of the law, under apartheid, was that of being subjected to draconian measures such as detention without trial. The current high levels of crime, including the less-publicised, but equally abhorrent, white-collar crime, and corruption in public life quite dramatically illustrate the extent to which disregard for the law has increased within the country at large.

Clearly, these and other instances of socially destructive practices reflect a deep-seated ethos whereby basic human worth was simply trampled upon in the process

---

16 I find it rather disappointing that ANC parliamentarians, who in the past were severely critical of the excesses of the previous regime, have merely settled into a parliamentary pattern of privilege, status and power. Those of us who voted the new government into power were surely hoping for the introduction of a new model of political and civil leader, not one whereby the luxury chauffeur driven cars, the fat-cat salaries and life-styles, the myriad of body-guards, and other tax-free perks are still the order of the day.

of maintaining power and privilege by an ethnic minority and its surrogates. The lives of black people in South Africa became cheap, exploitable and expendable under apartheid. While it is not valid to ascribe all the present social evils to Apartheid, there is a real sense in which the perpetuation of social and political violence within black communities is merely an inevitable consequence of the grim seeds that were sown in previous years. And the inordinate number of people losing their lives, their possessions, or even their sanity as a result of being dehumanised through continued exploitation, robbery, abuse and rape – to mention but a few socially destructive practices – is, in fact, a consequence of an ethically bankrupt apartheid moment in our history.

The New Constitution clearly does not have all the answers or solutions. However, such affirmations as contained in the Bill of Rights declaring, for example, that, regardless of race, religion or creed we are all equal in the eyes of the law could only set us on the right road to a mutually acceptable norm of social equality.[17] As a country we have a long way to go because many South African citizens are still being unjustly treated, discriminated against, excluded, or having their basic rights violated. Furthermore, the vast majority of such people do not have the means and the knowledge to access the avenues of justice. In this regard a great responsibility rests on the shoulders of social institutions, including the religious communities, to bridge the gap between the theory and practice of a genuine human rights culture where basic human values are affirmed.

An ethic of human mutuality

The quest for commonly accepted basic human values through the exercise of ethical norms does not only find expression through the avenues of political integrity and socio-economic equity. These are undoubtedly the arenas in which such basic values become visible and concrete, but these can only be held in place because of a prior recognition, that is, the primacy of *human dignity*. It comes therefore as no surprise that in the *Founding Provisions* of the New Constitution human dignity is listed as one of the essential values upon which the new South African democracy is founded.[18] The centrality of human dignity in the Constitution is certainly a factor which should be underscored by all the religions in the country. In this regard Lourens du Plessis (1996:62) anticipates that, given the history of our apartheid past, Christians should be inclined to welcome this emphasis:

> Christians will probably welcome the stronger emphasis on human dignity in the final Constitution. Freedom and equality are Christian values too but, politically speaking, they are means to ends rather than ends in themselves. Neither pure *libertarianism* nor undiluted *egalitarianism* seem to be Christian

---

17 It is precisely in the context of the Bill of Rights that such controversial issues as *affirmative* action, for example, need to be understood.

18 Chapter 1, *Founding Provisions*, p 3.

options; freedom and equality must achieve a higher purpose, such as the real-isation of human dignity, in recognition of humans' createdness in the image of God. This is particularly true in a society which endeavours to overcome an era where the humanness of most of its citizens was held in contempt by an oppressive regime.

If South Africans at large were to give due recognition to the fact that the human dignity of all citizens should not be compromised, as it was the case in the past, a sound basis could be established for mutual respect and acceptance. Of special in-terest to the religious communities would be the reference in the Bill of Rights to religious freedom. Section 15(1) states that "Everyone has the right to freedom of conscience, religion, thought, belief and opinion".

Du Plessis picks up on the significance of religion being grouped with conscien-ce, thought, belief and opinion in the Constitution, noting that the freedom of reli-gion clause protects more than freedom of religion in the strict sense of the word; it also guarantees freedom of conscience and thought and belief and opinion and probably includes the right not to observe any religion and not to believe (Du Plessis 1996:66).

Furthermore, the recognition in the New Constitution of as many as 11 official languages is an important signal about the need for reversing past trends whereby the languages of African people were disregarded. The Constitution gives implicit recognition hereby that language is not merely a means of communication but also a bearer of cultural values, and by affirming the cultural value one is allowing for expressions of a group or human community's collective dignity.

It is one of the anomalies of South African society that while we are geographi-cally part of Africa, our cultural expressions and systems are Eurocentric rather than Afrocentric. This culturally alienating phenomenon has been largely responsi-ble in the past for creating misconceptions and fostering mistrust amongst South Africans of different cultural backgrounds. The separate development policies of apartheid, instead of affirming different languages and cultures as it claimed, used these differences to justify and perpetuate the divide and rule intentions of its crea-tors.

Challenge to the churches

The overall provisions in the Constitution of the Republic of South Africa, and the specifications in the Bill of Rights, by declaring that all citizens have a legal, social and moral right to be treated fairly and equitably, set us on the right road to estab-lishing inclusive and acceptable moral principles and ethical norms. In the final analysis, the quest for a transformed and transforming social order is contingent thereupon. What then, are some of the major challenges facing the churches and Christians in this regard?

The first is to come to terms with the new status of Christianity under the emerg-ing secular state. This means a full recognition that the churches and Christians no longer have the monopoly in matters of ethics and morality in society, and can therefore no longer impose their will upon other religious and even non-religious communities. This realisation constitutes a fundamental paradigm shift for the churches in particular, and for the religious communities in South Africa in general. One of the more obvious implications of this shift is the need for a much greater degree of co-operation and collaboration amongst the religious communities in responding to such ethical issues as AIDS, abortion, capital punishment, etc. It is incumbent on the churches, by virtue of their historical privilege and advantage, to take the initiative in this regard.

The second major challenge facing the churches is that of resisting the threat of being marginalised in matters of socio-political and economic influence and policy-making. The fact that Christianity no longer enjoys a religious monopoly under a secular state does not mean that the churches now have to take a backseat in the ongoing process of social reconstruction in South Africa. The prophetic voice and the pastoral presence of the church in matters of social justice can never be compromised, and certainly not on the pretext of being in solidarity with the new regime.

Third, perhaps the most formidable contemporary challenge facing the churches is the awakening, or re-awakening of the moral conscience of a nation which, by many accounts, finds itself on the slippery slope of widespread moral decay. The discipling or teaching ministry of the church is going to be subjected to one of its greatest tests, namely that of shaping sound moral character amongst its own constituencies. Unless virtues such as honesty, integrity, dignity and accountability in public life are more visibly demonstrated by Christians themselves, the churches' efforts towards the moral transformation of society will simply flounder.

SELECT BIBLIOGRAPHY

Du Plessis, L. 1996. 'A Christian Assessment of Aspects of the Bill of Rights in South Africa's Final Constitution'. *Journal of Theology for Southern Africa*, 96: 59–74.

Du Toit, CW. (ed). 1994. *Sociopolitical changes and the challenge to Christianity in South Africa.* Pretoria: University of South Africa.

Froise, M. (ed). 1996. *The South African Christian Handbook.* Cape Town: Christian Info.

Goba. B. 1995. 'Searching for a New Moral Identity', in B Pityana and C Villa-Vicencio (eds), *Being the Church Today.* Johannesburg: South African Council of Churches.

Pityana, B. and Villa-Vicencio, C. (eds). 1995. *Being the Church In South Africa Today*, Johannesburg: South African Council of Churches.

Ronge, Barry. 1996. "Inside Spit 'n Polish", in *Sunday Times News Magazine*, 15 December.

Villa-Vicencio, C. 1992. *'A Theology of Reconstruction – Nation Building and Human Rights'.* Cape Town: David Philip.

Villa-Vicencio, C. 1994. 'Are we still of any use? A question of social significance', in CW du

Toit, (ed). *Sociopolitical changes and the challenge to Christianity in South Africa*, Pretoria: UNISA.

Constitutional Talk: Official Newsletter of the Constitutional Assembly, 17 September 1996, No 4.

Know Your Rights: Fundamental Rights under the New Constitution. Macmillan Boleswa, Manzini, 1994.

The Constitution of the Republic of South Africa, 1996. Act No 108, 1996. (Published in the Government Gazette, 18 December 1996).

10 Racism in the post-apartheid South Africa

Nico Koopman

A major element in the history of South Africa has been racism. In the recent past it was written into our laws. These laws have now been repealed, but the question remains whether racism still exists in the new non-racial South Africa. We will examine the question initially by defining racism as an ideology. This approach to racism will help us to grasp the nature, character, origin, manifestations, magnitude and presence of racism.

This chapter is divided into two main parts. In the first part we do an analysis of racism as an ideology and investigate the various elements of our definition. This first round of analysing this phenomenon paves the way for concrete proposals for combatting it and building a new society free of racial discrimination.

What are we dealing with?

Racism – towards a definition

For various reasons it is not ideal to speak about a definition of racism. First, racism is an inflated concept which is used with a variety of meanings. The concept must do justice to various elements, such as biological, ethnic, cultural, religious, political, economic, educational and social differences amongst people. It is therefore difficult to find one single definition of racism which is adequate and comprehensive. The second reason why it is difficult to define racism is because no definition can sufficiently describe the pain and destruction racism causes to so many people and societies. In fact, any definition of racism runs the risk of underestimating the magnitude and the mystery of the suffering this evil has had on millions all over the world. Therefore, it is wise that the direct victims of racism play a prominent role in defining racism.

Despite the difficulties surrounding attempts to define racism, it is important to arrive at a working definition of racism in order to come to a level of understanding which would enable us to take up the challenge to combat it effectively.

A decade ago two Dutch scholars, Hans Opschoor and Theo Witvliet, offered a definition of racism which can assist us in this endeavour. According to them racism is

> the specific ideology which organizes and regulates the exploitation and de-
> pendence of a specific 'race' on the basis of the assumed cultural and/or bio-

logical inferiority of that 'race'. In this way actual differences in power are maintained and intensified (Opschoor and Witvliet 1983:563 – translation NNK).

This definition offers a suitable outline for our analysis of racism and the consequent proposals for addressing the problem.

Racism – an ideology

In this chapter we define ideology as "a world-view or mind-set" (Kretzschmar 1992:47) which:

(a) serves the vital political, economic, social and psychological interests of my own group (Nürnberger 1983:49) – often at the expense of the other group;

(b) is embodied in concrete societal structures;

(c) is often supported or justified in terms of religious convictions.

Ideology, like racism, is a wide concept which is used in a variety of ways. Ideology derives from the Greek word, *eidos*, which can be translated with the words picture or image. Ideology, therefore, refers to the picture, image or idea that people have about reality, how they understand reality, how they respond to it and structure it. Ideology functions on a conscious level as the self-determined way in which people understand and respond to reality. It also functions on a subconscious level in the sense that it influences and conditions people to think in a specific way about reality. Since this conditioning process takes place on a subconscious level (through the continuous influence and peer pressure of the group that you belong to as well as the effect of the societal structures which you start to take for granted), people are often not aware of their ideological thinking. In this regard the South African theologian, Johan Kinghorn, refers to the "blinding" (translation – NNK) effect of ideology. Hereby he means that ideology brings people under the impression that they know the full reality, also the reality of the other groups, without even having been exposed to that reality (Kinghorn in Kinghorn J (ed) 1986:191–193).

An ideology can be formulated in a sophisticated way and as such become a blueprint for the future. It can indicate how reality should be altered and simultaneously suggests methods and strategies to achieve the changes which is required. Sometimes, however, an ideology functions to protect the status quo and to prevent changes to the current reality, thus protecting group self interest. Ideologies, therefore, do not remain as ideas in the minds of people, but become manifested in concrete structures. In the 20th century in particular, ideologies have been formulated as well-defined thought- and idea-systems or blueprints for the future with concrete strategies and methods. Capitalism, socialism, communism, nazism and racism are examples of ideologies in this century.

As mentioned earlier ideologies are sometimes justified by religion. This fact will be illustrated with regard to the ideology of racism. The societal structures which are erected in terms of an ideology and the arguments, specifically the religious arguments, which are offered in support of the ideology serve to condition people to think in terms of that ideology.

All ideologies should always be evaluated critically, no matter how noble their aims might be – and there are indeed ideologies with good intentions. Christians should evaluate all ideologies in the light of God's Word since we know how imperfect, and contaminated by selfishness, our best efforts as human beings can be. Being critical however does not imply that we become passive and negative about human endeavours for change, but it means that we expose our ideas and ideologies to, and accompany all our action with, the guiding light of the Word, knowing that the specific meaning of the Word for a concrete situation is not always that easy to ascertain. We should also be aware of the fact that our ideologies not only predetermine how we think, and how we view other ideologies, they even influence our interpretation of God's Word.

Although scholars are in agreement that racism was only formulated as a sophisticated ideology in the 20th century, this phenomenon has been with us for much longer. The South African theologian, Allan Boesak, refers to the German scholar, Helmut Gollwitzer, who traces the roots of racism back to the beginning of the period of slavery, which according to Gollwitzer was developed and legitimised theologically by white Protestant Christians as part of their so-called capitalist revolution (Boesak, in De Gruchy et al. 1983:3). Here the ideological nature of racism was already present.

In the following sections we will apply the above explanation of ideology to our understanding of racism. Racism as an ideology means that a specific group of people with more or less the same physical and biological features and attributes and the same cultural affiliation view society in a way which implies that the group to which they belong is superior to other groups and that society should be structured in terms of this perceived superiority and inferiority. A group must acquire the political and economic power to enable it to implement its ideological thinking and racism is one of the ideologies which is strongly supported by religious arguments. Understanding racism as an ideology helps us to recognise the different levels on which it functions. It is a personal matter of thinking, feeling, attitude and prejudice. However, it is also an impersonal matter which is manifested in the structures and institutions of society. Lastly, where it is supported by religious belief, it is a matter of faith. To combat this evil adequately all these levels should be addressed.

Racism and race

The concept race was originally used to distinguish between people in terms of biological differences. In 1952 and 1965 the task group of the United Nations for Education, Science and Culture (UNESCO) described race as a biological concept. Their comprehensive research concluded that all human beings belong to one type, namely *homo sapiens* and with the same origin. However, through the ages, due to factors like geographical and/or cultural isolation as well as changes in the genes of people – which control, amongst others, the inherited physical characteristics – differences between groups of people evolved. Amongst these differences are those in skin colour, hair texture and the shape of the face. Consequently, various ethnic or racial groups came into being. Race therefore refers to a group of people which is characterised by specific concentrations of genes and by specific physical attributes. The genetic make up of people and genetic changes are influenced by factors like geographical and/or cultural isolation.

Most cultural anthropologists divide homo sapiens into three races, namely the Caucasians, Mongoloids and Negroids. The Caucasians consist of people from Northern India, Northern and Central Europe and the peoples around the Mediterranean Sea; the Mongoloids are, amongst others, the Chinese, Taiwanese, Malaysians, Indonesians and Indian Americans; the Negroids are the black people originating from Africa. Some scholars add a fourth racial group, namely the Austroloids which include, amongst others, the Australian Aboriginals and the people of Northern Japan. Other scholars like Franz Boas distinguish only between the Negroids and Mongoloids. He includes the Caucasians with the Mongoloids. The consensus is, however, that there are three main racial divisions.

There is also agreement that the division of human beings into various racial groups does not imply the existence of pure races. The majority of scholars reject the idea of racial purity. They indicate that through the ages the mixing of races has taken place. The South African historian, Hans Heese, has shown this mixing process in the history of those Afrikaner families who claim to be racially pure, in a publication titled *"Groep sonder grense: Die rol en status van die gemengde bevolking aan die Kaap 1652–1795"*.

On the basis of the belief that there are pure races, the race concept was eventually used not only to distinguish amongst various groups, but also to classify groups in terms of superiority and inferiority and to stereotype and stigmatise them. Especially the Negroids were stigmatised. They were portrayed as inferior to other races in every way. It was asserted that psychologically they are underdeveloped and are like children and adolescents when compared to adults of other races. They are also more prone to abnormal and maladjusted behaviour. Sexually they are more lustful and promiscuous and are capable of overwhelming other races with their strong passions. White females, in particular, should be protected against the seductive power of black males. Morally they have poorly developed consciences and are therefore less capable of morally good behaviour. Merely on the basis of physiological differences their religion and cultures are portrayed as inferior. The white, Western civilization with its scientific and technological progress was sketched as the ideal. In comparison, the civilizations of other races are seen as inferior or underdeveloped. The imperialism of the 19th century was part of this belief in superiority expressed in the colonisation of "backward" peoples. Lastly we must mention the unfinished debate about the question whether different racial groups do in fact have different degrees of intelligence. The English ethicist, John Stott, refers to the debate between H Eysenck who holds the view that differences in IQ amongst various racial groups are determined by heredity and L Kamin who attributes the lower IQ levels of black people to the educational, social and economic discrimination to which they have been subjected (Stott 1984:204–205).

In the afore-mentioned passage we can see how the term race acquired a negative connotation. It was used to propagate the idea of a pure, superior group whose interests are of greater importance than those of others. By means of the ideology of racism these interests were protected and promoted, not only in the minds of people or with the assistance of religious arguments, but also in the structures and institutions of oppression that were erected in terms of this ideology. The continued use of this word should be reconsidered in the light of the gross abuse thereof. The biological and historical-anthropological evidence against the idea of pure races also supports this plea for a re-evaluation of this specific term. Other, less discredited, terms for distinguishing between people should be considered. Simultaneously, the danger of categorising and stigmatisising people on the basis of physiological differences, no matter what terminology is used, should be seriously reconsidered.

It is also necessary to refer to the negative, painful use of the word race, because it reflects the way so many people still think about their own and other groups. In this chapter we indicate how these old stereotypes resurface in newer, more subtle forms today – despite the explicit expression of non-racism in our own country.

Ethnicity might be considered as a category of distinction amongst people which does not have a negative connotation like the concept race. According to Kenneth Leech, this term is conventionally used to describe a group of people with some degree of coherence, common origins and shared experiences. Ethnic identity, he states, can be passed on from one generation to another and may include distinct languages, religions, political and cultural styles (Leech 1996:320–322). These distinctions are not as contaminated with biological factors as in the concept of race. However, when ethnicity is linked to nationalistic conflicts, as in Eastern Europe, the stress on innocent distinctions like culture, customs, language and religion, might, as Leech puts it, raise the same concern and have the same negative effect as the stress on blood and descent (Leech 1996:321). Below we indicate how distinctions like culture are used afresh in a racist way.

Racism and religion

In this section we will not deal with the phenomenon that certain racial groups view their religion as superior to that of others. In the past, the white race of Europe viewed their religion, that is the Christian religion, as superior to the religion of, for instance, black races in Africa as well as Judaism and Islam. The Dutch theologian, Theo Salemink, in an article titled *De Kleur van de ziel en de kleur van het liggaam,* states in strong language that in this context the Christian religion was seen as part of the broader so called more civilised culture of the European world. Judaism was stigmatised as the religion of those who killed the Messiah of the Christians and

Jews were seen as people who always abused Christians economically. Muslims were identified with fundamentalism, violence, sexual promiscuity and prejudice against women.

In our description of ideology we have mentioned that an ideology is often supported by religious arguments. For most people religious belief – not necessarily institutionalised religion – functions as a final meaning-giving entity, the ultimate definer and strongest motivating force of their lives. In South Africa, the ideology of racism functioned with religious roots. The white Dutch Reformed Church, more than anyone else, proclaimed this ideology, which was concretely manifested in the political system of apartheid, as gospel, as God's good news, as God's solution for the South African society with its racial diversity. Although some DRC theologians like B B Keet, Ben Marais and Beyers Naudé differed, the DRC in this century developed the so-called "Apartheidsteologie". The research of the Reformed theologian, Andries Botha, with the title *Die evolusie van 'n volksteologie* offers valuable information on the arguments the proponents of "Apartheidsteologie" used.

Apartheid theologians argued that God had chosen the Afrikaner people as his elect just as God had done with the people of Israel, who were the church of the Old Testament, to proclaim his kingdom amongst the heathen of Africa. In order to fulfil their superior vocation, they had to preserve themselves by separating themselves from other groups. Here we see how the unique situation of Israel as both a national entity and the "church" of the Old Testament is not properly understood and how it is illegitimately applied to justify the presumed superiority of Afrikaners over not only other races, but also over other cultural groups – which included groups of the same race, but who held different views on race.

To support the apartheid paradigm for church and society the biblical principle of diversity was also used. In the 1974 policy document of the Dutch Reformed Church, *Ras, Volk en Nasie*, the biblical principle of diversity was elevated to the status of a God-given principle on a par with the unity of the church and of humanity with an appeal to the episode of the tower of Babel. This could happen because the specific salvation-historic context of Babel was not taken into consideration, but the text was merely applied as if it consisted of general principles. The impression is hereby confirmed that Scripture was only used to justify a prior nationalistic position. Their presuppositions, determined by their racist ideology, enabled the authors of *Ras, Volk en Nasie*, both to interpret the Bible in a way which suited their presuppositions and to conclude that the Bible supported apartheid. The idea of diversity received such emphasis that it caused a situation where the reconciliation of people on the basis of Christ's redemptive work was questioned.

Precisely this questioning of the essence of the gospel opened the way for the 1978 declaration of apartheid as a sin by the Dutch Reformed Mission Church, and its 1982 statement that any theological support of the ideology of racism and its political manifestation, apartheid, is a heresy. Simultaneously the Dutch Reformed Mission Church, in the *Confession of Belhar* which was adopted in 1986, confessed the unity of all believers in the midst of their diversity. It also stressed reconciliation amongst all believers on basis of the redemptive work of Christ and also the fact that God is, in a situation of injustice, the God of the oppressed. The Dutch Reformed Mission Church was not alone in its critique, but other churches and ecumenical bodies both here and abroad shared these views.

In 1986 the Dutch Reformed Church, in its policy document *Kerk en Samelewing*, revised in 1990, distanced itself increasingly from the old "Apartheidsteologie". In fact, today it is almost an impossible task to find a supporter of racism in mainline church and theological circles. Such support will still be found mainly in extremist right wing circles.

Nevertheless, to address the racism crisis effectively this close link between the ideology of racism and religion must be thoroughly taken into account. Freedom from racism also involves a major theological shift for many. Since religion is such a powerful force which played such a key role in the racial history of this country, people from all groups in our society should be aware of that role and also of how religion may have influenced their own thinking about others and themselves. Christians in particular will have to proclaim the message of the gospel with specific reference to the construction of a society free from racism.

Racism and culture – new racism

Our analysis up to now has made it clear that supporters of racism on explicitly biological or religious grounds are hard to find today. In this section, however, we make the point that these arguments are still alive, but that they are put forward in a concealed form in the name of culture.

Culture is used here as referring to the habits, customs, way of life and values of a group of people. It also denotes the way people view, represent and name reality in their art, literature, architecture, technology and science, symbols, language, religion and other facets of their lives as a group. In the so-called *postmodern* era we are experiencing worldwide a re-appreciation of the various cultures. Much more room is made for the particularity and identity of one's own group than was the case in the modern era with its emphasis on universality and individualism. On the one hand, the recognition of diversity and plurality as well as the acknowledgement of the rights of various groups, also minority groups, is to be applauded. On the other hand, the emphasis of particularity runs the risk of creating negative manifestations of nationalism, tribalism, sectarianism, patriotism, isolation and alienation which can lead to new racial prejudices or which can strengthen old ones. So the shift to the celebration of plurality might prove to be ambiguous, as will be shown below. Theo Salemink distinguishes between primitive and new racism. Primitive or old racism was aimed at people living outside Europe and against the marginalised Jews in Europe. It was based on biological and religious differences as discussed above. The scenario in Europe has changed drastically in recent decades. Europe is now flooded by people from other continents for economic reasons, many of whom are Moslems. They came looking for employment, but European economies are now dependent on their labour. In this new context, racism has re-emerged and new right wing parties have been formed and are growing in countries which were opposed to the so-called old racism. In this new racist thinking, people are no longer classified in terms of biological differences, but rather in terms of factors like region of origin, nationality, language and other forms of cultural expression.

The new category of discrimination is no longer based on biological evolution which makes people into one common race, but on the historical and cultural evolution which divides them into various discrete communities. This historical development is not coincidental, but it is suggested that it is an essential part of human nature to form distinct communities which differ from others. These communities which developed over time are given the status of unchangeableness and the fact that the Dutch people are a combination of other groups and peoples is ignored. These "accidents of history" are seen as divinely sanctioned. From this it becomes clear that the new racism, like the old one, gives supernatural status to coincidental, historical and cultural differences.

Another resemblance with the old racism is the fact that the European peoples as well as European migrants who have shared in the historical evolution of the European peoples are mainly white people. They are perceived as superior to the other peoples. Hence, the subtle presence of the old biological racism is clear. Furthermore, racially motivated religious enmity has also re-appeared in the guise of the so-called "Islamic danger" with its perceived religious fundamentalism and lack of democracy.

As indicated in the introduction to this section, the new racist thinkers respect both plurality and particularity. They are committed to the cause of democracy and human rights. However, they apply these noble liberal ideas only to their own people and only use them for the protection and the advancement of the interests of their own "superior" people.

This brief discussion of the new racism in Europe makes it clear that it is derived from the same ideology as the old racism. Although it explicitly refers only to seemingly neutral historical and cultural differences, in the end it uses these differences to legitimise the comprehensive superiority of European peoples and advance the interests of those groups which are homogeneous in biological characteristics and often also in religious affiliation.

In the diversified South African society, with its history of racism and of the ongoing anti-racism struggle, the risk of this new racism emerging is very strong. As has been the case in Europe, regional origin and especially cultural differences between various groups can be used as a new rationale for the old racism which is now officially rejected in South Africa. White people, in particular, and other groups in South African society who identify with the European culture, which has previously been portrayed as the superior culture in the history of this land, should guard against this new racism. On the other hand, this warning also applies to

African and Asian cultures. Any emphasis on ideals like multiculturalism should be investigated for hidden new racist motives.

Racism, structures and power

We have indicated that racism as an ideology is often supported by religious convictions and that it consists of specific ideas about reality and of the relationships between various groups. In this section we want to show that these ideas are embodied in concrete structures through specific methods and strategies. On the one hand, racism as an ideology functions to create new structures and, on the other hand, it later justifies these new structures. South Africa is one of the supreme examples of how the ideology of racism, which functioned on both conscious and subconscious levels in the thoughts of groups of people and which was supported by their religion, manifested itself in all the structures of the apartheid society.

This ideology determined where people could live, the type of work they could do, the amount of money they could earn, the quality of their education, the health, welfare and housing services and even the leisure facilities to which they were entitled. It also determined which political and other rights they could exercise. All of these societal arrangements were written into and enforced by law. It is well documented how these racial developments led to major injustices and shocking imbalances which still continue in our society.

To embody a specific ideology in concrete structures, political and economic power is required. The North American author, Joseph Barndt, reasons that we can only talk about racism when you have the power to exercise your racial prejudices. In fact, he defines racism as follows:

> Racism goes beyond prejudice. It is backed up by power. Racism is the power to enforce one's prejudices ... It is not only the control of one individual over another, but also a collective power expressed through political and economic systems, through educational, cultural, religious and other societal institutions. It victimizes entire racial or ethnic groups for the purpose of maintaining the benefits and privileges of another group (Barndt 1991:28–34).

In opposition to Barndt one would rather state that racial prejudice is part and parcel of the racist ideology as shown above. This implies that even powerless people can be racist in the sense that they have racial prejudices and in the sense that they adhere to a racist ideology. However, with reference to the prejudices of black people one should ask to what extent their prejudice is a reaction to the experience of racial discrimination from white people and also to what extent the ideology of racism adopted by black people functions as a means of liberating them from white racism.

On the other hand, I agree with Barndt that racism can only be expressed in concrete structures when the power to implement the racial ideas is present. This, in turn, implies that economically and politically powerful people are the only ones who are able to practise their racial beliefs structurally and formally. Since this power, viewed globally, resides mainly with white people in the Western world, Barndt speaks of racism as referring only to white racism. Barndt is correct when he argues that structural racism can only be practised by powerful people – and therefore mainly by white people.

In the history of racism in South Africa it is clear that white people obtained political power and acquired most of the economic resources at the expense of other groups. This enabled them to implement their racial ideas and to structure the society according to those ideas. Structural racism in South Africa is, therefore, according to Barndt's analysis, exclusively white racism.

As wielders of political and economic power, white people were able to give structure to the ideology of racism in the form of the political system of apartheid. The apartheid structures, on the one hand, were the product of the ideological thinking which presupposed that white people were superior to others who could even be oppressed and abused for the sake of white interests. On the other hand, the apartheid structures protected the privileged position of whites and kept other groups in political and economic subjugation. The scenario in South Africa has, in the meantime, changed drastically. Political power now resides with political parties which are predominantly black. This could lead us to think that the white structural racism will be replaced by reactionary or reversed black structural racism. However, the fact that economic and related power is still in white hands, and will be so for decades to come, makes this impossible. The immense imbalances in this country will not be rectified overnight. Having the vote does not ensure good housing, health, education and general well-being. Political measures, like the so-called affirmative action policy, which are taken to rectify the unjust conditions should not be confused with reverse racism. The new South African constitution suggests a way of addressing imbalances and of achieving equality which opposes reverse racism:

> Equality includes the full and equal enjoyment of all rights and freedoms. *To promote the achievement of equality, legislative and other measures designed to protect or advance persons, or categories of persons, disadvantaged by unfair discrimination may be taken. (Constitution of the Republic of South Africa 1996, Chapter 2, point 9(2) – italics NNK)*

The above analysis makes the point: people of all colours can have racial prejudices and can support a racist ideology. In this sense all people can be racist. However, only those who have political and especially economic and related powers are able to convert their ideology of racism into social behaviour and concrete structures. In the Western world, this structural racism can largely only be practised by white people since economic power resides mainly with them. Although black people in South Africa have obtained political power, and although they can be racist in attitude, they are not able to practise structural racism, since they are far from the point of having sufficient economic power to put this ideology into practice.

Simultaneously, the racism which was built up over the years into the structures and institutions of South African society should be recognised. In my view, only the political institutions have started to reflect non-racialism, but all the other institutions still reflect the racist ideology of the apartheid era.

Liberation from racism

In the first part of this chapter we offered an analysis of racism. We have concluded that racism is alive in the new South Africa because as an ideology it functions in the thinking of people on a conscious and even a subconscious level. As an ideology it was driven and supported by religious belief and this led to the creation of the apartheid societal structures within which we still live. Hopefully, this analysis will facilitate a better understanding of this complicated problem and enable us to formulate ways of addressing this evil. In the last part of this chapter we endeavour to propose ways of building a society free of racism.

Liberation from ideology – story-telling

We have defined racism as an ideology. To have any chance of being liberated from the bondage of racism we must be freed from our ideological thinking. Freedom from ideological thinking would imply the right answers to the following questions:

> How do we see or view ourselves and people from other groups?

> How does God see or view us and people from other groups?

> Do our societal structures and institutions correspond with God's view of all people?

These questions provide a good framework for the proposals we would like to offer for addressing the issue of racism. First, people from different groups must listen to each other. Second, they must together listen to God and, last, they must together bring the social structures in which they live into correspondence with their new joint views and beliefs.

The groups that we refer to are the white and black people of South Africa. During the years of the struggle against apartheid "black" was for many an umbrella term which included Coloureds, Indians and Africans. A further distinction was the fact that Africans included groups like Tswanas, Zulus and Xhosas.

Although the black people (as defined above) were united in the goal to break down apartheid, they were separated from each other by the apartheid laws and they enjoyed different levels of rights and privileges. Moreover, even racial prejudices existed amongst them. In the current post-apartheid South Africa, this racism has come ever more to the fore. The story-telling process for which we plead should, therefore, also include these finer nuances and should not only be a dialogue between black people on the one hand and white people on the other hand. There is, of course, a unique element in the dialogue with white people, namely the fact that they, unlike the black people, had the political and economic power to embody their racial beliefs and prejudices in the apartheid structures.

Listening to each other – story-telling

A few years after the first democratic elections South Africans are still deeply divided and alienated from each other along racial lines. This suggests that the older racial prejudices are still alive. These racial stereotypes can only be broken down if sufficient genuine opportunities are created for members of the various groups to be exposed to one another.

Churches, other religious communities, institutions of education at all levels, work places, sports and cultural bodies and other social institutions should run formal, well-planned and structured programmes which will facilitate opportunities for people of various backgrounds to meet each other in their various habitats and to share the stories of their lives in apartheid South Africa. In an atmosphere of openness, honesty and constructive confrontation people can share their deepest pain, hurt, anger, hatred, fear, shame, guilt and feelings of hopelessness which were caused by racism. This is happening in some measure in the Truth and Reconciliation Commission. Different groups will give different contents to these emotions, but in the end it will become clear how all of us are victims of racism. Where this happens, people will – many for the first time – develop real empathy with others. This means that for the first time they will look at reality through the eyes of other people and not only in terms of their own ideology. For the first time many people will see reality as it really is and not as their ideologies portray it to be. Consequently, the doors will be opened for a thorough and common – not one-sided – understanding of our situation, for the confession of guilt, for the dealing with the above-mentioned emotions, for the achievement of forgiveness and for the joint construction of a new life story of non-racism, peace and justice.

These opportunities for exposure should be created intentionally, because in a society with such a high degree of alienation and suspicion they will not occur spontaneously. Friendly, kind interactions where people just have to tolerate each other, without honest, constructive confrontation are rather the order of the day. In the end, the latter type of relationships can be just as detrimental to the ideal of a society free of racism – if not more so – than relationships marked by naked racism. However, the formal story-telling processes can encourage people to create such opportunities spontaneously.

In an excellent theological comment on the Truth and Reconciliation Commission in South Africa, the South African theologian, Dirkie Smit, stresses the value of story-telling by referring to various famous theologians. To strengthen and further clarify my point I gladly make use of his references (Smit 1995:3–5).

Amongst others he refers to the black North American theologian, James Cone, who stresses that we can only bridge our ideological divides if we tell stories, share experiences and share memories. In this regard the famous ecumenical theologian, Dietrich Ritschl, is also quoted:

> We only love those with whom we are prepared to share our story and in whose story we want to have a share. Only those who share memories and hopes really belong together.

Last, it is also valuable to refer to the comments of the famous North American theologian, H Richard Niebuhr, to whom Smit refers. In our stories, we reveal our separate pasts to each other. Only this revelation can help us to interpret the past, present and the future properly. Without revelation we interpret the past, present and future in terms of the evil images – or negative ideologies – in our hearts. It is only through revelation that the past can be saved from meaninglessness. Revelation helps us to deal with the past, not to suppress and bury it, but to deal with its shame, guilt and pain. It helps us to develop a common memory, to take ownership of each other's pasts. And common memory leads to real community where there is no room for the divisions and prejudices of the past. Niebuhr reasons that this process of story-telling should be ongoing, since sin always enters anew to separate people from God and from each others' pasts.

In the South American context, where the past has been swept under the carpet as a result of the measures for general amnesty and impunity from prosecution for human rights violations, the plea, as indicated in the following quote of Jan Sobrino, is for people to be able to tell their stories and to be listened to:

> Truth gives [people] back dignity and honour ... Telling the truth, not forgetting it, is absolutely essential for the building of a new country (Harper 1996: 127).

Only by dealing with the past can the social pathology be healed.

The relevance of the above-mentioned insights to the problem of racism is clear. Racism can only be broken down if we are willing to face the past together, to work through it together and to jointly embark on the journey to the future. Only through this revelatory story-telling process can we adequately deal with the past, present and the future.

Listen to the story of the faith community

Christians from the broad spectrum of South African society will also have to listen together to the story of the Christian faith. Although the Scriptures do not give blue prints for our societal problems, our ideologies are corrected by the light the biblical principles provide. In South Africa, where the race factor has also determined how people understand the Bible, it is of utmost importance that people listen jointly to the Word to discover God's will for us today. This joint listening to the Word will help us to develop a common story which belongs to all of us. This common heritage corrects our racial ideologies, but also liberates, encourages and energises us to work for a new society which reflects something of the biblical ideals.

Where Christians embark on this joint listening to God's Word, they cannot but commit themselves to work for a church life and church structures free of racism and eventually for a society free of racism.

Making a new story

The process of listening to each other and of listening to God's Word as explained above is not mere talking and listening. Nor is it merely an endeavour to create good attitudes without addressing structural racism. On the contrary, it is an essential, indispensable part of the making of a new common story. The telling of stories is already the confession of guilt and therefore the opening up of new possibilities and the entrance into the sphere of the renewal and transformation of the structures of society. The apartheid structures which exist in every sphere of the South African society are the products of the ideology of racism. Therefore, not only the political structures of government on all levels, but also the economic and related structures in the fields of land ownership, housing, health and education need to be transformed into structures which are free from racism. The church can provide an example by creating structures on all levels of church life which reflect non-racism.

The breaking down of the apartheid structures and the construction of new structures will be a successful and fruitful venture only if this process is accompanied by the ongoing story-telling process sketched above. Only within this framework will we succeed in the tremendous task of defining what we mean by: a society free from racism, affirmative action, by justice and by transformation, and will we be able to erect new structures to replace the old ones. If this task of defining and reconstructing is isolated from the story-telling process we will again end up with the old story, namely oppressive, racially divided definitions and structures. Through story-telling we can face the past and simultaneously embark on the making of a new story of a society free of racism.

Although racism is well and alive in the so-called new South Africa, there is hope. The discovery of the stories of fellow-citizens and a renewed discovery of the story of the Christian faith can pave the way for the joint making of a new story of a country free from the bondage of racism.

BIBLIOGRAPHY

Balia, DM. 1989. *Christian resistance to apartheid*. Braamfontein: Skotaville.

Barndt, J. 1991. *Dismantling racism: The continuing challenge to White America*. Minneapolis: Augsburg.

Boesak, A. 1978. *Farewell to innocence: A socio-ethical study of Black Theology and Black Power*. Johannesburg: Raven.

Botha, AJ. 1984. *Die evolusie van 'n volksteologie*. Bellville: UWK.

De Gruchy, J and Villa-Vicencio, C (eds). 1983. *Apartheid is a heresy*. Cape Town: David Philip.

Harper, C. (ed). 1996. *Impunity: An ethical perspective. Six case studies from Latin America*. Geneva: WCC Publications.

Heese, HF. 1984. *Groep sonder grense: Die rol en status van die gemengde bevolking aan die Kaap 1652–1795*. Bellville: UWK.

Kinghorn, J. (ed). 1986. *Die NG Kerk en Apartheid*. Johannesburg: Macmillan.

Kretzschmar, L. 1992. *The privatization of the Christian Faith amongst South African Baptists*. PhD thesis, UCT.

Nürnberger, K. 1983. "Socio-political ideologies and Church unity". *Journal of Theology for Southern Africa* 44: 47–57.

Leech, K. 1996. "Ethnicity", in PB Clarke and A Linzey (eds). *Dictionary of Ethics, Theology and Society*. London: Routledge.

Opschoor, J. and Witvliet, T. 1983. "De onderschatting van het racisme", in *Wending*, pp 554–565.

Salemink, T. 1995. "De kleur van de ziel en de kleur van het liggaam," in E Schillebeeckx et al. (eds). *Tijdschrift voor Theologie* 35: 24–47.

Smit, D. 1995. "The Truth and Reconciliation Commission – tentative religious and theological perspectives". Journal of Theology for Southern Africa 90: 3–15.

Stott, J. *1990. Issues facing Christians today*. London: Collins.

Verkuyl, J. 1971. *Breek de muren af! Om gerechtigheid in de rasseverhoudingen*. Baarn: Bosch.

Verkuyl, J. 1975. *Inleiding in de Nieuwere Zendingswetenschap*. Kampen: Kok.

West, C. 1988. *Prophetic Fragments*. Grand Rapids: Eerdmans.

West, C. 1994. *Race matters*. New York: Vintage.

OTHER DOCUMENTS

Ras, Volk en Nasie 1974. The Confession of Belhar 1986.

Kerk en Samelewing 1986 and 1990.

The Constitution of the Republic of South Africa 1996.

Gender, women and ethics

Louise Kretzschmar

It is a striking feature of societies world-wide that while women make up at least half of the population, it remains a man's world in terms of the way in which these societies are organised. If the numbers of women and children are taken into account, we need to ask why it is that the majority of the earth's population enjoy only a fraction of the wealth, freedom, pleasures and power generated by these societies. Within the context of the attempt to build a "new" South Africa, we need to ask not only how South Africa can become "non-racial" but also how it can become "non-sexist". Put differently, what role should gender analysis play in terms of the attempt to effect a transformation of attitudes and structures in the political, economic, socio-cultural, family and ecclesiastical spheres of life? Before this task can be undertaken, clarity concerning some of the terms used below needs to be attained.

Definitions and methodological considerations

Generally speaking, ethics is concerned with issues of right and wrong norms as well as good and bad motives and consequences. A distinction can be made between ethos and ethics. Ethos refers to the "way things are", that is, what is customary and generally accepted within a society. Ethics, however, is a critical reflection upon the ethos of our society (Botha, in Villa-Vicencio et al. 1994:36). Ethical enquiry asks whether those ideas, practices and structures which are generally accepted should be accepted. Are they essentially right? Are they based on good intentions and do they have positive consequences? Christian ethicists, in addition, need to ask the even more difficult question as to whether our personal and family lives as well as our political, economic, socio-cultural and ecclesiastical contexts conform to the purpose and will of God.

Ethical analysis involves the identification of what people consider to be valid norms and why they are considered as being valid. This involves an analysis of both ethical criteria and approaches as well as the contexts within which ethical (or unethical) attitudes, behaviour or social structures are experienced by a variety of individuals and groups. Theological ethics is a particular species of ethics which attempts to do all of this from within a Christian framework or paradigm:[1]

---

1 These debates are not restricted to Christian theological ethics. Within African Traditional Religion, Islam, Judaism and Hinduism, for example, gender analysis and women's analysis in particular are also at issue.

Theological ethics, then, is not a matter of abstract theorising: it is a process through which believers seek to provide answers to the real questions that people are asking about their faith and its application to their personal and social existence (Kretzschmar, in Villa-Vicencio et al. 1994:3–4).

This does not mean that all are agreed concerning what constitutes either the Christian faith itself or how it should be lived out. Instead, the ongoing and interconnected process of the identification and exercise of the Christian faith is an essential part of the theological ethical enterprise. "Doing ethics involves participation in an action-reflection-action continuum" (Villa-Vicencio et al. 1994:xi).[2]

Feminism and/or womanism can be defined as the attempt to see that justice is done with regard to women. That women should be liberated from oppression and subjection. That they be regarded with respect, accorded dignity, be given opportunities (including educational, political and employment opportunities), and that they be accorded full human rights similar to the rights enjoyed by men. Women should be free, for example, to make career choices, inherit property, own and manage farms and businesses, and be legally independent. Further, women seek not simply to obtain a better position within the present structures, but to engage in the transformation of the very structures themselves. Despite certain commonalities, it is not true that all women are equally oppressed or that they are oppressed in the same way. Nevertheless, all women share the experience of being treated with indifference or contempt, and are often forced to submit to a variety of forms of suppression or oppression.[3]

Since the modern feminist debates of the 1960s, the very definitions of what constitutes feminism have been hotly debated. Liberal, Radical and Marxist feminists have critiqued each other's positions.[4] Womanists in North America have rejected the use of a generalised description of women, arguing that the Liberal, Radical and Marxist feminists are white and cannot speak for black women.[5] More recently, African and Asian women have also made their own contribution to the debate (eg Oduyoye and Musimbi 1992).

What is at issue here is the fact that while women do share some experiences, they also come from very different backgrounds. This means that it is a perilous task to embark upon a discussion of women and gender. Certainly, all formulations remain provisional and contain but aspects of the whole, and contested aspects at

2   In Part 3 of this book, M Motlhabi speaks in terms of "see-judge-act" which implies an ethical process of "analysis-evaluation-action".

3   For a discussion of the similarities and differences of Western and African feminism see S Bazilli 1991: 4ff.

4   See Caroline Ramazanoglu (1989) *Feminism and the contradictions of Oppression*, (London and New York: Routledge) pp 3–23 for further discussion.

5   See Susan Brooks Thistlethwaite (1989) *Sex, Race, and God: Christian Feminism in Black and White* (New York: Crossroad) and Roxanne Jordaan (1987) "The emergence of Black Feminist Theology in South Africa", *Journal of Black Theology in Southern Africa* 2:1, 42–46.

that. This chapter, however, proceeds on the assumption that a contribution to the debate is preferable to a paralysed silence.

Feminist and/or womanist theology is similar to feminism in that it is concerned with the nature, status and roles of women. In contrast to liberal, secular humanist, socialist or Marxist feminism, it has a theological base, although different Christian feminists draw on a variety of these and other political ideologies. Feminist and/or womanist theology seeks to re-interpret (or reject) traditional male approaches to theology, the Bible, church history and tradition, worship and liturgy, and contemporary theological praxis.[6]

Whereas the "sex" of a person refers to their male or female biological differences, the meaning of the term "gender" is wider and more complex:

> The word *'gender'* extends these physical attributes to create an ideological construct which is based on the way that society understands those biological differences between men and women. What we recognise and experience as 'masculine' and 'feminine' is socially and culturally constructed as our 'gender', which involves a whole constellation of roles, expectations, social and sexual behaviours (Bazilli 1991:8).

Gender Studies, then, is the attempt to study society from the perspective of gender differences and relations. But because the personalities, status and roles of women have, for centuries, been either ignored or subsumed beneath the interests and power of men, gender studies often leads to an emphasis on the needs and rights of women. Inasmuch as this puts women's issues "on the agenda", this is a valuable development. However, we must not reduce gender studies to "women's issues" especially if the concerns of women are perceived in a narrow fashion. Women certainly are concerned with particular issues within the "private" sphere such as domestic responsibilities, maternity leave, child care, and family conflicts. But it would be a mistake to ignore the fact that women are also vitally concerned with the "public" sphere such as constitution writing, the promulgation and implementation of laws, access to education and the economy, and the processes of national, regional and local government.[7] In fact, it is a myth that the "private" and "public" spheres of life can be compartmentalised. Furthermore, women need to be engaged not simply in a process of seeking to be absorbed into a male-dominated society, but rather to engage in the development of a non-sexist society. As Ginwala puts it, "we have to build our democracy as a gender-neutral society, one whose institutions, patterns of behaviour, values and norms are people-shaped rather than man-shaped" (F Ginwala, in Bazilli 1991:64).

The importance of feminist analysis, especially within the context of theological ethics, lies in the fact that it has been estimated that over 70% of South African women belong to one or another church or parachurch organisation (Bazilli 1991:3).

6   See Kretzschmar in Ackermann et al. 1991, pp 106–121 as well as the other articles in this book.
7   For a discussion of the restriction of women to the "private" sphere see Catherine Hall (1992) *White, Male and Middle Class: Explorations in Feminism and History* (Cambridge and Oxford: Polity Press).

This means that women, simply by force of numbers, are in a position to play a major role in both the church and the society at large. However, if women remain uneducated, acquiescent and unempowered, this numerical preponderance will have no effect upon the churches or the country as a whole. This is, in fact, often the case. Even though the active membership of the church is female, because they are not represented proportionally in the church leadership, they exercise less influence than their numbers would suggest. A process of conscientisation within this group would have a very dramatic effect on the self-understanding of the church and its role within the wider community.

Gender analysis is also vital because it has only recently begun to receive attention and much still needs to be done on both a theoretical and practical level. There have been a number of conferences held in recent years that have served to begin to "put women on the agenda" in South Africa. On the theological and ecclesiastical front, a number of conferences were held over the years hosted by a number of different bodies including the South African Council of Churches (SACC), the Institute for Contextual Theology (ICT), a number of churches, and various university departments.[8] Also, the Institute for a Democratic Alternative for South Africa (IDASA) hosted women's conferences in Harare in April 1989 and in Cape Town in August 1989, while in May 1990 a statement was released by the ANC concerning the rights of women (Bazilli 1991:2–3). Also the Women's National Coalition has produced various drafts of the *Women's Charter for Effective Equality*. Some of these initiatives have concentrated on Theology and the Church, others on history and sociology, still others have been overtly political in nature.

Gender analysis, because it gives particular attention to gender, and particularly to the lack of women's participation, is urgently required in our socio-theological analyses. This is because patriarchy (male-rule) is entrenched, both in the structures of most societies and in the inner consciousness of both women and men.[9] Because of the widespread impact of patriarchy, gender analysis cannot be pursued in isolation from other analyses such as race and class. For, if these analyses are isolated from each other, one misses the interrelation between these and the way in which the different levels of oppression accumulate; each intensifies the oppression that women suffer. In other words, gender analysis cannot be effectively pursued in a vacuum. Instead, when feminist/womanist analysis reveals the accumulation of discrimination and oppression experienced by women on the basis of their gender, as well as on the basis of their race, culture and class, a clearer picture begins to emerge. It is for this very reason that black women, for example, have often claimed that they are triply oppressed: on the basis of their race (black), their class (poor) and their sex (female). As indicated above, cultural analysis also needs to be added

---

8   Early examples include the report on the *Women's struggle in South Africa, Feminist Theology Conference* 1984 (Institute for Contextual Theology) 43 pp and WS Vorster (1984) (ed), *Sexism and Feminism in Theological Perspective*, (Pretoria: UNISA).

9   E Schüssler-Fiorenza uses the term "kyriarchy" (rule of lords).

to this list. This is because culture, though not static, can in some instances add to the oppression experienced by women, whilst in other instances, culture can act as a vehicle of liberation and empowerment (Kretzschmar 1995a).

Gender analysis also draws upon the insights of both the sociology and psychology of religion in its attempt to understand the way in which both church and society function with respect to women and men. Other disciplines such as history, philosophy, anthropology, political, and religious studies, and many more, are also important. In this regard, it is vital to understand the impact of social ideologies, structures, and change on gender perceptions and relations. What is the relative status of women and men, how are femininity and masculinity defined, and what roles are women and men expected to play within the context of our societies?

Instances of gender discrimination and oppression

There are a variety of spheres in which discrimination occurs against people on the basis of their gender. These include the realms of politics, the economy, culture, the family and the church. More extreme forms of discrimination are rightly termed oppression. At least two types of oppression may be identified at this point: external and internal oppression.

Types of Oppression

External oppression encompasses both exclusion and androcentrism. Exclusion prevents the access of women to influential areas such as politics, church government, and the economy and restricts women to service in the context of home and family. Androcentrism, on the other hand, is

> ... the habit of thinking about the world, ourselves, and all that is in the world from the male perspective ... Androcentrism drowns or silences women's voices and perceptions by the continual outpouring of male perceptions into the world (Wehr 1987:16).

Internalised oppression occurs when the oppressed accept or internalise the negative perceptions that those in power have of them. The powerful develop the systems and define the roles that they wish others to play in these systems. Once the weak, poor, or marginalised (who are often women) accept these roles, they have allowed themselves to be conquered. This acceptance is not simply verbal or intellectual, it requires that the oppressed pattern their behaviour on what is regarded as generally accepted and proper. Once the oppressed accept the legitimacy of these perceptions, customs and systems, they have internalised the system that is oppressing them. Thus, it is so that women sometimes defend "the system" and react aggressively to those who question or attack it.

In this regard it is apparent that many women are not aware of the evils of gender discrimination and sexism. Thus, within the context of the churches, for example, many women are unable to distinguish between the gospel of Christ and the male version of the gospel of Christ:

They accept sexist beliefs as an integral part of Christian teaching. They derive security from the stereotypes projected upon them, and willingly conform to these stereotypes. The self-denigration created in them by sexism causes them to admire and even adore the male leaders of their church. To break away from the old stereotypes is frightening to them; liberation demands authentic self definition, and offers little short-term security. It is easier to accommodate the expectations of the oppressor groups than to defy that group and enter the uncharted territory of self-knowledge and free self-identification (Swart-Russell, in Ackermann 1992:299).

One consequence of this internalised oppression is the persistent and chronic feelings of guilt experienced by many women. A distinction needs to be made between genuine and neurotic guilt. Genuine guilt is a consequence of the work of the Holy Spirit who leads us towards repentance, confession and forgiveness. Neurotic guilt is a false guilt which is imposed upon certain people by those who wish to maintain control over them. Thus neglected and abused children often feel that what is happening to them is "all their fault". Similarly, physically or emotionally battered wives, of whom there are a frighteningly large number, somehow feel that they have "provoked" their husbands to violence. In both instances the victims take on board a false and neurotic form of guilt whilst the actual aggressors balk at accepting responsibility for their own actions. The oppressors refuse to admit their real guilt, instead they project it onto the oppressed who then experience a neurotic (and paralysing) form of guilt.

Women often feel "stupid, helpless, inadequate" either because they are made to feel this way by others, or because they lack the esteem, skills, opportunities and experience to achieve any of their dreams. The sad irony is that very often it is women who hold households, families, churches and communities together, and yet they feel inferior and useless.

In this regard, a re-reading of the Bible and a questioning of the traditional interpretations of the biblical text is vital. This will involve, at the very least, a radical revision of traditional interpretations of the relevant Pauline texts, the stress on a more biblical mutual submission as opposed to female submission, and a questioning of the hierarchical paradigm of church leadership as opposed to that of servant leadership (eg Tucker 1992). Women also need to investigate and reinterpret the history of the Church and the way in which societies function (Kretzschmar 1991:106–121 and Kretzschmar 1995c). All of these will be invaluable ways in which many women can escape the cloying toils of internalised oppression.

Having identified the differences between external and internalised oppression, attention can now be turned to the identification of some key instances of political, economic, socio-cultural, family and ecclesiastical gender disparities and oppression.

Gender and Political Power

It cannot be denied that there is a huge disproportion in terms of the access of women and men to political rights and power. While some countries in the world, and more recently South Africa, have begun to address this disproportion, it remains a stark fact. Several questions can be raised at this point. What is the role of the state (at national level) and that of regional and local authorities with regard to gender relations? Are men and women treated equally? Do they have equal access to government, the law, and education? Do our legal and political systems protect the rights of women and children, for example, with reference to laws relating to child maintenance, alimony, domestic violence and rape? Do the various structures of society make it possible for women to participate fully in the various decision-making bodies? What avenues exist through which women can critique and transform those structures that oppress them?

Another important factor is the dissonance between theory and experience. For example, with respect to the Constitution and the legal system: it is not enough that women's equality and rights be enshrined in the Constitution, if those forces, practices or laws which perpetuate inequality cannot be removed or transformed. Similarly, unless women have access to the law and it can in practice protect them, it is of no use to them at all. Similarly, if only the rich can afford to take someone to court, the poor have no actual access to the law.

It is clear that women of all classes and races, both rural and urban, need to take a greater share in the decision-making and implementation of political transformation. White women need to examine to what use they have put their limited access to political power in the past and to ask what their role is in the present context. Those previously marginalised need to develop strategies to effect genuine change. Men, too, need to ask themselves whether their first loyalty is to their own gender group or to the cause of justice. Are they governed by selfish group interests or by ethical considerations of what is right and good for the population as a whole? Thus, men who are governed by personal or group self-interest need to have their selfish motives exposed. Equally, men who believe that patriarchy operates for the good of society need to be challenged and convinced of the fallacious and unjust nature of this viewpoint.

Gender and the economy

At the outset it needs to be asked what values are attached to the economic contribution of women and men. Why is it that different values are attached to so-called "men's work" compared to "women's work"? Why is it that work done outside the home (eg in the mines, industries, manufacturing and commercial sectors) receives remuneration while work done inside the home (eg child care, parenting, housekeeping and cooking) receives no remuneration? "Women's work" done in the home is not regarded as contributing to the economy of the country. Often, it is said of a woman who is a homemaker and is caring for her family that "she is not working". This popular saying is a reflection of a negative attitude to the labour of women. We need to ask what constitutes paid labour and what constitutes unpaid labour and who makes these decisions? As the Women's Charter for Effective Equality puts it:

> We claim recognition and respect for the work we do in the home, in the workplace and in the community. We claim shared responsibilities and decision-making in all areas of public and private life (1994:2).

This means that definitions of economic activity need to be radically revised. Rather than being restricted to the formal economy and to "men's work", they must also now include subsistence labour, economic activities within the informal sector, community service and all forms of "women's work" which have been hitherto both unrecognised and unpaid. In South Africa today, a great many women are either the sole bread-winners or contribute a large portion of the monthly income. At both a family and national level, due recognition needs to be given to the significant economic contribution made by women.

A second major issue is that of the exclusion of certain groups from the economy, the basis of gender. Women have limited access to the economy because many lack the education and skills to effectively compete in the labour market. Because the education of boys has been, and often still is, regarded as more important than the education of girls, those families with limited resources tend to use their funds to educate boys. Furthermore, women are for both biological and cultural reasons regarded as those who care for children, the sick and the aged.[10] This also limits their access to the economy. For this reason women are beginning to put pressure on employers to provide crèches, for example, for their employees.[11]

Because women, and particularly black women, are at the bottom of the socio-economic ladder, they suffer the worst forms of economic exclusion and deprivation. Millions of black women suffered as a result of migrant labour, influx controls and forced removals. Many now live in shacks and literally bear the burden of fetching water and fuel. The highest levels of illiteracy are found amongst women. There can be no doubt that poverty, hardship, malnutrition and intense suffering are experienced more by black women and children than any other group in our society (Wilson and Ramphele 1989:169–185).

With respect to conditions within the workplace, a number of issues can be listed which pertain to the exploitation or neglect of women within the economy. The first of these concerns the debate about what constitutes a "living wage".[12] It is a simple fact that employers continue to avoid paying women the same rate for the same job. Women also tend to be promoted with reluctance and are generally regarded as less capable of filling executive positions. In addition to direct forms of

---

10 "Professional" care for such persons in crèches, hospitals and "old-age homes" costs the relevant family money, but if a wife, mother, sister or daughter provides the care, she is unpaid.

11 Conversely, attention also needs to be given to the long-term effects of children not receiving sufficient emotional nurturing from their parents.

12 This needs to be balanced with a discussion of what constitutes a "proper day's work". Thus wages and productivity are two sides of the same coin.

remuneration, other forms of payment such as pensions, medical aid and subsidies need to be considered. Thus, those who occupy part-time positions (generally women) as well as domestic workers, very often do not receive these additional payments at all.

In addition to the factors already mentioned, several others can be noted. These include sexual harassment in the workplace, limited access to all levels of training, the conflict of expectations between domestic workers and employees, and increased participation of women in the leadership of the trade unions. In short, women should resist the artificial separation between the forces of production and the forces of reproduction within our economy.[13]

The status and roles of women within the socio-cultural sphere

Within some churches in South Africa there has been a tendency to be overly critical of aspects of African culture while failing to be sufficiently critical of aspects of Western culture. With regard to the position of women, some white men are quick to point the finger at black men while failing to recognise their own sexism. Thus, it needs to be stated that Western culture cannot escape the criticism of being sexist. For centuries women have been subjected to exclusion and androcentrism. They have been ignored, patronised and abused. Girls and women have been socialised in such a way that they have internalised the oppressive "order systems" of men. Though claiming to be objective and fair, those in power have sought to ensure that their power is maintained at the expense of women. Equality before the law is preached, but not practised, since women have traditionally been regarded as legal minors. Within the context of the advertising media, sexist portrayals of women are often used to sell products, reducing women to useful objects. Pornography, too, perpetuates sexist stereotypes and the sexual abuse of women. As pointed out earlier, gender oppression has co-existed with racial, political and economic oppression within our country.

With regard to traditional African culture, there is also a tension between the affirmation of women (especially mothers) and the lack of gender equality. With respect to customary law, questions need to be asked about whose interests are being served. Do both women and men benefit equally from the various provisions that operate within customary or traditional law?[14]

It has been widely argued that because women were (and often still are) defined within the context of the family in general and marriage in particular, they are accorded little status outside of this framework (Oduyoye 1986:122). Prior to marriage, the woman's life is governed by the traditions of the tribe or clan and she is

13 Ramazanoglu discusses the debate concerning biological and social causes of women's oppression on pp 28–33.
14 Concerning traditional and colonial patriarchy, see Nhlapo in Bazilli 1991:112ff and Walker and Guy in Walker 1990:1–47.

subject to the authority of her father and the other male members of the family, clan or tribe. After marriage, she is subject to her husband and, after his death, to his brothers or her sons. The purpose of marriage, in turn, is perceived primarily in terms of procreation and the alliance between two kinship groups (Oduyoye and Kanyoro 1992:9–73). Customary law is thus inimical to women's rights because it is based on

> ... an attitude to women in marriage and in the family which sees them solely as adjuncts to the group, a means to the anachronistic end of clan survival, rather than as valuable in themselves and deserving of recognition for their human worth on the same terms as men (Nhlapo in Bazilli 1991:114).

Other elements of customary law that have been subjected to critique include: polygamy, the levirate, the payment of lobolo, the sororate, child betrothal, mourning rituals, the perpetual childhood of women in terms of the law, proprietary incapacity and inequality in relation to divorce (Nhlapo in Bazilli 1991:120–121).[15] For this reason the Women's Coalition issued this statement:

> Women and men shall have equal legal status and capacity in civil and customary law, including, amongst others, full contractual rights, the right to acquire and hold rights in property, the right to inheritance and the right to secure credit (Women's Charter for Effective Equality: 3).

With reference to both Western and African culture, a number of points can be made. Firstly, that socio-cultural traditions and structures must be understood and evaluated in terms of the contexts within which they originated. Secondly, as neither society nor its customs are immutable, the effects of change upon these customs need to be assessed. Are these customs, for example, still providing the same social function as was previously the case and is this function morally defensible? Thirdly, it then becomes necessary to ask whether these traditions and structures should be totally abandoned, fully adopted, or radically revised. There are many elements of both Western and Traditional African culture that are inherently valuable and which provide the necessary social functions of giving identity, providing stability and group cohesion to a people. These aspects need to be identified and embraced, but in such a way that the creation of morally defensible and non-sexist basis for a genuinely "new" socio-cultural context within a presently fragmented and violent South Africa is possible.

The family

Closely related to issues just discussed above, is that of gender relations within the family. As several issues pertinent to the family are discussed elsewhere in this volume, only three areas of concern are outlined here: perceptions concerning the nature and status of women and men; role expectations; and arenas of struggle.

Concerning the relative status of men and women, the majority of cultures have perceived men as superior to women in one way or another. Although this myth has

---

15 See also Oduyoye and Kanyoro (eds) 1990:106–108, 131–138, 187–213 and Oduyoye 1992:87–179.

been questioned and disproved by a great many women over the centuries, such notions have only relatively recently fallen into disrepute in certain areas of the world. Although often weaker in terms of muscular strength, women not only live longer on average, but are physically stronger, for example, in terms of endurance to pain and cold. While certain thinkers have held that women are intellectually and spiritually inferior to men, there are a great many in our contemporary world who hold rather different views. (I return to this point in the next section on the church.) The next point to be considered is that of role expectations. What does society expect from males and females and why do these expectations differ? Are these due to biology (nature) or society (nurture) (see Ramazanoglu 1989:24–42 and 174–192)? Obviously, biological differences do play a role in the development of gender stereotypes and socialisation processes. Thus, women are usually responsible for the care of small infants. Indeed, the vast majority of women are either mothers and/or wives at some point in their lives. But does this mean that their identity is to be completely subsumed within these roles? Why is it that men, while often fathers and/or husbands are not perceived purely in terms of these roles? Surely socialisation plays a role in this process in which gender inequalities are perpetuated to the detriment of women. Although few women wish to forsake child care and parenting responsibilities, they do not wish these to assume such proportions that it determines their identity or that child care and parenting be the sole responsibility of women.

One final comment with regard to roles. The greater participation of women within the formal economy has meant that a woman is often the only or a substantial "bread winner" within the family. Naturally enough, this has impacted upon the family and resulted in some men feeling threatened or even refusing to work themselves, but assuming control over all the money earned by their wives. This raises the question of how role expectations regarding family responsibilities need to be changed and definitions of "work" radically rethought. Why is it that women often bear the brunt of the responsibility for family life, but seldom receive appreciation or assistance in this regard?

A third major area of concern can be identified as the arenas of struggle. The first of these is that of widespread domestic violence. Marital rape, emotional abuse and physical battering are widespread as are cases of the abuse of children within the family. In cases of divorce, teenage pregnancy, and other single parent situations, women are usually left, literally, holding the baby. Although the system of forcing fathers to make maintenance payments has greatly improved in some sectors, much still needs to be done to extend this legal protection to the entire population.

With respect to medical care, access to health facilities such as clinics and hospitals is a factor of major importance. Furthermore, far more attention needs to be given to preventative medicine and nutrition than is presently the case. Thousands of women are inadequately informed concerning AIDS, breast and cervical cancer and the implementation of family planning. Debates concerning abortion, counselling services, and welfare services remain firmly on the agenda.

In the interim, a number of other practical steps can be taken immediately such as the construction of shelters and the provision of counselling services, police and legal aid for women and children who are in dire straits. With regard to rape, for example,

> Appropriate education and training must be provided for police, prosecutors, magistrates, judges, district surgeons and other people involved in dealing with cases of rape, battery, sexual assault, incest and other forms of abuse (*Women's Charter for Effective Equality 1994:8*).

The Church

Mention has already been made of the controversial issues of the relative status and roles of women and men. In the past, "orthodox" theology has supplied the divine legitimation of male headship over women and the subsequent construction of social, family and ecclesiastical hierarchies. However, a persistent minority of women have consistently critiqued this dominant and "official" theology.[16] Both in earlier centuries and, particularly, during the 20th century, biblical interpretations that justify the subjugation of women have been widely criticised.[17]

Within many churches, women are presented with a confusing double message. On the one hand their acceptance by God, even their equality in God's sight, is affirmed. On the other hand, their roles are restricted and their nature as equally God-created is denied in practice. Passages such as Galatians 3.28 are spiritualised (ie they are regarded as not applicable to historical, earthly reality) while passages such as 1 Timothy 2:12 are taken out of context and regarded as universally binding. Arguments based on questionable interpretations of "orders of creation" and male "headship" are usually advanced to perpetuate male domination in church and society.[18] More often than not, women are silenced, excluded, ignored, laughed at, and marginalised within the Church. Understandably, this experience impacts negatively on the spiritual growth of women who, given their experience, find it difficult to actually believe in a (male) God who loves them and regards them as valuable and important.

Another important factor that requires attention is the process of socialisation, particularly gender socialisation. Women and men need to pay attention to the way in which girls and boys are socialised in the Church. If this is not done, the oppression presently being experienced will simply be perpetuated.[19]

---

16 See Ruth A Tucker & Walter L Liefeld (eds) (1987) *Daughters of the Church: Women and Ministry from the New Testament Times to the Present*, (Grand Rapids: Academie).

17 See Margaret Fell, *Women's speaking justified by the scriptures* (1666) and, much more recently, Ruth A Tucker (1992) *Women in the Maze: Questions and Answers on Biblical Equality*, (Downers Grove: Inter-Varsity Press).

18 For a discussion of these see Tucker 1992:33–38 and 112–125.

19 See Caroline Tuckey, (1994) "Sexist socialising of children in the Sunday Schools of the Church of the Province of Southern Africa: A Theological Ethical Study", (Pretoria: UNISA, unpublished MTh thesis).

In all these instances, a tension emerges between God and the Church; between the Christian faith functioning as a means of generating salvation, freedom and growth or as a means of legitimating religious patriarchy.[20]

Some concluding comments on the way ahead

This chapter has highlighted the very significant inequalities that exist between men and women in our contemporary society. In many cases, women are not only ignored, they are actively oppressed and abused. If Christians believe that both women and men are created in God's image, and that in Christ there is neither male nor female, how can they resist the conclusion that part of their witness to the world is to live out these realities in obedience to God? This being the case, how can the churches make a constructive contribution to the building of a more just and less sexist society?

To begin with, the issues raised here need to be widely discussed, not just within academic circles, but also within our homes, churches, places of work and study, in short, wherever people gather together. It would be naïve to expect easy and complete agreement to be reached, but unless a process of conscientisation ensues, the points made in this chapter would be equally relevant in ten year's time. How can churches talk glibly about Jesus calling the children to himself (Mk 10:14) while they do not simultaneously enter the struggle to end child abuse, in whatever form it takes? How can we preach about the women that Jesus noticed, healed and taught (eg Lk 8:1–3; 10:38–56; Jh 11:1–54) while we ignore, oppress, and fail to teach or empower the women in our churches and wider society? To preach one thing and practise the opposite is nothing but blatant hypocrisy.

In addition to the task of conscientisation and thinking through our faith in relation to the multitude of needs around us, we need to make the attempt to analyse the causes of gender inequalities and oppression. To what extent are these due to biological differences and why have these differences been exploited rather than celebrated? Why is it that so many children grow up without proper appreciation, love and care from their fathers? (While not all mothers are good mothers, the absence of fathers, both geographically and emotionally, is far more widespread).

As far as the topic of ethics, women and gender is concerned, conscientisation involves becoming aware of the way in which the male and female genders interact at a number of levels. The various spheres touched upon in this chapter include: politics, economics, socio-cultural matters, the family and the church. Empowerment takes place when people, in this instance women, have access to information, are enabled to assess this information, and develop paradigms that can make sense of their experience and insights. Further, they need to personally appropriate and internalise these insights and go on to develop the necessary personal and structural strategies that can serve to promote the application of these insights.

20 See Kretzschmar in Ackermann et al. (1991); Kretzschmar in Villa-Vicencio (1995a); and Kretzschmar (1995b).

Patriarchy may be defined as the rule by the fathers; the socio-economic, religious, legal and political legitimation of male sovereignty. It has operated within a number of different political systems within South Africa including that of traditional tribal rule, colonialism and apartheid. Within all of these women have experienced exclusion and oppression. What are the root causes of the common experience of patriarchy and its abuse of power in our societies? Is sin at the base of this abuse of power and authority? What can be done to create family, church and social customs and structures that are just and life-giving rather than unjust and oppressive?

Another important matter is that of identifying and removing false religious legitimations of male domination. The all too common distortions of biblical teachings on submission linked with the tendency of women to acquiesce to and seek approval from men, can make a devastating mixture. A process of "depatriarchalising" is necessary:

> Depatriarchalizing is not a matter of imposing one's own values and beliefs on Holy Scripture but a dynamic process within Scripture itself (Govinden in Ackermann et al. 1991:291).

As women gain greater access to education and theological education in particular, a range of previously unconsidered issues can begin to be placed on the agenda. This makes it possible for the entire issue of gender perceptions and relations to be reviewed and the androcentric paradigms that have previously excluded women to be critiqued and transformed. Thus, a process of deconstruction must take place by and for those in positions of power, and a process of construction initiated by and for those who are marginalised. Within the churches, in addition to the deconstruction of patriarchy, a creative process of devising alternative symbols, liturgies, theological paradigms, and ecclesiastical structures is urgently required.

Women also need to examine their own internalisation of oppressive attitudes, actions and structures. Part of this process is an examination of the process of socialisation, particularly gender socialisation. Women and men need to pay attention to the way in which girls and boys are socialised not simply within the context of society, but also within the church. Furthermore, external oppression can only be effectively counteracted if the social structures that perpetuate sexism are themselves reviewed and transformed.

A number of areas have been identified in this chapter. In essence, women wish not simply to be permitted to participate on the fringes of a male-dominated society, they insist upon both deciding what form a particular society is to take and participating in its reconstruction. In short, gender stereotypes and gender-based oppression need to be challenged and overcome.

SELECT BIBLIOGRAPHY

Ackermann, Denise, Draper, Jonathan and Mashinini, Emma (eds). 1991. *Women Hold Up Half the Sky: Women in the Church in Southern Africa*. Pietermaritzburg: Cluster.

Bazilli, Susan. 1991. *Putting women on the Agenda*. Johannesburg: Ravan Press.

Fell, Margaret. 1666. *Women's Speaking Justified*. Reprinted in Christine Trevett (ed). 1989. *Women's Speaking justified and other seventeenth century Quaker writings about women*. London: Quaker Home Service.

Hall, Catherine. 1992. *White, Male and Middle Class: Explorations in Feminism and History*. Cambridge and Oxford: Polity Press.

Jordaan, Roxanne. 1987. "The emergence of Black Feminist Theology in South Africa", *Journal of Black Theology in Southern Africa* 2:1, 42–46.

Kabira, Wanjiku Mukabi and Nzioki, Elizabeth Akinyi. (eds). 1993. *Celebrating Women's Resistance*. Nairobi: African Women's Perspective.

Kretzschmar, Louise. 1991. "The Relevance of Feminist Theology within the Southern African context", in D Ackerman, et al.(eds). *Women Hold up Half the Sky*. Pietermaritzburg: Cluster 106–121.

Kretzschmar, Louise. 1995a. "Women and Culture: Ecclesial and Cultural Transformation" in C Villa-Vicencio and Carl Niehaus (eds). *Many Cultures, One Nation: Festschrift for Beyers Naudé*. Cape Town: Human and Rossouw pp 90–104.

Kretzschmar, Louise. 1995b. "Gender and Oppression: A South African Feminist Underview", *Missionalia* 23:2: 147–161.

Kretzschmar, Louise. 1995c. "History, Authority and Ministry: An analysis of the implications of lives of 17th century English Baptist women for contemporary women in South Africa", *Journal of Theology for Southern Africa* 93: 17–31.

Lipman, Beata. 1984. *We make Freedom: Women in South Africa*. London and Boston: Pandora.

Oduyoye, Mercy Amba and Kanyoro, Musimbi RA. (eds). 1992. *The Will to Arise: Women, Tradition and the Church in Africa*. Maryknoll: Orbis.

Oduyoye, Mercy Amba. 1986. *Hearing and Knowing: Theological Reflections on Christianity in Africa*. Maryknoll: Orbis.

Oduyoye, Mercy Amba and Kanyoro, Musimbi (eds). 1990. *Talitha, Qumi: Proceedings of the Convocation of African Women Theologians 1989*. Ibadan, Nigeria: Daystar.

Ramazanoglu, Caroline. 1989. *Feminism and the contradictions of Oppression*. London and New York: Routledge.

Thistlethwaite, Susan Brooks. 1989. *Sex, Race, and God*. New York: Crossroad.

Tucker, Ruth A. 1992. *Women in the Maze: Questions and Answers on Biblical Equality*. Downers Grove: Intervarsity Press.

Tucker, Ruth A. and Liefeld, Walter L. (eds). 1987. *Daughters of the Church: Women and Ministry from the New Testament Times to the Present*. Grand Rapids: Academie.

Tuckey, Caroline. 1994. "Sexist socialising of children in the Sunday Schools of the Church of the Province of Southern Africa: A Theological Ethical Study". Pretoria: UNISA, unpublished MTh thesis.

Villa-Vicencio, C. and De Gruchy, J. (eds). 1994. *Doing Ethics in Context: South African Perspectives*. Cape Town: David Philip and Orbis: Maryknoll.

Walker, Cherryl. 1990. *Women and Gender in South Africa to 1945*. Cape Town: David Philip.

Wehr, Demaris S. 1987. *Jung and Feminism: Liberating Archetypes*. London: Routledge.

Institute for Contextual Theology, *Report on the Women's Struggle in South Africa, Feminist Theology Conference, 31 August–2 September 1984* 43 pp.

Report of the Commission on the Ordination of Women Church of the Province of South Africa, January 1989 58 pp.

Papers offered at the *Conference on Women and Gender in Southern Africa*, University of Natal, 30 January–2 February 1991.

Women's Charter for Effective Equality. Issued by the Women's Coalition 25–27 February 1994 9 pp.

12

The burden of moral guilt: its theological and political implications

Charles Villa-Vicencio

A crime is atoned for; political liability is limited by a peace treaty and thus brought to an end. As far as these two points are concerned, the idea is correct and meaningful. But moral and metaphysical guilt, which are understood only by the individual in his community, are by their very nature not atoned for. They do not cease. Whoever bears them enters upon a process lasting all his life (Karl Jaspers, Germany 1947:117).

First we are asked to sacrifice justice. Now, in the name of reconciliation, some ask that we sacrifice truth. The burden of truth will not disappear. We demand to know. This much is not negotiable (Michael Lapsley, South Africa 1995).[1]

Two observations from opposite ends of the globe, fifty years apart. There are vast similarities and differences between Nazism and apartheid. As ideologies, they died different deaths, although the legacy of both continue to weigh like nightmares on their respective societies. The collapse of Nazism came with the defeat of Nazi forces by the allied armies. The Nuremberg Trials followed. The collapse of apartheid was otherwise. The apartheid state was not defeated on the battlefield. The South African Interim Constitution requires that there "shall be" amnesty for perpetrators of "acts, omissions and offences associated with political objectives and committed in the course of the conflicts of the past." At a recent conference on the Truth and Reconciliation Commission,[2] established to deal with South Africa's past atrocities, a human rights lawyer observed: "In post World War ll Europe people paid with their lives for past deeds. In South Africa state torturers could walk away with a pension."[3]

The Nuremberg Trials continue to be a symbol of what is politically right, morally just and socially decent among many who have survived the atrocities of Nazism, Latin American dictatorships, Eastern European forms of state oppression and

---

1 Father Michael Lapsley is a survivor of a political assassination attempt in 1990.
2 The Truth and Reconciliation Commission was established by Act of Parliament, commencing its work on 15 December 1995.
3 At a consultation on the Truth and Reconciliation Commission, sponsored by Justice in Transition. Cape Town, May 1994.

apartheid. Criminal and political justice are dimensions of the reconciliation process that cannot be avoided without social, cultural, moral and spiritual consequences. South Africa is yet to face these consequences. Equally important, however, are questions of moral, metaphysical and corporate guilt – without which there can be neither serious national reconciliation nor serious political renewal. Moishe Postone suggests that Germany has, at one level, been "quite successful in overcoming the legacy of National Socialism" (Postone in Harms, 1990:223). The Nuremberg Trials did not, however, equip the German people to deal adequately with the legacy of moral guilt. Lutz Reuter shows that the burden of Nazi rule continued to be the dominant paradigm of political analysis in Germany in the late 1980s (Reuter in Harms et al. 1990:155). Post 1990 reunification is, in turn, being challenged by two different understandings of Nazism. The past continues to be central to the German present. A recent *New Yorker* article notes that the German people continue to be driven by "a duty to remember and a longing to forget, as if duty and desire were the thesis and anti-thesis of a dialectic of destiny" (Kramer 1995).

Consideration is given in what follows to the importance of acknowledging moral culpability and corporate responsibility – in Germany and South Africa. Karl Jaspers' distinction between different levels of guilt is addressed. Secondly, the need to transcend both moral and cultural morbidity and indifference in pursuit of human and political reconstruction is considered. Finally, the question of spiritual healing is discussed.

Acknowledging guilt

To limit culpability to those who can be tried and convicted of monstrous crimes is to allow others to excuse themselves. To mitigate the crimes of monstrous perpetrators of violence on the basis that all are culpable is, on the other hand, to allow evil to prosper. It is within the ambits of these extremes that Jaspers' different levels of guilt provide clarifying insight.

Writing shortly after the institution of the Nuremberg Trials, Karl Jaspers, an existentialist philosopher who himself narrowly escaped the concentration camps, warned that only "a transcendently founded religious or philosophical faith" (Jaspers 1947:21) could provide a basis for the "new world now waiting to be built" (Jaspers 1947:59). He saw this possibility as being directly related to the acknowledgement of guilt. "The guilt question," he argued, "is more than a question put to us by others, it is one we [must] put to ourselves. The way we answer it will be decisive ... for the German soul" (Jaspers 1947:59). Yet, he realised that it was humanity itself that needed to be renewed: "Unless a break is made in the evil chain, the fate which overtook us will overtake the victors – and all mankind with them." Yet, refusing to allow the notion of "original sin" to be used as a "way to dodge German guilt", he insisted that Germans had "fallen into a peculiar, terrible incurring of guilt [which] exists as a possibility in man as such" (Jaspers 1947:100). Recognising the dangers involved in tampering with the past and exposing the raw ends of guilt, he spoke, nevertheless, of the need for a "spiritual-political venture along the edge of the precipice" (Jaspers 1947:16).

It is within the context of this interrelationship between the particular and the universal that Jaspers analyses human guilt. His concern is to discern the relationship between the guilt of the German leadership and the guilt of those who ignored "the warning signals which ever more shrilly, from 1930 until 1939, portended the hell to be loosed by the satanic forces of National Socialism" (Jaspers 1947:95). He recognises the need to expose the axis of guilt between the Nuremburg Trialists and those industrialists who fuelled the fires of the Third Reich, but escaped the Trials. His analysis impinges on the guilt of scientists, academics, doctors, pastors and passive observers who allowed evil to prosper, while enjoying the fruits of its prosperity. To this end Jaspers discusses four levels of guilt:

Criminal guilt, he argues, is the consequence of being tried and found guilty in court of breaking the law (Jaspers 1947:31). Criminal propitiation involves the judicial price exacted and the appropriate penalty paid.

Political guilt concerns the acts of politicians and others (bureaucrats, civil servants and citizens) who promote, support and allow government policy to succeed. Everyone is responsible for the way in which he or she is governed. Judgement and guilt is pronounced on the basis of natural, common and international law. Jurisdiction rests with the power and will of the new rulers – in the German situation, with the allies (Jaspers 1947:61ff). Political propitiation is via reparation, restitution and political reconstruction or settlement.

Moral guilt is wide ranging. It includes criminal, political and military actions as well as indifference and passivity (Jaspers 1947:31, 63ff). It includes a sense of responsibility and guilt which no amount of criminal or political propitiation can appease. For Jaspers it refers to that sense of remorse and responsibility which endures after the magnitude of the industrial, technological terrorism of the Nazi state had rendered the would-be resister impotent. It is grounded in what has been called the "subterranean unease ... of a repressed past" (Postone 1990:234). It is an unease that contradicts the "aggressive silence" of those who, in their "self-isolating pride" refuse to admit culpability of any kind (Jaspers 1947:112).

While guilt cannot be nullified, its "purification," Jaspers suggests, is only possible via a willingness to face the agony of culpability. This alone provides a basis for "political liberty" and the opportunity for a new national beginning (Jaspers 1947:82, 121). Recognising that not all are capable or willing to face their guilt, he contends:

> The morally guilty are those who are capable of penance, the ones who knew, or could know, and yet walked in the ways which self-analysis reveals to them culpable error – whether conveniently closing their eyes to events or permitting themselves to be intoxicated, seduced or bought with personal advantages, or obeying from fear (Jaspers 1947:63).

Martin Niemoller, a U-Boat commander in World War l, who later became a Lutheran pastor and leader of the Confessing Church, was imprisoned in Sachenhausen and Dachau for opposing Nazism. He repeatedly sought to relate the crimes of the Nazi regime and core moral guilt of the entire nation, without equating the two: "We have let all these things happen without protest against these crimes and without supporting the victims" (Niemoller, in Reuter 1990:175). "We should not blame the Nazis [alone]. They will find their prosecutors and judges, we should blame ourselves and draw logical conclusions."[4] For Jaspers the choice was decisive: "Either acceptance of guilt ... in which case our soul goes the way of transformation, or else we subside into the average triviality of indifferent, mere living" (Jaspers 1947:117).

The propitiation of moral guilt, Jaspers writes, "rests with my conscience, and in communication with my friends and intimates who are lovingly concerned about my soul" (Jaspers 1947:32). It is a deeply spiritual and profoundly personal possibility. The burden of such guilt does not cease (see Jaspers 1947:117). The memory of our personal and collective involvement in the past continues to weigh upon us.

Metaphysical guilt takes the notion of moral guilt a step further. It involves human solidarity. "There exists a solidarity among men as human beings that makes each co-responsible for every wrong and every injustice in the world, especially crimes committed in one's presence or with one's knowledge" (Jaspers 1947:32). Jaspers' concern is not to accuse others. Indeed, it would be quite wrong to impose guilt and culpability on the victims of Nazism, apartheid or any other atrocity. His concern is rather that each person acknowledge his or her own place within the drama of evil, as a basis for addressing the underlying potential for evil which resides within humanity itself. Jaspers, the existentialist, becomes overtly theological: "Before God it is not a case of some, or the majority, or many, or most, but all who are guilty." Without acknowledging the capacity for evil in all humanity as well as the responsibility of all humanity to correct what is wrong, Jaspers sees no hope to tapping into what he calls "a new source of active life" (Jaspers 1947:120).

Collective guilt involves the recognition that no sector of the human race is beyond the possibility of committing the gruesome and shameful acts of others. Dr Josef Garlinski in his book *Fighting Auschwitz*, written as a memorial to the victims of Auschwitz, reminds us that the young SS men "could have been your sons or mine" (1994:139). They were brainwashed, trained to be brutal, to follow orders, coming to believe that to show human compassion or remorse was to be a bad German and a bad soldier. To metaphysically exclude oneself from the evil of others is for Jaspers to fail adequately to deal with the problem of human evil. He acknowledges that "our [German] national tradition contains something, mighty and threatening, which is our moral ruin". He at the same time insists that it is important not to identify Germans as "the evil people" (Jaspers 1947:80, 96). To do

---

4   Letter of the Council of the Evangelical Churches in Germany to the Allied Control Council and the German State Governments, May 2, 1946. Published in Friedrich Soehlmann (ed), *Wort zur Verantwortung der Kirche Für das Öffentliche Leben* (Freysa 1945–1946).

so is to fail to deal radically enough with the problem of human evil – which history suggests knows no national, racial nor time constraints.

As with moral guilt, the propitiation of metaphysical guilt is more difficult than is the case with criminal and political guilt. To the extent that propitiation is possible at all, it comes through acceptance of corporate responsibility. It involves a commitment to a new option for humanity itself. By acknowledging collective guilt we accept responsibility for "renewing human existence from its origin." This is a "task which is given to all men on earth but which appears urgently, more perceptibly ... when our own guilt brings us as a people face to face with nothingness" (Jaspers 1947:81). In the face of the abyss the demand for a new beginning – for radical change, is most pertinently felt. We are challenged to "take ourselves seriously". In so doing we are required to accept responsibility for the history of which we are part (Jaspers 1947:115). We are compelled to rise above the "triviality of indifferent, mere living" (Jaspers 1947:117).

Beyond morbidity and indifference

Jaspers' reflections on the post-Nazi situation are highly relevant to the present situation in South Africa. The proposed Truth and Reconciliation Commission's task is to enable the nation to deal with its past – considering requirements for political amnesty, listening to the stories of victims and survivors, and addressing claims for reparation and healing.[5] This is a task located within the continuum that extends from morbid acknowledgement of past atrocities by some perpetrators, passive observers and victims, to denial, acceptance of responsibility to redress (where possible) past wrongs, and moral indifference. The latter comes to expression in a new found willingness to acknowledge guilt and appropriate a cheap form of reconciliation. It constitutes a refusal to undergo the kind of change that is required to initiate a new beginning. As in Germany "people turned from Nazis into democrats in five minutes after 1945" (De Gruchy 1993:10) so in South Africa it is increasingly difficult to find whites who actually supported apartheid!

Jane Kramer speaks of what she calls the Victim Germany Syndrome. "It is the Germany Hitler 'seized' in 1933 and 'occupied' for twelve dark years: the Germany that was 'liberated' in 1945, as if it were Holland, or a concentration camp" (Kramer 1995:48). It constitutes an attempt to get back to a romantic notion of pre-Nazi national identity and culture that is seen to constitute all that is decent, good and noble. It ignores within that tradition what Jaspers defined as "something mighty and threatening, which is our moral ruin" (Kramer 1947:89). It constitutes a refusal

5   The Truth and Reconciliation Commission (established by parliament) makes provision for three separate committees: an amnesty committee which considers the application for amnesty from perpetrators of gross human rights violations; a human rights commission which will, inter alia, hear the stories of victims of human rights violations; and a reparations committee which seeks to provide reparation to victims where this is possible.

to place the existing order (or what is defended as its 'essential goodness') under the spotlight of prophetic critique. Steve Biko captured this desire among liberal (anti-apartheid) South Africans, who have resolutely refused to address the indecencies of a liberal culture that tolerated and often promoted an ethos that gave rise to the apartheid monster: "If by integration you understand ... acceptance of blacks into an already established set of norms and codes of behaviour set and maintained by whites, then YES I am against it," he wrote (Biko 1987:24).

It is the identity of South African culture itself – in all its different mutations (liberal, apartheid, black, non-racial and any other) that needs to be scrutinised. More than that, it is our mental constructs of what constitutes human decency and what is morally acceptable that needs to be reassessed in order that "a new source of active life" may be discovered (Jaspers 1947:120). It involves the opportunity of "taking ourselves seriously", to rise above the "triviality of ... mere living" (Jaspers 1947:115). Like Germany in 1945, South Africa in 1990 stared into the face of nothingness. The facing of this crisis has provided the opportunity to create something new. For this to happen two profoundly theological exercises are required. Only then can the equally theologically important exercise in reconciliation and healing take place.

Acknowledgement of guilt

The inter-relationship and distinctions between Jaspers' different levels of guilt need not be reiterated here. "Our moral ruin" (Jaspers) needs to be plumbed. A culture that has generated racism, gender discrimination, economic deprivation and the horrors of apartheid needs fundamental renewal. It contains structures of oppression and habits of moral degradation that will perpetuate themselves and continue to produce people capable of evil. A society within which lies, aggression, violence and moral defeat are accepted as the norm is a society deeply in need of rebirth.

This realisation, although never fully addressed, lies at the heart of progressive Protestant theological thought in Germany, with the critique of German culture occurring long before the rise of Nazism. Friedrich Nietzsche (among others) rejected the theological paradigm itself: "As long as your morality hung over me I breathed like one asphyxiated," he observed. "That is why I throttled the snake. I wished to live. Consequently it had to die" (1908:123). Karl Barth, in turn, initiated a new theological paradigm in his *Epistle to the Romans* (1918), defining established German culture as a "morality ... that turns out to be a lie". He described the self-confessed piety of German bourgeois Christianity quite simply as "the night". He instinctively supported the socialist challenge to this order. "The revolt of Prometheus is wholly justified once Zeus, the 'No-God', has been exalted to the throne" (Barth 1960:43). Years later he became a formative member in the Confessing Church and an author of the Barmen Declaration (1934). Again it was the dominant culture that he called into question (Barth 1965:42). The Confessing Church was divided against itself (it included conservatives, moderates and radicals – even some who regarded themselves as German Christians). The Barmen Declaration, in turn, reflected many limitations. Eberhard Bethge writes of the church's reluctant involvement in an "unwanted political struggle" which moderated the intensity of its resistance (Bethge 1974:167–184). Frederick Bonkovsky explains the ecclesial focus of the Confessing Church in showing that "resistance grew precisely when the Nazi upheaval challenged the positions and status of the religious elite" (Bonkovsky in Little and Locke 1974:167–184). Pinchas Lapide has exposed the extent to which the Confessing Church failed to address the Jewish question in an adequate manner (Lapide 1985:37–51). This having been said, for Barth, Barmen was but a first step.[6] He was deported to Switzerland shortly after the publication of the Barmen Declaration, and it remains an open question what the level of his involvement in Germany would have been had this not occurred. He was at the same time hesitant (due perhaps to a latent ambiguity in his thought) to relate, in a concrete and explicit manner, the radical insights of his theology to some of the most pressing social realities of his time.

It was not until October 1945, in the first post-war Synod of the Evangelical Church, that the next step was taken. This resulted in the Stuttgart Confession of Guilt. Franklin Littell describes it as one of the most remarkable confessions of church history, primarily because it was people who had fought against Nazism and suffered its persecution who were confessing their guilt (Littel 1961:49). The central sentence reads:

> We have caused immeasurable suffering in various countries and peoples. Even if we fought against the awful ideology of National Socialism, we accuse ourselves of not confessing more courageously, not praying more devotedly, not believing more cheerfully, and not loving more urgently.[7]

Ultimately, however, the Stuttgart Confession was not a confession of guilt by the German Christians. It was a public declaration to members of the Ecumenical Movement present at the Stuttgart meeting by those who were most deeply engaged in the church struggle against Nazism. Important as this was, the Confession lacked specificity and it failed to mobilise the support of grassroots Christians. It was essentially the confession of a group of courageous leaders. Few understood its theological significance. The Darmstadt Declaration of Guilt followed in 1947.[8] It was a more concrete statement – addressing the nature of corporate and moral guilt. It enjoyed the support of many within the Confessing Church, but again failed to attract the support of grassroots Christians in Germany.

The history of theological confession against apartheid in South Africa contains

---

6   See essays in Karl Barth, *Barmen Theologischen Erklaerung* (Zurich: Theologischer Verlag, 1984). Also *Eine Schweitzer Stimme 1938–1945* (Zollikon-Zurich: Lutterworth Press, 1965).

7   The text of the Stuttgart Confession can be found in Martin Gerschat (ed). *Im Zeichen der Schuld. 40 Jahre Stuttgart Schuldbekenntnis: Eine Dokumentation* (Neukirchener-Vluyn: Neukirchener Verlag, 1985).

8   *Ibid.*

several contours, reaching a turning point in the World Alliance of Reformed Churches' (WARC) declaration on apartheid as a heresy – subsequently adopted by most member churches of the South African Council of Churches (SACC).[9] *The Kairos Document* was published in 1985, stating that the affirmation of reconciliation was being widely abused in the church as a means to obviate the need for fundamental change.[10] It called Christians to radical disengagement from the state and other forces of apartheid both within and outside of the church. Other statements followed, including the *Harare Declaration* (1985) which called for support for liberation movements fighting against the apartheid regime and the *Lusaka Statement* (1987) which went a step further in declaring the South African government to be illegitimate.[11]

The unbanning of political organisations and the release of Nelson Mandela and other political prisoners in 1990 resulted in a different kind of church response to the apartheid state. This response included the statement of the Rustenburg Conference held in November 1990, which brought together the most representative gathering of churches ever in South Africa. The statement included a confession of guilt for the sins of apartheid.[12] Also important is the revised position of the Dutch Reformed Church regarding their support for apartheid.[13] In October of the following year (1991) the South African member churches of the WCC met in Cape Town, committing themselves to the eradication of apartheid and other forms of exploitation in South African society.[14]

In pursuit of these goals, various churches have committed themselves to programmes of renewal and structural change. The Methodist Church of Southern Africa has, for example, adopted a programme entitled "Journey to a New Land". The United Congregational Church continues to address the structural implications of the Kairos Document for renewal in church and state. The SACC has, in turn, established several task forces on renewal. Drawing on both Christian theological and African Traditional Religious resources, these include a programme on healing. Plans are being made for ecumenical services of confession and purification.

In brief, the South African church, not unlike the German church in the wake of World War ll, has recognised the need to acknowledge its complicity in apartheid

9   See John de Gruchy and C Villa-Vicencio (eds.), *Apartheid is a Heresy* (Cape Town: David Philip; Grand Rapids: Eerdmans, 1983).

10 *The Kairos Document* (Braamfontein: Skotaville, 1985). For documents on church-state relations culminating in the Kairos Document see appendices in C Villa-Vicencio, *Between Christ and Caesar* (Grand Rapids: Eerdmans, 1986).

11 See C Villa-Vicencio, *Trapped in Apartheid* (Maryknoll: Orbis Press, 1988).

12 Louw Alberts and Frank Chikane (eds), *The Road to Rustenburg: The Church Looking Forward to a New South Africa* (Cape Town: Struik, 1991).

13 C Villa-Vicencio, "South Africa: Piety and Politics," *Africa Report*, Vol. 36, No. 1, January/February, 1991.

14 "Cape Town Statement," October 1991. *Journal of Theology for Southern Africa*, 77, December, 1991: 84ff.

and the need to rise above it. What it has not done is face the full theological and moral implications of the confession of guilt. To do so in a manner akin to the discussion generated by Jaspers could lay the foundation for the kind of renewal, grounded in "a new source of active life" without which what Kairos theologians have called "a moment of grace" requiring "decisive action" could pass the church and nation by. In the words of *The Kairos Document*: "This is a dangerous time because if this opportunity is missed and allowed to pass by, the loss for the Church, for the Gospel and for all the people of South Africa will be immeasurable" (Kairos 1985:1). Pertinent in this regard is whether the church has the will and capacity to lead the nation in an act of national confession.

Historical adjustment

Related to this confession is the need for a new understanding of historical identity. It is an understanding that needs to transcend the partisan interpretations of the past, while being enriched by these differences. The struggle for memory in Germany has taken on new meaning with the coming down of the Berlin Wall. A visit to the imposing Treptow Memorial to Soviet soldiers in former East Berlin recalls the price paid by the Soviet people for the defeat of fascism. The House of the Wannsee Conference Centre (where the technical details of the extermination of Europe's Jews was worked out), in former West Berlin, focuses the mind on the anti-semitic centre of Nazi ideology.

Controversy raged around Lea Rosh's plans to build a multi-million dollar holocaust memorial in the shadow of Brandenburg Gate. It vividly illustrates the place of memory in the quest for healing and nation-building.[15] It is a question of what to remember where. "Is Berlin worthy of a memorial to Jews at all?" ask Rosh's detractors. "Why not let it stand on the ruins of the number 8 Prins-Albrecht Strasse, the nerve-centre of Nazi terror, within eyeshot of the new Reichstat, the Brandenburg Gate and other symbols of the 'old' and 'new' Berlin?" The rejoinder of those who support the idea seems to make equal sense. Historian Reinhard Ruerup (somewhat mechanically) suggests that the way to reclaim the past is to dig for it.[16] He has done precisely that in uncovering the ruins of the Gestapo, the SS and the Nazi state-security police headquarters in Prins-Albrecht Strasse, in which is housed the Topography of Terror archives and exhibition. "Not memory but history," is his axiom.

The inherent link between memory, history, interpretation and political point-scoring could be lost in the banter. History is almost as fluid as memory. Memory cannot be turned into a monument, but monuments do shape the character of memory. Theology is about memory, primarily the memory of victims. It is this that makes the debate about monuments of struggle and memory in the South African theology so important.

15 *New Yorker*, pp 48–65.
16 *Ibid.*, p 51.

Equally important in the process of historical adjustment is story-telling. James Cone, the American black theologian, suggests it is perhaps only by sharing our stories with one another that we can hope to transcend the boundaries of our past and reach towards a shared future:

> Every people have a story to tell, something to say to themselves, their children, and to the world about how they think and live, as they determine their reason for being ... When people can no longer listen to the other people's stories, they become enclosed within their own social context ... And then they feel they must destroy other people's stories" (Cone 1975:102–103).

H. Richard Niebuhr has, in turn, reminded us that:

> Where common memory is lacking, where men do not share in the same past there can be no real community, and where community is to be formed common memory must be created ... The measure of our distance from each other in our nations and our groups can be taken by noting the divergence, the separateness and the lack of sympathy in our social memories. Conversely, the measure of our unity is the extent of our common memory" (Niebuhr 1941:115).

South Africa still awaits a unifying memory which incorporates provincial memories and partial pasts. This struggle, for symbols that unite and stories that bind, has only just begun. These are stories and symbols encapsulated in song, in dance, in poetry and art. They are spoken and unspoken. They are written and oral. They are pre-oral and some are so deep within the human psyche that they cannot be adequately articulated – at least not yet, while the pain is still so acute.

The parochial memory of a battle won, of a defeat suffered, of a celebration or a funeral, of an engaging event or bitter conflict often does more to unite and motivate a people than the most sacred events of established religion. At times these stories override the importance of established sacred symbols; at times they give established religious stories new vitality and contextual meaning. The memory of the Great Trek, Blood River and the suffering of Boer women and children in concentration camps are memories that unite many Afrikaners. Sharpeville, the 1976 Soweto rebellion, Umkhonto we Sizwe (for some) and Apla (for others) unite blacks. These same stories, memories, symbols and culture are at the root of the alienation that exists between most whites and most blacks. Nation-building of the inclusive kind that underpins the goals of the present era of South African politics, requires that we transcend these memories. However, such memories will and must remain. They cannot simply be expunged from the collective memory.

The need is to fit these partisan memories into the greater story that unites. The exercise involves more than a careful analysis of what contributed to these different memories, although analysis is important. It involves sharing our recollections of the past. It involves telling our stories to one another and listening intently to the stories we are told – which involves reaching beyond the words and the 'facts' to what lies behind the words. Herein lies the possibility of 'cracking the code' – of gaining an understanding from the perspective of another's lived experience. It is a process that involves more than empathy. It involves hermeneutical relocation whereby we see, hear and understand in a different way. The exercise involves more than the surrender of one's own perception of truth. It involves what Gadamer called a fusion of horizons. His words deserve repeating:

> ... [The fusion of horizons] always involves the attainment of a higher universality that overcomes, not only our own particularity, but also that of the other. The concept of the 'horizon' suggests itself because it expresses the wide, superior vision that the person who is seeking to understand must have. To acquire a horizon means that one learns to look beyond what is close at hand – not in order to look away from it, but to see it better within a larger whole and in truer proportion (1988:272).[17]

"If you cannot understand my story, you do not accept me as your neighbour," notes Ellen Kuzwayo, "I am an African woman. I've tried to share my soul, my way of seeing things, the way I understand life. I hope you understand." "Africa is a place of story-telling," she continued, "We need more stories, never mind how painful the exercise might be. This is how we will learn to love one another. Stories help us to understand, to forgive and to see things through someone else's eyes."[18]

It takes time for true stories to be told. Stories that reveal the sacredness of life, that point to events that have hurt and healed, given life and death are not easy stories to tell. Reconciliation cannot be forced. True stories are rarely told to strangers. "It was not easy for me to write my story. It was not easy to tell my story to people who I did not know. Sometimes I do not fully understand it myself," Kuzwayo says. This is what makes the Truth and Reconciliation Commission's task of hearing stories of victims a strained, albeit necessary exercise. It is necessary to spring the trap that has prevented people from telling their stories and thus prevented them from being understood (Kuzwayo). This has, in turn, prevented us from broadening our national horizon (Gadamer). It has imposed an ideologically closed memory that has excluded and alienated the majority of South Africans. It is this partisan memory that needs to be reconstructed.

"Scream as loud as you want; no one will hear you," torture victims in apartheid jails were often told by tormentors who were confident that knowledge of their crimes would never go beyond the cell walls. The defeat of the apartheid regime, offers the opportunity for the suppressed anguish of these victims to be heard. "Now there is a chance for the whole world to hear the victims scream," Marlene Bosset, of the Cape Town-based *Trauma Centre for Victims of Violence and Torture*, told The South African Conference on Truth and Reconciliation organised by the Justice in Transition project.[19] People must be allowed to tell their stories. The nation is

---

17 I am grateful to Mieke Holkeboer, a graduate student, for her work on Hans-Georg Gadamer.
18 In personal conversation with Ellen Kuzwayo, 16 October 1994. See also her book, *Call Me Woman*. (Cape Town: David Philip, 1985).
19 *Democracy in Action*, Vol. 8, No. 5, 31 August 1994, p 16.

obliged to hear them. It is in the encounter of telling, hearing and understanding that the reconciliation process can begin. Mike Nicol's remarkable account of South Africa in psychic transfiguration, *The Waiting Country*, defines stories as "the footnotes of history." "These [are] days," he suggests, "when history is so much with us. I suppose that in the end all we really have are the stories" (1995:12). We need to listen. We need to hear.

The relationship between the confession of guilt and historical memory is complex but inherent. The one feeds off the other. Some who claim "we never knew" still do not want to know. It is they, suggests Jaspers, who cannot/do not want to repent. They deny themselves access to a future – grounded in "a new source of active life".

Healing

Memory that transcends morbidity is ultimately a memory that heals. Anger and aggression, bitterness and resentment, hostility and revenge are at the same time understandable responses in the wake of the kind of suffering that has characterised apartheid.

Ultimately, however, healing serves the victim and survivor. In Jaspers' terms, it concerns the creation of a new future – within which the "evil chain" of inhumanity is broken. Healing memory is about dealing with the past in a manner that facilitates the creation of a new future.

The House of the Wannsee Conference museum in Berlin, captures this link between past and future in a powerful manner. It was here that Reinhard Heydrich, head of the Reich Security Head Office, chaired a meeting of fourteen high-ranking civil servants and SS officers to ensure the efficient elimination of Europe's twelve million Jews in a 'final solution'. Jews, and other designated undesirables, had to be located, rounded-up and transported to work camps and extermination. Paper work was necessary to ensure that trains ran on time, concentration camps were planned, gas ovens manufactured and crematoria built. Germans speak of Schreibtischtaeter or desk criminals, who simply did their jobs. The Wannsee Conference prepared the way for all this to happen in a single morning, over a cup of coffee on the banks of the tranquil Wannsee.

The Centre today houses a harrowing photographic collection extending from the rise of Nazism to the liberation of death camps. Within this context history is employed as a 'learning setting', relating the past to the present. In addition to housing a multi-media library, the Centre offers workshops and seminars on professional and personal ethics, sensitising people to the message of Nuremberg – that to simply follow orders and do one's job is no valid excuse. Healing, in addition to all else, is about taking moral responsibility. This constitutes an important ingredient of what it means to be human. If we can learn this much as a result of the Truth and Reconciliation Commission, the nation-building exercise will have been well served.

Reconstruction includes many facets. Restitution and reparation necessarily involve a strong material component. They ultimately involve the empowerment of people to create for themselves a better future. This includes educational, cultural, economic and political empowerment. The church has a responsibility with regards to each one of these dimensions. Ultimately, however, it has a special responsibility to provide moral and spiritual access to "a new source of active life". It is here that its particular contribution to nation-building begins, with a special obligation to endure the long struggle for renewal that has only just started. In the words of President Nelson Mandela:

> The truth is we are not yet free; we have merely achieved the freedom to be free, the right not to be oppressed. We have not taken the final step of our journey, but the first step on a longer and more difficult road (1994:617).

BIBLIOGRAPHY

Barth, Karl. 1960. *The Epistle to the Romans*. London: Oxford University Press.

Barth, Karl. 1965. "The Confessing Church in National Socialist Germany", in Allchin AM, Marty Martin E and Parker THL. (eds) *The German Church Conflict*, London: Lutterworth Press.

Bethge, Eberhard. 1974. "Troubled Self-Interpretation and Uncertain Reception in the Church Struggle", in Littell, H and Locke, G (eds). *The German Church Struggle and the Holocaust*, Detroit: Wayne State University Press: 167–184.

Biko, Steve. 1987. *Steve Biko (1946–1977): I Write What I Like*, London: Heinemann, 1987.

Bonkovsky, Frederick O. 1974. "The German State and Protestant Ethics", in Little FH and Locke G (eds) *The German Church Struggle and the Holocaust*. Detroit: Wayne State University Press 124–147.

Cone, James. 1975. *God of the oppressed*. New York: Seabury Press.

De Gruchy, John W. 1993. "Guilt, Amnesty and National Reconstruction", *Journal of Theology for Southern Africa*, 83: 3–13.

Gadamer, Hans-Georg. 1988. *Truth and Method*. New York: Crossroads.

Garlinksi, Josef. 1994. *Fighting Auschwitz*. London: Orbis Books.

Jaspers, Karl. 1947. *The Question of German Guilt*. New York: The Dial Press. First published as *Die Schuldfrage: Zur politischen Haftung Deutschlands*. Heidelberg: Verlagen Lambert Schneider, 1946.

Kairos Document, 1985. Braamfontein: Skotaville.

Kramer, Jane. 1995. "The Politics of Memory", *New Yorker*, Vol. 71, No. 24, 14 August.

Lapide, Pinchas. 1985. "No Balm in Barmen: A Jewish Debit Account", *Journal of Theology for Southern Africa*: 50, 37–51.

Littell, Franklin. 1961. "From Barmen (1934) to Stuttgart (1945): the Path of the Confessing Church in Germany", *Journal of Church and State*, Vol. 3.

Mandela, Nelson. 1994. *Long Walk to Freedom*. Randburg: Macdonald Purnell.

Moishe, Postone. 1990. "After the Holocaust: History and Identity in West Germany", in Harms, K, Reuter R and Durr Volker (eds). *Coping with the Past: Germany and Austria after 1945*. Wisconsin: University of Wisconsin Press.

Nicol, Mike. 1995. *The Waiting Country*. London: Victor Gollancz.

Niebuhr, H. Richard. 1941. *The Meaning of Revelation*. New York: Macmillan, p 115.

Niemöller, Walter. 1967. *Neuanfang 1945: Zur Biographie Martin Niemöllers*. Guttersloh.

Nietzsche, Friedrich. 1908. *Thus Spake Zarathustra Vl*. London: Fisher Unwin.

Reuter LR. "Political and Moral Culture in West Germany: Four Decades of Democratic Reorganisation and Vergangenheitsauseinandersetzung", in Harms K, Reuter LR and Durr Volker (eds). *Coping with the Past: Germany and Austria after 1945*. Wisconsin: University of Wisconsin Press.

PART 4

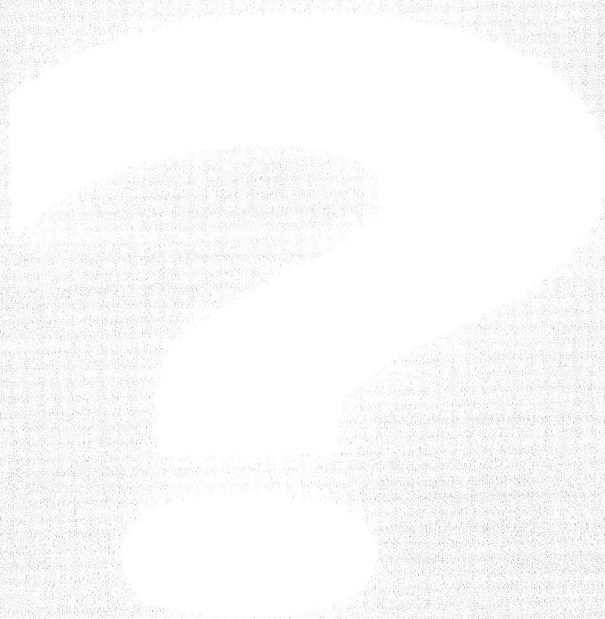

Ethical issues in ecology, development and business

13 The Gold Fields Faith and Earthkeeping Project: a theological and ethical discussion

David F. Olivier

The Gold Fields Faith and Earthkeeping Project (GF F&E) was two and a half years old on the 30th of June, 1997. This five year project, made possible by a grant received from the mining house, *Gold Fields*, through the *Gold Fields/World Wide Fund for Nature (SA) Benefactor Scheme*, is a project run under the auspices of the *World Wide Fund for Nature (SA)* and under the administrative wing of the University of South Africa's *Research Institute for Theology and Religion*, in this university's *Faculty of Theology and Religious Studies*. As its name indicates, religions and environmental care define its field of interest as well as the main thrust of its activities.

A project of this nature naturally raises many varied questions – some of these questions quite fundamental theological and ethical questions. In the short period of time that I have had the privilege of heading the GF F&E Project at the University of South Africa, I have time and again experienced just how closely knit "theological" and "ethical" questions are! I am convinced that any attempt to make a watertight distinction between "theological" and "ethical" could only lead to a greatly impoverished "theology" and "ethics" – "theology" here referring to what some would call "systematic theology" and "ethics", "theological ethics". The one is rooted in the other. A second point must also be made. Kretzschmar's comments on the "critical and creative interplay between reflection and action" and her statement that "Theory needs to be informed by action, and action by theory" (Kretzschmar 1994:3) have relevance for both "systematic theology" and "theological ethics" as disciplines. Much of the sterility in both disciplines boils down to the fact that much of the "reflection" is not rooted in "action". Whether my "interplay between reflection and action" within the context of the GF F&E Project has been "critical and creative", others will have to judge.

The issues dealt with in this chapter touch upon "basics" as far as this project is concerned: (1) the relevance of environmental care for Christian life; (2) a multi-faith approach to environmental care; (3) calling for a change to a sustainable lifestyle and (4) the issue of capacity building. Each of these have been questioned as to their relevancy for Christian life. I have not tried to say the last word on these issues. I have only indicated a few lines of thought – lines of thought based on what has so far been experienced in the context of the GF F&E Project. Hopefully they will be taken up in further discussion.

Let met now provide some background information concerning the Gold Fields Faith and Earthkeeping Project.

The principal objective

In short: *the principal objective of this project is to conscientise, empower and support communities and individuals at a grass roots level to create and implement their own activities and policies for local, regional and national environmental protection, conservation and sustainable resource use through the promotion of a religious engagement in ecological issues and with a view to improving their quality of life.* Allow me to elaborate on this rather 'full' statement.

At the root of this project lies the conviction that we now are facing a global as well as regional environmental crisis that is beginning to seriously effect the quality of life of millions of people, and which, if not effectively dealt with, in the long run will prove fatal for much of life on this planet – human and otherwise. This project shares the view that our present generation "is the first one that can irreversibly transform our planet for the worse" and that it is "also the last generation with the capacity to introduce the changes required to avert environmental disaster" (Huntley, Siegfried and Sunter 1989:1). We have developed the capability to affect "the entire global environment, not just a particular area" says Gore (1993:30). We have become "the dominant cause of change in the global environment" (Gore 1993:30).

Within the boundaries of South Africa, we have a "microcosm of the challenges facing the world" (Huntley, Siegfried and Sunter 1989:1). This is true. Claude Martin, director general of the World Wide Fund for Nature sketches the basic problem we face well. He states (Yeld 1997:7; cf. Cock and Koch 1991:v; and more in general Clarke 1991):

> South Africa is challenged to meet the basic housing, educational, health and employment needs of its growing population, while maintaining the capacity of the natural environment to support this development in the longer term. The fact that South Africa also possesses a treasure of biological diversity, and has the responsibility to preserve this genetic, species and ecosystem diversity on behalf of the global community, considerably heightens that challenge. This requires a development process which provides real improvement in the quality of human life and at the same time conserves the vitality and diversity of the natural world.

The GF F&E Project is sensitive to the needs of not only animals, plants and their habitats, but also to the needs of humankind. The project seeks an integrated approach to conservation and development. It endeavours to help, where possible, towards creating and providing lasting healthy habitats for the diverse fauna and flora of our country, but it also actively supports development programmes that would lead to the improvement of the quality of life of all South Africans, as long as these programmes reflect environmentally sound principles. Development needs to be sustainable and, therefore, within the carrying capacity of supporting ecosystems, if the needs of present as well as future generations of humans, and other species, are to be met.

This project is also grounded on the belief that there can be little hope of effecting any meaningful and lasting action against environmental degradation and destruction unless an environmental ethic develops among the broad public. "No survival without a world ethic", Küng (1991:xv) rightly says. Environmental problems can only be effectively dealt with if actions are backed by an informed and committed community that will take full responsibility for its environment through earth-healing and earth-caring activities (cf IUCN/UNEP/WWF 1991:57–63).

The GF F&E Project targets religious communities – primarily (in alphabetical order), African Traditional, Baha'i, Buddhist, Christian, Hindu, Jewish and Muslim communities – in the Southern African region. Most religious groups have an enormous potential in effecting a greater awareness of the many and varied environmental problems experienced world-wide. They also have a major role to play in the development of environmentally friendly lifestyles and the values and attitudes such lifestyles reflect. Core values that can form the basis of a global ethic exist in the teachings of the world's religions. With global and regional networks and the potential to influence people of all walks of life, the GF F&E Project claims that religions cannot be ignored in the struggle to save our world.

It is only when each and every community in our country is actively involved in environmental care on a regional and national level, and the various religious bodies within these communities understand their role in such an endeavour as well as play a meaningful part in such care, that the GF F&E Project would have no more reason to exist.

Towards accomplishing the objective of this project

Three basic interrelated activities define attempts to realise this project's aim or goal. These are:

- *research* in the field of environmental theology, philosophy and ethics;
- the *conscientisation* of communities and individuals with regard to ecological issues and problems; and
- the *mobilisation* of communities and individuals with a view to various projects geared to environmental protection, conservation and sustainable resource use.

A few notes must be added to each of these points:

Research in the field of environmental theology, philosophy and ethics

The aim of this research is to:

- stimulate interest in environmental theology, philosophy and ethics in various religious communities;

* enhance the knowledge of individuals and communities concerning environmental issues (global and local) and the role religious and philosophical belief systems play not only in the development of ecological problems, but also in creating a lifestyle compatible with the ecological realities of the world in which we live;
* strengthen the ability of individuals and communities to assess such religious and environmental problems as there might be in their communities and regions, and develop, implement and evaluate measures to counter them; and
* stimulate interdisciplinary interaction and co-operation in research related to the above-mentioned. A sustained effort is made in the research undertaken to understand issues as they relate to Third World countries, specifically South Africa.

The GF F&E Project endeavours to stimulate interest in environmental theology, philosophy and ethics primarily through discussion groups, workshops, pamphlets, posters, slides, videos, newsletters, lectures, courses, reports, articles, books and conferences.

The conscientisation of individuals and communities

The aim of the process of conscientisation of individuals and communities is to:
* develop a specific group of individuals' awareness of environmental problems and associated threats;
* generate a sense of responsibility and urgency with respect to these problems;
* strengthen their social values towards a greater stewardship in regard to the environment – a strengthening which is ultimately intended to increase their motivation to take action in the form of environmental protection and improvement; and
* where necessary, make the environmental movement aware of the great potential that belief systems of a religious nature have for combatting environmental degradation and destruction.

The conscientisation of communities and individuals is done through: workshops on various issues, the establishment of different environmental projects, networking between communities and groups and communities and groups with environmental organisations, degree, certificate and personal development courses which take into account local environmental and socio-cultural conditions and priorities, conferences and seminars, religious ceremonies, retreats and, occasionally, environmental tours for specific groups.

The mobilisation of individuals and communities

The aim of the mobilisation of people is to:
* develop their skills for solving environmental problems;

- stimulate appropriate action in this regard;
- help and empower people through various projects to develop a more environmentally friendly lifestyle; and
- contribute to the improvement of people's quality of life.

Where a need is identified, the GF F&E Project, through religious groups and their networks, aims to mobilise people in that area for community projects that will, in their particular situation, stimulate environmental protection, conservation and sustainable resource use.

The following are examples of the kind of projects the GF F&E Project would want to see communities develop in their region and propagate further afield:

Tree-planting

There is a great need for planting trees for conservation purposes as well as personal (fuel wood, fruit trees etc) and commercial use. Indigenous species have priority, but exotic species that are not invasive are also planted.

Veld management and land-use

The poor condition of much of the veld and arable land in such areas as communal/tribal lands is widely known. Overgrazing and over-utilisation of croplands are primary factors in the environmental degradation of many of these regions. The GF F&E Project would want to see projects developed that would help people to better manage their veld and lands as well as take care of the fauna and flora in their region. This implies helping people to become more self-sufficient in providing for their needs through better methods of gardening and the rearing of animals, etc.

The development and preservation of water resources

South Africa is an arid country that cannot afford the mismanagement of one of its most precious resources, namely, water. In the communities where the GF F&E Project is involved, it would want to see projects develop that will help in establishing points where good clean water for household and gardening use can be obtained. It would also want to help in establishing effective measures in communities for the care and preservation of existing water resources.

Cleaning-up operations

One of the most basic of activities that needs to be undertaken in many of the townships and informal settlements before anything else of an environmentally constructive nature has any real chance of rooting itself in a community, is the collection of garbage and other forms of litter in streets and other public places. The GF F&E Project endeavours to stimulate such action through awareness campaigns, and it also actively participates in such actions by mobilising volunteers in the various religious groups.

Urban greening

The greening of townships, new housing projects for low income groups and informal settlements, as well as in any other urban region in need of it, is another priority of the GF F&E Project. This involves not only the planting of trees, but also grass, shrubs and flowers in school grounds and in church properties, parks, playgrounds and other public places.

Urban agriculture

The GF F&E Project negotiates for the productive use of urban open spaces by the community. Where permission is granted by the authorities, the GF F&E Project primarily concentrates on projects such as communal vegetable gardens, orchards (fruit trees) and poultry production to provide food for the community.

Nurseries

The establishment of nurseries in the communities is also on the GF F&E Project's list of possible projects. Nurseries are essential for such projects as tree-planting, vegetable gardens, orchards and the greening of the townships. We endeavour to establish nurseries through the involvement of religious groups and to have them care for these nurseries as part of their involvement in the care for and upliftment of their communities.

Recycling projects

Recycling, among other things, reduces waste, saves energy and landfill space, creates jobs and helps towards conserving natural resources in communities. The GF F&E Project endeavours to establish the practice of collecting, sorting and preparing material for sale to recycling companies.

It is within this context that the four issues identified in the introduction will now be discussed.

Four basic issues

The four basic issues dealt with here, namely, the relevance of environmental care for Christian life, a multi-faith approach to environmental care, calling for a change to a sustainable lifestyle and the issue of capacity building, are fundamental, but closely related issues. They are basically four strands of thought woven into the thought-structure supporting much of what this project is all about.

In dealing with each of these issues, the emphasis is on understanding their importance for environmental care in general and then, more specifically, within the context of the project. Once again, I wish to point out that in this chapter I am here doing little more than indicating a few lines of thought for possible further discussion. This I do from an Evangelical Christian perspective.

The relevance of environmental care for Christian life

Two and a half years of involvement with the GF F&E Project and hundreds of discussions with spiritual leaders and various groups in Christian circles have confirmed what I have sensed for a long time: there is a dire need for good and sound *teaching* and *training* in the field of environmental care.

Christian theology, whether of a Catholic, Orthodox or Protestant leaning, has seen several attempts to come to grips with what Grove-White (1992:13) calls "green questions" and Elsdon (1992:13) "green issues" (cf Regenstein 1991:154–175). Reasons for addressing these "questions" or "issues" differ.[1] What could not be denied is that a flood of literature (no more than a mere trickle of books and articles two or three decades ago![2]) witnesses to the endeavours of a large number of people within Christian circles who have taken up Lynn White's challenge, as far as religion and environmental care is concerned, to 'rethink' their 'old one' instead of looking for another (cf White 1967:1206).[3] In this process of rethinking, many have, in a variety of theologies of creation,[4] of the earth,[5] ecology,[6] nature,[7] the land,[8] the environment[9] and geo-justice,[10] as well as in a wide range of topical studies in Old and New Testament studies and in the propagation of various forms of spirituality,[11] offered religious and theological insights which they have perceived as envi-

1 A real concern for the environment underlies most of these endeavours. While this is certainly also true of Elsdon's work, he adds to this concern a further dimension. Green issues are for him not to be seen as "red herrings", but as "golden opportunities" in the endeavour to evangelise people (cf Elsdon 1992). His view is also shared by, for example, Sider (1993:26).
2 Within the English speaking world the works of Moule (1964), Bonifazi (1967), Elder (1970), Engel (1970), Froehlich (1970), Santmire (1970), Schaeffer (1970), Rust (1971), Barnette (1972) and Derrick (1972) could serve as examples of the kind of books and articles which marked the beginning of a steady flow of theological literature addressing the ecological problems. In German circles, Altner (1971) and Amery (1972) could be mentioned. In no way is one to deduce from the above that no theological work of relevance for theological reflection on what we are confronted with in the ecological crisis was done besides the above-mentioned. Barnette (1972:xx) draws attention to the works of process theologians such as, for example, Williams (1968), Cobb (1965), Ogden (1966) and Pittenger (1968).
3 Many of these attempts have, however, not gone unchallenged within Christian circles. Sider (1993:26), for example, claims that "in today's environmental movement there is a lot of theological confusion" and Bandow (1992:57ff) states that "the hysteria fueling the synthesis of religion and ecology is often either unwarranted or misdirected" and that much of "the greening of the church" is "theologically flawed". In his opinion, some strands of this "new ecotheology" are clearly no more than a "sacralization of nature that verges on pantheism" and this to him poses a risk to Christian life and theology. See also in this regard Milbank (1993).
4 Examples of attempts of such theologies of creation are McDonagh (1986:107–128) and Thiemann (1981).
5 Reference could here be made to, for example, the works of Dubos (1973) and Jäger (1983).
6 Barnette (1972:62–81) and McPherson (1986) are two good examples.
7 References to theologies of nature could include such works as, for example, that of Carmody (1980:32–61), Daecke (1979), Hendry (1980), McCoy (1985), McFague (1990), Meye (1987) and Santmire (1986).
8 References to theologies of the land could include such works as that of Hart (1984).
9 Here one could point to, for example, Biggs (1991), Derrick (1972), Engel (1970), Fackre (1973) and Zinger (1992).
10 See, for example Conlon (1990).
11 The name of Matthew Fox (see among others his works of 1983, 1988 and 1991) has become synonymous with creation spirituality. For a short discussion of his views, see Ruether (1990) and Smith (1992:292–305). Some also are proponents of a cosmic spirituality [cf Nolan (1992)].

ronmentally relevant responses to the many, but extremely complex, problems constituting the ecological crisis. We have little to compare with that which has already happened elsewhere in the world as far as theological and ethical reflection is concerned. Yes, in our own country there has been a small but steady growth in interest in this field of study over the past decade, but on the whole South African theology and ethics still have a long way to go before one can say that all is well with environmental theology and ethics in this part of the world.

Of course there are the exceptions. I have over the years met with individuals in Christian circles who are well informed concerning environmental issues and many of them were also well versed in relating their faith to the issue of environmental care. Among them are the bird-watchers, the campers, the hiking trail enthusiasts, the lovers of the open veld, the mountains, the sea and the blue sky. I would not dare say that those persons do not "love" nature! Yes, most of them would certainly condemn the way nature is treated by humans. But, sad to say, among them the number of those who have trod the "narrow road" and have entered the "small gate"[12] of actual involvement in environmental projects, is, however, few. Is this not the acid test for true love of the environment? Environmental consumerism is alive and well! Real environmental care is struggling to make ends meet!

What has been most disturbing in my dealings with many of the ministers of religion, and some of the other leaders in congregations in predominantly 'white'[13] circles, is the fact that although many of them acknowledged the need for environmental care, and for themselves and their people to be involved in relevant ways to stem the tide of environmental degradation and destruction, they themselves seem to be the bottleneck in getting congregations environmentally active! It is not uncommon to experience (after much explanation and discussion and then promises!) that they, and others from their congregations, do not arrive for meetings and events that were planned. In quite a few cases, ministers of religion did not even bother to inform people of such meetings and events – and that after they were asked to do so, and undertook to do so. Enquiries have also brought to light that in some case events and meetings were brought to the attention of people, but in such a way that people were given the impression that their time could be spent better doing something else rather than attend and get involved in such activities. It also came to light that some fear social gospel, liberal theology, New Age, activism, politics, creeping into their congregations.

Among the very poor in 'black' circles the response has been overwhelming! In most cases it is not the issue of environmental care as such that is the main drawing card, but the possibility that projects such as food gardens and the recycling of glass, paper, tins, plastics and so forth offer in the struggle against a growing poverty, malnutrition and abject living conditions. As in the case of 'whites', better socio-

---

12 To use the imagery of Matthew 7:13–14.
13 I must apologize to the reader for the use of such racial terms as white, black etc. Although a new South Africa, many of our structures still carry *apartheid's* marks.

economic conditions among 'blacks' also do not automatically spell out a greater concern and care for the natural environment. My exposure to preaching and teaching in 'black' churches seems to confirm a suspicion that also among them environmental care is seldom, if ever, addressed.

I suppose that many reasons could be given for why environmental care is low on the list of priorities of the many ministers of religion and their parishioners. The one that troubles me most is that there seems to be no clear conviction about the importance of environmental care as far as living our lives as *followers of Christ* is concerned. Environmental care has not become a issue of conscience for many of them. For people to be really sensitive to environmental issues and to act in an environmentally responsible way, these issues must be matters of *conscience*. They must become *personal issues*. Conscience is aroused or stirred only when one's own *moral values and moral welfare* are at stake.

The primary objective in the GF F&E Project's conscientisation drive is the development of people's *conscience* with regard to environmental issues – *conscience* here understood as that personal sense of the moral goodness or blameworthiness of one's own intentions and conduct as measured against that which one feels is the right or good thing to do in a given situation. Conscientising a person is initiating and stimulating a process aimed at bringing that person to adopt a specific pattern of behaviour as part and parcel of his or her lifestyle. Part and parcel of that which he or she believes, thinks and feels as being the morally right thing to do, and which he or she also wants to do and tries to do, when confronted in a given situation with a choice between various other possible patterns of behaviour.

Conscientising people certainly involves raising their levels of *consciousness* or *awareness* with regard to a specific issue. Knowledge of an issue and of that which constitutes morally good or right behaviour or conduct are of the utmost importance in the conscientisation process. Information therefore certainly plays a role – a very important role – but one should never equate being aware of (or even knowing much about) an issue with an issue being a matter of conscience for a person. Conscience implies consciousness, but consciousness does not necessarily imply conscience.

If effective, the conscientisation process will in most cases lead to a change in lifestyle. Where such a change in lifestyle, and thus a change in the values and attitudes at the root of a lifestyle, takes place, it implies that basic commitments have to change – and they do not change without a person's basic philosophy of life changing. The switch from merely being conscious or aware of an issue, to that of a specific issue becoming a matter of conscience, in essence boils down to a reorientation of basic beliefs and commitments concerning that issue within the cadre of a person's specific philosophy of life. It is only when this orientation takes place that a person will develop a conscience concerning a specific issue, for that issue now becomes part and parcel of his or her basic beliefs about what life is all about. It is now part of the experiential core of that person's life – his or her philosophy of life which is a comprehensive frame of reference functioning in his or her life as an interpretative, value-creating and supporting belief system.

One has to acknowledge that, although many experiences of conscience have a religious basis (in other words, are based on definite religious experiences), a religious life-experience is not a necessary condition for conscience to function. Conscience is not of necessity a religious phenomenon. The history of the development of the many and varied lifestyles to be found among humans, however, clearly points to the fact that religious beliefs have over the ages profoundly influenced people. Lifestyles, in essence expressions of conscience, in most cases reflect a specific religious life-experience at the root. The religions of the world have proven to be major role players in conscientising people with regard to various issues (cf Olivier 1995b:1–2).

For environmental care to become a matter of conscience and a priority in our lives, we need to be clear on the relevance environmental care really has for Christian life.

Environmental care is the very root of true Christian service in this world and it reflects in our "groaning" world (Rm 8:18–25) – God's basic concern for the *total well-being and renewal of the whole of creation* (Rev 21:1; 2 Peter 3:13; Is 65:17; 66:22). It touches the heart of the Gospel in that it testifies, in human actions, to the reconciliation with God of "all things, whether things on earth or things in heaven" in Christ (cf Col 1:15–20). It is the proclamation by all saved by God's grace in Christ of this Gospel "to every creature under heaven" (Col 1:23 within the context of verses 21–23). We, all humans, are called to serve this purpose: God's renewal of every facet of life and existence! We succeed or fail, in terms of the Gospel, in so far as we (within our own time and sphere of existence) reflect (in Christ and under the guidance of the Holy Spirit) this purpose in everything we do.

The challenge posed to much of our present day myopic theology and spirituality should be clear. A Gospel proclaiming salvation for humans, without placing this salvation within the broader context of God's concern for the whole of creation, is just not bringing the "full" Gospel! Caring for the "souls" of people without caring for their total well-being (which includes the environment in which they live!) witnesses to a "dead" faith (cf James 2:14–17; 1 John 3:16–18). The Spirit of Christ is revealed in the lives of people who seek to create conditions in which God can be "all in all" (cf 1 Cor 15:20–28) and people can experience life "to the full" (John 10:10).

In short, a church that does not share God's concern for *the total well-being and renewal of the whole of creation* and, as a result of it, does not teach and train its ministers and people accordingly, has a greatly impoverished ministry!

A multi-faith approach to environmental care

In Christian circles, the fact that the GF F&E Project also works with other religions – mostly African Traditional, Baha'i, Buddhist, Hindu, Jewish, Muslim and Pagan –

has raised a number of questions. Many fear that such an approach opens the door for the creation of a syncretistic "green" religion. Others claim that it compromises the Christian faith because it creates the impression that the Christian faith is acknowledged as just another faith among many others. It is said that working hand-in-hand with these other faiths affords them some legitimacy.

I acknowledge the fact that working with different faith groups raises many fundamental theological questions – one of which is surely whether we are not, in the end, really serving one and the same God, only in different ways. I, however, sense behind much of the concern expressed in Christian circles, a great uncertainty as to how to relate to the other faith groups now that Christianity has lost the privileged position it had under the previous regime. Once again, I experience this more in 'white' than in 'black' circles. Cradled, in the past, in socio-political favour, Christianity in the South African context has, in many instances lost touch with the world of religious pluralism and its challenges. Ill prepared for the new situation, many shy away from it, and hide behind what seems like legitimate and worthy objections, but in reality these objections are no more than a camouflage for their own inadequacy to deal with the situation. Real evangelical concern would jump at the opportunity to witness in word and deed to the liberating reality of the Gospel of Jesus Christ!

The multi-faith approach to environmental care is dictated by the realities of the environmental crisis we are presently facing. It is global in the full sense of the word. It knows no boundaries; certainly not political, social, economic or, for that matter, religious. It poses a treat to the whole of humankind and to all forms of life on this planet *and it is caused by us humans!* We have lost our environmental balance. Efforts – whether of a political, economic, scientific or technological nature – if not supported by a *fundamental change in how we relate to the natural environment*, will do little to stop our plunge into life-threatening environmental chaos. The religions of our world, woven into the fabric of societies all across the world, each have a vitally important role to play in helping to create a *global environmental ethic* in their sphere of influence, that is, values and attitudes that enhance life in all its diversity. Core values that can form the basis of a global ethic exist in the teachings of the world's religions (cf Küng 1991). With global and regional networks and the potential to influence people of all walks of life, the religions of our world cannot be ignored in the struggle to save our planet from an ecological catastrophe (Olivier 1995c:4).

It cannot be denied: in the world of religions and beliefs one encounters what one would call "exclusivists", "inclusivists" and "pluralists". The *exclusivists* would, while acknowledging the existence of other beliefs, see their specific religion, and their understanding of it, as the only legitimate way to live a religious life. Only they have the "truth" and no one else. *Inclusivists*, again, would accept the spiritual power and depth manifest in other faiths and might even include in theirs many of the views and practices of other faiths but, in the end, they would reject the other religions as not being sufficient for an understanding of what is involved in a religious life. The others, in other words, have elements of "truth", but these have to be interpreted and understood in the light of what the inclusivists perceive to be the "truth". They thus attribute to their specific religion and views an ultimacy and normativity meant to embrace and fulfill that of all others. *Pluralists*, in contrast to exclusivists and inclusivists, would maintain that all religions, their's included, are equally paths for experiencing what one might perceive as "God". They, in other words, recognise the independent validity of the various religions, but eschew any views claiming to be the only and absolute "truth" concerning "God" and a religious life.

The GF F&E Project does not have as its objective the judging of what is true or false when it comes to religions and religious life. Neither does it wish to choose to work with, for example, only pluralists or exclusivists. It wants to work with all people irrespective of what they claim to believe (or not to believe). Its aim is to help, where needed and also possible, religious people of all faith groups to understand the many and varied environmental problems they face in their own communities. The GF F&E Project also wants to help them – once again if needed and possible – to see what the implications are of what they believe *as far as caring for the earth is concerned*. It wishes to motivate and guide such people in becoming involved in creating and implementing their own activities and policies for environmental protection, conservation and sustainable resource use, and nothing more. No syncretism, no "green" religion, only the different faiths and how they relate to environmental care (cf Olivier 1995a:7).

God's concern for *the total well-being and renewal of the whole of creation* is at the root of our outreach to others – even if they should belong to another faith. Environmental care is practical testimony to the loving care and goodness of our Creator God for all creatures (cf Mt 5:45–48).

Calling for a change to a sustainable lifestyle

Sustainable living is said to depend upon "accepting a duty to seek harmony with other people and with nature" (IUCN/UNEP/WWF 1991:8). What is important to understand is that each and every form of life on earth is part of one vast interdependent system of biotic and abiotic entities which create conditions that either favour life, and its further development, or impede such life. This "community of life" must be respected and cared for. The earth's vitality and its diversity must be protected. To live sustainably we will have to develop lifestyles that ensure that we stay within the earth's "carrying capacity" (cf IUCN/UNEP/WWF 1991:8–10). Not to do so, would just invite further disaster. Already the signs of environmental fatigue and, in many instances, environmental collapse are clearly to be seen. It all boils down to the fact that we are overtaxing the earth's life-support systems.

While negative aspects could be identified in most present and past cultures (cf Hughes 1975), the Western industrialised world, effected primarily by developments in various fields of science and technology, is singled out by many as environmentally the most devastating of all cultures. Ambler (1990:45) expresses this view when writing the following:

> Not every ecological problem is to be laid at the door of modern industrialism. There were many ecological disasters in the world before the onset of the modern era. But in surveying the areas of greatest concern today we cannot avoid the conclusion that they derive from the impact of industrial processes which are unsympathetic to the processes of nature.

The global problems that presently most worry us are, according to Ambler (1990:4), closely connected with the spread of Western civilisation. A relative latecomer to the ranks of civilisations, Western civilisation has proved itself "incomparably dynamic" (Artigiani 1987:109). It has, in a relatively short period of time, become the dominant culture in much of our present world. It is this "present domination of modern Western culture" which Ambler (1990:4) sees as "the greatest single factor in bringing our world problems to a critical state". De Klerk's (1979:82) remark that the ecological crisis should not be seen primarily as a "natuurkrisis" but as a "kultuurkrisis" clearly reflects what many see as the core of the environmental problems we presently face.

Placing the emphasis on Western culture's environmental impact greatly focuses the debate as far as the question of the nature of the ecological crisis is concerned. We should not, however, lose sight of the fact that although the emphasis is placed on Western culture's environmental impact, one is dealing with a global problem which has drawn into it all the cultures of this world. In the search for an understanding of what this crisis situation entails, this emphasis has led to the identification of at least six basic interrelated and interdependent factors which, interacting upon one another, have led to the development of this globally life threatening situation. These factors are demographic, scientific-technological, geo-agricultural, economic, political and religio-philosophical in nature (cf Olivier 1989:24; 1991:20). Each of these factors or spheres of interest highlight a variety of issues.

Of the many possible *demographic issues* which could come into play when discussing the environmental crisis is that of exponential population growth and its impact (globally and regionally) on the environment. Resource use and resource depletion along with such issues as, for example, pollution, population distribution, urbanisation and population regulation through, for example, economic development, family planning and migration, are often dealt with when discussing the ecological relevance of population growth.

It is widely recognised in discussions of *scientific-technological factors* within the context of the environmental crisis that advances in the fields of science and technology have indeed improved the conditions under which many in this world live. But they have also produced many unforeseen effects which have proved to be detrimental to environmental health. Air, water and ground pollution, waste, the rapid depletion of non-renewable and renewable resources and various imbalances created in natural processes by human manipulation, are but a few examples of effects of many of these advances. The view which, however, seems to have won the day in this debate is that research and the development of technology are much needed in the struggle to counter environmental degradation and destruction. Advances in these fields cannot be done away with because of the environmentally negative effects some developments have had in the past. Research presently undertaken and the development of new technology, it is stressed, will have to be guided by values which enhance environmental integrity.

The debate on *geo-agricultural factors* centres around the natural potential of a region, country, or for that matter, the world, as it relates to the exploitation of it by humans for their continued existence and for their quality of life. Such issues as climate, the distribution of fauna and flora, the quality of soil and water and the presence of various minerals come into play in discussions of this nature. So too do issues such as the rate of exploitation of resources, the influence of possible climatic changes, the loss of productive land (through, for example, salinisation, desertification or urbanisation), land degradation through pollution, the influence of possible water shortages, mining activities and the threat of the rise of the sea level.

The debate concerning the environment in the s*phere of economics* highlights the issues relating to sustainable development and growth. It is very much concerned with the environmental impact of the production, distribution and consumption of goods and services in a world of limited resources. It is also concerned as such with issues such as the state of the global economy, poverty, inequalities and the growing gap between rich and poor, aid and the debt crisis, inflation, the costs of improving environmental quality and conserving resources.

In the *political sphere* the concern is with, among others, the role of governments on a national and international level in combatting bad environmental practices and stimulating actions that will enhance efforts to bring about a more environmentally friendly lifestyle among the peoples of this world. It is concerned with political inertia, with laws, treaties and the enforcement of them. In this debate, the existence of nation states has also been questioned as something that has greatly contributed towards creating an "ours-theirs" mentality which for its part has led to much exploitation of other people and parts of the world.

The discussion of *religio-philosophical issues* brings to the fore the influence of various philosophies of life through the values and attitudes they promote in the lives of people in their interaction with their environment. Cultures are seen as specific expressions of different philosophies of life. Western culture is no exception and when analysed exposes those elements of it that have led to much of the environmental devastation presently experienced in the world. Attention is often called to the aspects of a world view that would bring about a much more ecologically harmonious lifestyle and it is in this regard one frequently finds people propagating a biocentric as opposed to a anthropocentric world view.

The call to change our lifestyles to be ecologically sustainable is of fundamental importance in environmental care. It is evident that all human behaviour that violates such principles as respecting and caring for all forms of life and protecting the earth's vitality and its bio-diversity, is unethical. It is sin! It clashes with God's concern for the total well-being and renewal of the whole of creation. It reflects a lack of true love, of *agape*, without which life loses much of its meaning.

Capacity building

The challenge Christianity faces in environmental care is one of truly being a servant to one's fellow humans and to all of God's creation. It reflects an acceptance of our responsibility towards God and fellow creatures – human and otherwise – and a *dedication*, a *commitment*, of ourselves and everything we have towards meeting the many and varied challenges such a life poses in a "groaning" world (Rm 8:22; cf Rm 8:18–25). In essence: as Christians – followers of Christ – we are called to serve (Mt 20:26–28; Mk 9:35; 10:43–45; Lk 22:24–27; Gal 5:13; Phil 2:5–8).

What is suggested here is a *basic lifestyle* when speaking of "service". A Christian way of life cannot but be a life of service – a pledging of oneself to serve God in Christ and a giving of oneself to others because of a deep-rooted love of Christ and everything He stands for. As I see it, it is not an optional facet of Christian life. For Christians it is a basic attitude to life. "Service" is characteristic of a true follower of Christ.

"Service" of the kind Christ embodies exists only where there is Christ-like "love". It is a fact of life that people are prepared to give much – in some cases even their lives – for that which they truly believe in and care about. People are prepared to sacrifice much for that which they are committed to. James is right in claiming that there is a link between a person's beliefs or commitments and a person's deeds (cf James 2:14–26). In other words, the way we live reflects much of what really matters to us in life.

It is also true of us humans that in "everything that we think, say and feel, do and suffer, we tend quite naturally to protect, shield, advance ourselves, to cherish ourselves" (Küng 1976:257). There is a basic "self-ishness" in all of us, a tendency to focus upon our own interests and well-being. Christ acknowledges this fact of life when he spells out clearly that we should "love" our neighbour *in the same way we "love" ourselves* (cf Mt 22:39). It certainly boils down to doing to others *what we would like them to do to us* (cf Mt 7:12). Christ's teaching clearly does not imply that "love" of self has no place in the lives of his followers. What is does suggest is that Christian love of self is guided by our love of God – a love of God with "all" our "heart", "soul" and "mind" (cf Mt 22:37). It is never a self-centredness at the expense of others! A life totally absorbed with love of God will be a life that wishes to love what God loves, as God loves. Such a life cannot be centred solely upon its own needs and wants, its own well-being, without any consideration for the welfare of others. The life of a person who has truly fallen in love with God cannot but be a life that echoes God's love for this "world"; a Christ-like life that is prepared to give itself for the well-being of others (cf Jn 3:16).

Serving God in the field of environmental care demands much of each person answering the call. It asks of one skills in many fields of expertise as well as knowledge of just about every facet of life, if not every facet of life! It is a life-long calling to serve and love what is dear to God: creation in all its fullness!

In reality, it is a calling one cannot but answer in collaboration with others! In Christ's body of "beings" it is in serving one another with that which one has, in seeing that life in all its many forms is cared for and the potential of such life is allowed to develop fully. Our capacity to serve continuously needs development. It has to grow. Expertise has to flow from the one to the other if the demand of life to develop its potential fully is to be met.

Conclusion

The *Gold Fields Faith & Earthkeeping Project*, in its own small way, wishes to answer to God's call to all who bear God's "image" and "likeness" (Gn 1:26) to work towards *the total well-being and renewal of the whole of creation.* These few lines of thought are presented in the hope that they will not only lead to further discussion but also, on further reflection, to a lifelong involvement in environmental care.

BIBLIOGRAPHY

Altner, G. 1971. *Grammatik der Schöpfung: Theologische Inhalte der Biologie.* Stuttgart: Kreuz Verlag.

Ambler, R. 1990. *Global theology: the meaning of faith in the present world crisis.* London: SCM Press/Philadelphia: Trinity Press International.

Amery, C. 1972. *Das Ende der Vorsehung: die Gnadenlosen Folgen des Christentums.* Hamburg: Rowohlt.

Artigiani, R. 1987. Cultural evolution. *World Futures*, 23, 1 & 2: 93–121.

Bandow, D. 1992. Ecoguilt. *Christianity Today*, 36(8): 57–58.

Barbour, IG. (ed). 1973. *Western man and environmental ethics: attitudes toward nature and technology.* Reading, Massachusetts: Addison-Wesley Publishing Company.

Barnette, HH. 1972. *The church and the ecological crisis.* Grand Rapids, Michigan: W.B. Eerdmans.

Biggs, J. 1991. Towards a theology for the environment. *The Baptist Quarterly*, 34(1): 33–42.

Birdh, C., Eakin, W. and McDaniel, JB. (eds). 1990. *Liberating life: contemporary approaches to ecological theology.* Maryknoll, New York: Orbis Books.

Bonifazi, C. 1967. *A theology of things: a study of man in his physical environment.* Philadelphia: Lippincott.

Carmody, J. 1980. *Theology for the 1980s.* Philadelphia: The Westminster Press.

Clarke, J. 1991. *Back to Earth: South Africa's Environmental Challenges.* Halfway House: Southern Book Publishers.

Cobb, J. 1965. *A Christian natural theology.* Philadelphia: Westminster.

Cock, J. and Koch, E. (ed). 1991. *Going Green: People, Politics and the Environment in South Africa*. Cape Town: Oxford University Press.

Conlon, J. 1990. *Geo-justice: a preferential option for the earth*. Canada: Woodlake Books.

Daecke, SM. 1979. "Auf den Weg zu einer Praktischen Theologie der Natur", in Meyer-Abich 1979:262–285.

De Klerk, WA. 1979. *Tyd van vernuwing: opstelle oor tyd en samelewing*. Kaapstad: Tafelberg.

Derrick, C. 1972. *The delicate creation: towards a theology of the environment*. Old Greenwich, Conn.: The Devin-Adair Company.

Dubos, R. 1973. *A theology of the earth*, in Barbour 1973:43–54.

Elder, F. 1970. *Crisis in Eden*. Nashville: Abingdon.

Elsdon, R. 1992. Green issues: golden opportunities. *Third Way*, 15(5): 13–16.

Engel, DE. 1970. "Elements in a theology of environment". *Zygon* 5: 216–228.

Fackre, G. 1973. *Ecology and theology*, in Barbour 1973:116–131.

Fox, M. 1983. *Original blessing: a primer in creation spirituality*. Santa Fe: Bear Publishing.

Fox, M. 1988. *The coming of the cosmic Christ*. San Francisco: Harper and Row.

Fox, M. 1991. *Creation spirituality*. San Francisco: Harper and Row.

Froehlich, K. 1970. The ecology of creation. *Theology Today*, 27(3): 263–276.

Gore, A. 1993. *Earth in the Balance: Ecology and the Human Spirit*. New York: Plume Books.

Granberg-Michaelson, W. (ed). 1987. *Tending the garden: essays on the Gospel and the earth*. Grand Rapids, Michigan: W.B. Eerdmans.

Hart, J. 1984. *The spirit of the earth: a theology of the land*. New York: Paulist Press.

Hendry, GS. 1980. *Theology of nature*. Philadelphia: Westminster Press.

Hughes, JD. 1975. *Ecology in Ancient Civilisations*. Albuquerque: University of New Mexico Press.

Huntley, B., Siegfried, R. and Sunter, C. 1989. *South African Environments into the 21st Century*. Cape Town: Human and Rousseau/Tafelberg.

IUCN/UNEP/WWF 1991. *Caring for the Earth. A Strategy for Sustainable Living*. Gland, Switzerland.

Jäger, A. 1983. Theologie der Erde: zur theologischen Funktion einer Schöpfungslehre. *Theologische Zeitschrift*, 39(3): 166–177.

Kretzschmar, L. 1994. "Ethics in a Theological Context", in Villa-Vicencio and De Gruchy 1994:2–23.

Küng, H. 1991. *Global Responsibility: In Search of a New World Ethic*. London: SCM Press.

McCoy, JD. 1985. Towards a theology of nature. *Encounter*, 46(3): 213–228.

McDonagh, S. 1986. *To care for the earth: a call to a new theology*. London: Geoffrey Chapman.

McFague, S. 1990. "Imaging a theology of nature: the world as God's body", in Birch, Eakin and McDaniel 1990:201–227.

McPherson, J. 1986. Towards an ecological theology. *The Expository Times*, 97(8): 236–240.

Meye, RP. 1987. "Invitation to wonder: toward a theology of nature", in Granberg-Michaelson (1987:30–49).

Meyer-Abich, KM. 1979. *Frieden mit der Natur*. Freiburg: Herder.

Milbank, J. 1993. Out of the greenhouse. *New Blackfriars*, 47, 867, 4–14.

Moule, CFD. 1964. *Man and nature in the New Testament*. London: Athlone Press.

Nolan, A. 1992. Cosmic Spirituality. *Challenge*, No. 8: 2–4.

Ogden, S. 1966. *The reality of God*. New York: Harper.

Olivier, DF. 1989. "The Role of Eschatology and Futurology in the Quest for a Future in the Light of the Ecological Crisis". *Theologia Evangelica*, 22,(1): 24–33.

Olivier, DF. 1991. "Ecology and Mission: Notes on the History of the JPIC Process and its Relevance to Theology". *Missionalia*, 19(1) 20–32.

Olivier, DF. 1995a. The Faith and Earthkeeping Project in a World of Religions and Beliefs. *Faith and Earthkeeping*, No. 2.

Olivier, DF. 1995b. Emphasising Conscience in Dealing with Environmental Issues? *Faith and Earthkeeping*, No. 3.

Olivier, DF. 1995c. Dialogue and co-operation are both needed! *Faith and Earthkeeping*, No. 3.

Pittenger, N. 1968. *Process thought and Christian faith*. New York: Macmillan.

Regenstein, LG. 1991. *Replenish the earth: a history of organized religion's treatment of animals and nature – including the Bible's message of conservation and kindness to animals*. London: SCM Press.

Ruether, RR. 1990. "Matthew Fox and creation spirituality: strengths and weaknesses". *The Catholic World*, 233, 1396, 169–172.

Rust, E. 1971. *Nature: Eden or desert?* Waco, Texas: Word.

Santmire, HP. 1970. *Brother earth*. New York: Nelson.

Santmire, HP. 1986. "Toward a new theology of nature". *Dialog*, 25, 1, 43–50.

Schaeffer, FA. 1970. *Pollution and the death of man: the Christian view of ecology*. London: Hodder and Stoughton.

Sider, RJ. 1993. "Redeeming the environmentalists". *Christianity Today*, 37(7): 26–29.

Smith, DL. 1992. *A handbook of contemporary theology*. Wheaton, Illinois: BridgePoint Books.

Thiemann, RF. 1981. "Toward a theology of creation: a response to Gustaf Wingren", in Vander Goot 1981:119–136.

Vander Goot, H. (ed). 1981. *Creation and method: critical essays on christocentric theology*. Washington D.C.: University Press of America.

Villa-Vicencio, C. and De Gruchy, J. (eds). 1994. *Doing Ethics in Context: South African Perspectives*. Theology and Praxis: Vol. 2. New York: Maryknoll/Cape Town and Johannesburg: David Philip.

White, L. 1967. "The historical roots of our ecologic crisis". *Science*, 155, 3767, 1203–1207.

Williams, DD. 1968. *The forms and spirit of love*. New York: Harper.

Yeld, J. 1997. *Caring for the Earth. South Africa. A Guide to Sustainable Living*. Stellenbosch: WWF South Africa.

Zinger, DH. 1992. "Lutheran reflections on nature: prolegomena to a theology of the environment". *Currents*, 19, 4, 281–287.

14 The ethics of sustainable development

David N. Field

The 1996 South African constitution affirms that:

> Everyone has the right ... to have the environment protected for the benefit of present and future generations, through reasonable legislative and other measures that ... secure ecologically sustainable development and use of natural resources while promoting justifiable economic and social development.

This ideal of sustainable development arises out of an awareness of both humanity's dependence on the earth[1] and of the disastrous consequences of humanity's exploitation of the earth. The ideal is best described as the attempt to promote human well-being in a manner that integrates ecological awareness and socio-economic development in order to prevent the well-being of future generations from being compromised.

The dilemma of sustainable development

Since 1980 the term sustainable development has been widely used in debates on the relationship between environmental concern and the need for socio-economic development. Attempts to give greater content to the term have resulted in a wide variety of concepts informed by diverse and often contradictory ideologies.[2] At its worst "sustainable development" has become a euphemism for business as usual with a perfunctory environmental impact study. It can also be used to mean that development must carry on unless there is an economically viable alternative that is more "environmentally friendly", such as eco-tourism. Or it can mean that development must go on, but attempts must be made to minimise its ecological impact. At best it refers to the attempt to integrate ecological concerns into the core of development projects. Unfortunately, this last option is not often followed and ecological issues are usually only addressed at late stages in the planning and implementation of development projects.[3]

---

1 The term "earth" refers to the planet, its atmosphere and all its complexly interrelated life forms, including human beings.
2 For a survey of these interpretations, see WM Adams, *Green Development: Environment and Sustainability in the Third World* (London: Routledge, 1990), pp 14–86, and David G Hallman, "Ethics and Sustainable Development" in David G Hallman, (ed), Ecotheology: *Voices from the South and the North* (Maryknoll: Orbis, 1994), pp 264–283.
3 See Adams, *Green Development*, pp 87–191.

This diversity of meanings is aggravated by a fundamental ambiguity that lies at the heart of the ideal of sustainable development. This ambiguity revolves around the recognition of the ecological limits on human economic activity implied by the term sustainable, and the need for economic growth implied in most definitions of development. Throughout history the over-exploitation of the earth's resources has resulted in ecological collapse leading to the demise of the socio-economic order responsible. Development understood fundamentally in terms of economic growth is thus ultimately unsustainable and will lead to socio-economic collapse.

Differences of opinion about the nature of sustainable development and the ambiguity about its goal reflect the divergent world-views and ethical values that inform the various conceptions of sustainable development. Thus the debate at its core is an ethical debate. Christian theological ethics has a significant contribution to make in redefining the ethical values that ought to inform the policy and the practice of sustainable development. A theological ethic of sustainable development will thus attempt to redefine the goal of and approach to development in terms of a Christian world-view. Before this can be done the context that determines the need for both development and sustainability must be examined.

The necessity of sustainable development

The need for sustainable development is determined by the deprived existence of millions of human beings and the finite character of the earth and its resources. This situation is not merely the case of too many people and too few resources. The population of the "developed" nations of the North consume vast amounts of the earth's limited resources, far in excess of their basic requirements. At the same time the exploding populations of the nations of the South are forced to engage in ecologically destructive enterprises in the desperate attempt to meet their most basic needs and repay their burgeoning debts. The necessity and the possibility of sustainable development are thus integrally related to issues of global political economy.[4]

Integral to the call for the development of a sustainable global socio-economic order is an ethical obligation. This obligation involves the interface of the ethical ideals of the establishment of a just and equitable human society, the empowerment and liberation of the poor and marginalised, and a respect and even reverence for creation. Only ethical development will be ultimately sustainable.

The South African context is shaped by our history of colonialism and apartheid. The ethical requirements of justice, equity and liberation will only be satisfied when there is a vast improvement in the quality of life of the majority of South Africans.

---

4 See Adams, *Green Development*, Michael Redcliff, *Sustainable Development*: Exploring the Contradictions (London: Routledge, 1987), pp 79–132, and Larry L Rasmussen, *Earth Community, Earth Ethics* (Geneva: World Council of Churches, 1996), pp 1–173.

This improvement is dependent on economic growth for it is only through such growth that the necessary progress can be made in meeting people's basic needs for food, energy, clean water, employment, education, peace and security. Yet there are limits to the resources that are available and the spectre of irreparable ecological degradation threatens the future viability of such development. Development that is only beneficial for the present generation and destructive for future generations is unacceptable. The pursuit of liberation and justice today must be carried out in a manner that is compatible with a respect for creation and the achievement of social and economic justice for future generations.

South Africa is confronted with a variety of ecological issues. Its population continues to grow. The possibility of expanding agricultural production is severely curtailed by the limited water resources and continued soil degradation. The economy is largely dependent on the exploitation of declining mineral resources. The presence of large coal reserves has resulted in the country's dependence on polluting coal power stations to meet its need for electricity. Over-fishing continues to severely deplete our coastal fish stocks. The apparent panacea of eco-tourism has proved to be full of pitfalls as a consequence of the conflict of interests between the needs of local marginalised communities, the imperatives of conserving bio-diversity and the interests of commercial tourist ventures. These issues cannot be put to one side while we concentrate on the imperative of social transformation. The ecological costs will be transformed into social and economic costs if they are not addressed and "[t]he environmental debt of society as a whole is always paid most by those least able to do so – the poor" (White 1995:3). A respect for creation and the ethical priority of the welfare of the poor and marginalised require us to pursue a policy of truly sustainable development.

The legacy of colonialism and apartheid has secured the most profitable resources for the white elite and deprived the majority of access to the most basic resources. The resultant injustice cuts through all the dimensions of the economy. Ecological degradation takes place on both sides of this divide. Agriculture provides a significant example. In the predominantly white commercial farming sector, the over-use of pesticides and chemical fertilisers combined with the farming of marginalised lands has led to severe soil degradation. In the over-populated former homelands, the struggle for survival has resulted in overgrazing and deforestation leading to soil erosion. Yet the blame for ecological degradation is not shared equally, for the marginalised communities have been forced to exploit their environment as a consequence of their marginalisation and oppression.

Apartheid had two further ecological consequences. First, it has resulted in pollution producing industries being located in predominantly black areas. Thus, black people bore the brunt of the health risks of South Africa's industrial development while white people enjoyed its benefits. Second, sanctions and disinvestment led to the development of a siege economy. Vast amounts of money were invested in industrial development that was neither ecologically sustainable nor of any long-term benefit to society. This includes the armaments industry and the Sasol and Mossgas petro-chemical projects.[5]

Theological perspectives on sustainable development

Christian theology can provide a particular vision of the earth and humanity's role as a member of the wider community of creation.[6] The ethical values embedded within this vision have a significant contribution to make to the theory and praxis of sustainable development.[7]

The earth as God's good creation

At its very beginning the Biblical witness affirms God's deep satisfaction with creation in the declaration that it was "very good" (Gn 1:31), Isaiah goes on to state that "the whole earth is full of [God's] glory" (Is 6:3). These affirmations of the goodness and glory of creation have important implications for our approach to the issue of sustainable development.

The first is that all of creation has value to God. All aspects of creation have value for their own sake and not merely as a consequence of their usefulness to humanity. This is not to affirm that they all have equal value but it is to reject a utilitarian view of the non-human world as mere resources to be used in the pursuit of human well-being. The second is to recognise that the complex and dynamic relationships between the various aspects of creation are the product of God's wisdom. Third, this good creation belongs to the God whose glory it displays. It can never be the private possession of finite human beings. The goodness of creation places the ethical demand on humanity to respect and even reverence creation.

5   For details of the South African context see Jacklyn Cock and Eddie Koch, (eds) *Going Green: People, Politics and the Environment in South Africa* (Cape Town: Oxford University Press, 1991), Alan B Downing, *Apartheid's Environmental Toll*, Worldwatch Paper 95 (Washington: Worldwatch Institute, 1990), Environmental Monitoring Group, *Towards Sustainable Development in South Africa: A Discussion Paper* (Cape Town: Environmental Monitoring Group, 1992), Mamphela Ramphele, (ed), *Restoring the Land: Environment and Change in Post-Apartheid South Africa* (London: Panos, 1991), and White, *Environment, Reconstruction and Development*.

6   The metaphor of "community" is used to describe the interdependent and interrelated character of creation. The metaphor is not, however, unproblematic as the often predatory character of this interdependence is incompatible with it. See James A Nash, *Loving Nature: Ecological Integrity and Christian Responsibility*, (Nashville: Abingdon, 1991), pp 146–148, and Rasmussen, *Earth Community, Earth Ethics*, pp 324–328.

7   For a more detailed presentation of the ecological significance of key theological themes see Dieter Hessel, (ed), *After Natures Revolt: Eco-Justice and Theology* (Minneapolis: Fortress, 1992), Nash, *Loving Nature*, pp 93–138, Rasmussen, *Earth Community, Earth Ethics*, pp 227–316, L Osborn, *Guardians of Creation – Nature in Theology and the Christian Life* (Leicester: Apollos, 1993), and Fred Van Dyk, David C Mahon, Joseph K Sheldon and Raymond H Brand, *Redeeming Creation: The Biblical Basis for Environmental Stewardship* (Downers Grove: InterVasity, 1996).

Shalom as the goal of creation

A theological evaluation of the development of human society must arise out of an understanding of God's purpose for creation. The different strands of the biblical witness combine to give us a vision of God's purpose for creation summed up in the Hebrew word *shalom*. *Shalom* is a vision of the flourishing of a peaceful, equitable and just human community living in fellowship with God and in harmonious relationship with a thriving non-human creation.[8] Human well-being is to be measured by the extent to which the human community experiences *shalom*. *Shalom* is, however, an eschatological goal that remains only partially manifested in history.

Genesis 1:26–27 proclaims that human beings are created "in the image of God". The "image of God" is best understood as both a status and a vocation. Human beings are created as God's representatives within creation and are called to represent God by reflecting God's character and advancing God's purpose for creation.[9] It is thus a vocation to promote the establishment of penultimate expressions of *shalom* in the present world. Human beings are thus called to the responsible care and enhancement of creation. This must be done in accordance with God's purpose for creation and in such a manner that the integrity of creation is maintained.[10]

Humanity as finite and sinful creatures

While human beings have been created in the image of God, they are finite creatures with limitations. As such they are called to live in humble recognition of their status and in accordance with God's dynamic and wise ordering of creation. The essence of sin is humanity's refusal to accept its identity as the finite bearers of the divine image. Powerful human beings have rejected their status as finite creatures and assumed godlike prerogatives over creation and their fellow human beings. God's creatures, both human and other, have thus been forced to become the tools and resources of the powerful in their selfish pursuit of comfort, wealth and power. Powerless human beings have been prevented from assuming their vocation of representing God and thus of promoting *shalom* within creation. In many cases the action of the powerful has instilled in the powerless a sense of apathy so that they seek their own security rather than assuming the costly vocation of promoting *shalom*. Sin thus shatters *shalom* and diverts creation from God's purpose for it.

---

8   See Ulrich Duchrow and Gerhard Liedke, Shalom: Biblical *Perspectives on Creation, Justice and Peace* (Geneva: World Council of Churches, 1987).

9   The phrase "the image of God" has been subjected to a wide variety of interpretations through out the history of Christian theology. A detailed discussion of these interpretations lies beyond the scope of this chapter. For further details see David Cairns, *The Image of God in Man* (London: Collins, 1973), Douglas John Hall, *Imaging God: Dominion as Stewardship* (Grand Rapids: Eerdmans, 1986), pp 88–112 and Anthony A Hoekema, *Created in God's Image* (Grand Rapids: Eerdmans, 1986) pp 33–65.

10 This ethical task has often been described through the symbol of stewardship (see Hall, *Imaging God*), however some contemporary scholarship has critiqued the use of this symbol as promoting a managerial and excessively anthropocentric approach to ecological ethics. See Nash, *Loving Nature*, pp 102–108, Rasmussen, *Earth Community, Earth Ethics*, pp 230–236.

Human beings ought to fulfil our vocation as God's finite representatives in a spirit of humble boldness. Human finitude and sinfulness require humility before God, our fellow humans and the grandeur of creation. Our status as bearers of God's image, however, requires boldness in the face of all that would deny us our dignity.

Redemption and the establishment of Shalom

The good news of the Christian gospel is that God has acted through the life, death and resurrection of Jesus Christ to redirect creation back to God's purpose for it. God has sacrificed God's very self for the sake of a broken creation. The Spirit of God is now active within creation, transforming human life and society in order to establish penultimate anticipations of the eschatological *shalom*. Redemption is therefore a multi-dimensional reality that transforms all of human life in its dynamic relationship with the rest of creation.

The core of redemption is God's gracious transformation of human persons which enables them to fulfil their vocation as God's representatives and thus promoters of *shalom*. This transformation involves inner spiritual renewal as a person, united to Christ through faith, is gradually empowered to overcome sin and is thus brought into closer conformity with the character of God revealed in Jesus Christ. God is also at work beyond the Christian community. God empowers oppressed and other peoples, enabling them to represent God by resisting oppression and promoting *shalom*. The consequence of both aspects of God's work is to transform society which in turn enables and allows people to carry out their vocation to represent God in the world.

God's redemptive action in establishing penultimate expressions of *shalom* is characterised by a fundamental restructuring of human power relations. Sinful human society is characterised by the use of power to dominate and oppress the other in the service of the self-interest of the powerful. God's redemptive action works through the empowerment of the powerless to enable them to represent God in creation. Power is thus transformed so that it may be organised and used in the service of all creation.

A theological ethic for sustainable development

An alternative goal for development

The theological framework outlined above shapes a particular understanding of the goal of development. The goal is the establishment of penultimate expressions of *shalom*. The symbol of *shalom* provides a holistic and multifaceted vision of an ideal human society that includes the following dimensions:

The flourishing of human community – In this vision, development is primarily about the creation of true human community. The success or failure of development is not to be measured by economic criteria alone. Economic growth often occurs at the expense of human community, and can be particularly detrimental to the marginalised members of a society. The flourishing of human community involves the flourishing of all aspects of human life. It begins with the meeting of the basic needs of clean air, nutritious food, pure water, adequate shelter and a basic energy supply. It extends far beyond that. A flourishing community is one in which good interpersonal relationships, family life, health care, education, employment, and recreational opportunities exist. In short, *shalom* includes all that contributes to a long, healthy and fulfilled human life in relationship with our fellow humans.

The establishment of justice, equity and peace – Inequality, injustice and violence are characteristics of our contemporary society. Even in the "developed" world there are increasing levels of inequality and violence. Development that results merely in the creation of a substantial wealthy elite while the majority of the population continues to exist in conditions of poverty and deprivation is unacceptable. We must reject development that is unjust, that is, development which under the guise of economic growth enriches the powerful while it underpays workers, employs child labour or has inadequate safety standards. From a theological perspective, justice is to be measured by the effect that development has on the poor and marginalised members of the community. Distributive justice is only achieved when they experience *shalom*.

The ideal of a peaceful community is particularly significant from three perspectives. First, war and preparations for war have been major causes of ecological destruction in the 20th century. Second, the armaments industry has consumed vast quantities of the earth's resources. Third, the economic and technological effort that has been spent on the development of arms could have been more profitably used in the development of ecologically appropriate technology. This would have contributed to saving humanity from the greatest threat to its survival – global ecological collapse.[11]

The facilitation of spiritual growth – Integral to the vision of *shalom* is the recognition that the needs of human beings extend beyond the merely physical. Central to this is the recognition that human beings find their ultimate fulfilment in fellowship with God. The growth of the human spirit is not, however, confined to this. It also includes the development of the cultural, intellectual and aesthetic dimensions of human life. Development that excludes these dimensions is inadequate and warped, and its long-term effects are detrimental to human community.

The flourishing of the non-human creation – The ideal of *shalom* recognises that human beings are part of creation and are dependent on the rest of creation for their survival and well-being. The durability of any project aimed at the development of the human community is severely undermined if it involves the major disruption of the delicate and dynamic balances of the created order. The over-exploitation, degradation or pollution of aspects of creation, in the pursuit of short term economic profit or survival, will in the long term severely undermine the flourishing of human community. It is only as a human community lives in relationship with a thriving non-human creation that its own well-being is assured. Even in this context, the non-human creation ought never to be treated as a mere commodity, it has value in and of itself.

This recognition imposes limits on the development and expansion of human society. The earth cannot possibly sustain the expansion of the affluence of the "developed" world over the entire globe. The average member of the earth's elite, whether a citizen of the "North" or an affluent citizen of the "South", consumes far more of the earth's limited resources than the average member of the powerless majority of humanity. The long-term

---

11 See Hallman, "Ethics and Sustainable Development", p 270.

flourishing of human community is dependent on a rejection of the wasteful consumer economy[12] as well as the reduction of the human population.[13]

An alternative approach to development

An understanding of sustainable development shaped by a Christian theological ethic results in an alternative approach to development. This alternative includes the following characteristics:

It empowers the powerless – Many development projects are motivated and shaped by the ethical norm of caring for the poor. While this is a core component of a Christian theological ethic, on its own it is insufficient. Fundamental to a Christian ethical approach ought to be the recognition that all human beings are called to represent God and to promote *shalom*. This cannot happen while the people most deeply affected by the development process are marginalised and powerless. Yet in most cases development planning is dominated by the "experts", that is, members of the powerful political, intellectual and economic elite. Development that promotes the establishment of *shalom* must begin with the empowerment of the powerless so that they can be the agents for establishing *shalom* in their own communities.

In practice this means that decision making with regard to the nature, methods, goals and consequences of a particular development project must be taken at a grassroots level.[14] This is not to say that there is no need for "experts", but rather that their efforts must be directed towards the empowerment of the powerless. Ultimately, the empowerment of the powerless is dependent upon the restructuring of the global economic order. This is not a mere development strategy it is an ethical requirement demanded by the recognition that all human beings are created in the image of God. Care for the poor is not enough. The poor must be liberated and empowered to act as God's representatives in the world.

It follows the patterns within creation – The confession that human beings are called to promote *shalom* involves a recognition that it is legitimate to use human power to alter aspects of creation. However, all such alteration must recognise that the dynamic patterns within creation are a product of the Creator's wisdom. Scientific, technological, economic and socio-cultural development must be carried out in an appropriate manner. A manner designed to reflect God's wisdom imbedded in creation. Scientific research is imperative if we are to discover these patterns and design appropriate technology. The manufacture of such technology would, in turn, be a stimulus to appropriate economic development and job creation.

The first pattern seen in creation is that everything is recycled. The waste products of one aspect of creation become the food of another. Development that follows the patterns of creation must seek to recycle as many of its waste products as possible. Second, the primary resources are renewable resources. In the 20th century, development has become totally dependent on the use of non-renewable mineral resources. In particular, our energy is derived

---

12 See Herman E Daly and John B Cobb, *For the Common Good: Redirecting the Economy Toward Community, the Environment and a Sustainable Future* (Boston: Beacon Press, 1989), Herman E Daly and Kenneth N Townsend (eds.), *Valuing the Earth: Economics, Ecology and Ethics* (Cambridge: MIT Press, 1993), and Bob Goudzwaard and Harry de Lange, Beyond *Poverty and Affluence: Toward an Economy of Care*, trans. by Mark R Vander Vennen (Grand Rapids: Eerdmans, 1995).

13 See Susan Power Bratton, *Six Billion and More: Human Population Regulation and Christian Ethics* (Louisville: Westminster/John Knox, 1992).

14 See Edward P Antonio, "Letting the People Decide: Towards an Ethic of Ecological Survival in Africa", in David G Hallman, (ed), *Ecotheology*, pp 227–234.

from the fast declining resources of fossil fuels. Truly sustainable development must depend on renewable resources particularly for its energy requirements. The development of clean sources of energy, such as wind, hydroelectric and solar power, is imperative. Third, creation is composed of complex interrelated networks and interdependent entities. What happens in one component of the biosphere affects other components often over great distances. All development plans must recognise this dynamic relatedness of all things and thus take into account the varied consequences of the proposed development, not only on the immediate context but also on contexts separated by distance and time. Finally, creation is characterised by dynamism and diversity. Most contemporary human development involves a reduction of this diversity often with disastrous social and ecological consequences. Mono-crop agriculture, for example, has impoverished the soil, led to the excessive use of chemical fertilisers and pesticides, denied local people a balanced diet and led to economic dependency on an unpredictable international market.[15]

Ethically, this following of the patterns of creation arises out of the interaction of two moral values. The first is that all our interaction with creation must be characterised by a respect and reverence for its goodness and value as that which God has created in God's grace and wisdom. The second is the vocation of human beings to care for and enhance creation. Enhancing creation means that we have a moral obligation to promote the well-being of the human community in its relationship with the rest of creation through the development of appropriate technology. The care of creation means that all our technology and development must protect the dignity and value of creation as creation. Hence it must seek to prevent the irreversible degradation of creation. These two moral values are informed by a third dimension, that is the recognition that we are responsible before God for the manner in which we interact with creation.

It recognises human finitude and sinfulness – Far too much contemporary economic and technological development assumes human ability to predict and control the non-human creation. It has also failed to take account of human greed and pride. We are discovering that creation is far more dynamic and unpredictable than had been previously anticipated. When this unpredictability interacts with greed the result is socially and ecologically disastrous. In the fishing industry, for example, fish stocks have demonstrated large scale and unpredictable fluctuations. This has often been combined with overfishing by large fishing companies resulting in the rapid decline of fish stocks and the resultant suffering of marginalised communities dependent on fishing for their survival.[16]

All development ought to be shaped by the moral virtue of humility. Humility enables us to recognise that we cannot fully predict the results of our actions. We ought thus to err on the side of caution in attempting to anticipate the ecological consequences of any development project.

Human sinfulness and capability for self-deception require that we evaluate development policy and projects with humility and boldness. Humility in recognising that our best intentions often disguise selfish interests. Boldness to actively counter the greed of the powerful who exploit creation at the expense of the powerless.

---

15 For examples of this kind of development see Rasmussen, *Earth Community, Earth Ethics*, pp 322–343, Calvin B De Witt and Ghillean T France, eds, *Missionary Earthkeeping* (Macon: Mercer University Press, 1992), and Wayan Wastra, "Environment and the Christian Faith: Holistic Approach from Bali", *Evangelical Review of Theology*, 17, (1993), 259–268.
16 See Rasmussen, *Earth Community, Earth Ethics*, pp 155–167.

It calls the elite to sacrifice their affluent lifestyle – The economic and political elite of human society consumes vast quantities of the earth's resources while the poor struggle for survival. Truly sustainable development cannot be premised on the extension of the consumer society of the "North" to the rest of the earth. The earth cannot bear this burden. Nor can the elite expect the poor to continue to sacrifice their lives and well-being in order for the elite to continue to enjoy their exploitative lifestyle. As long as the elite lifestyle of the "North" is modelled and promoted as the ideal for all human society, sustainability will remain a hopeless ideal.

If the members of the elite are to represent God in the world they can only do so when their lifestyle is characterised by self-sacrifice and a frugal use of resources. In response to God's goodness expressed in creation and redemption, they are called to an unselfish and sacrificial generosity for the sake of the earth and its inhabitants. This involves far more than charity, it is a reorientation of the fundamental direction of a person's life. It is an act of repentance resulting in a re-evaluation of one's life as one commits oneself to God who gave God's very self for the redemption of creation. Such a commitment will place one in opposition to the powers that dominate the present world order.[17]

Conclusion

In the contemporary world with its injustice and ecological degradation, Christians are called to pursue the ideal of sustainable development. If this pursuit is to be of any value it must be motivated by a vision of *shalom* and empowered by fundamental moral convictions. These convictions include a passion for a just and equitable society, a deep reverence for God's creation, an awareness of our human responsibility before God and a willingness to sacrifice our comforts and even our well-being for the good of our fellow creatures, both human and other kind.

The ethical obligations for the rich and powerful are different from those for the poor and powerless. While the powerful are called to self-sacrifice, the powerless are called to assert their rights and dignities as God's representatives in the world. In the South African context, this demands a radical reorientation in the lifestyles, expectations and demands of those who experienced the benefits of Apartheid. It also means rejecting an approach to development that merely changes the racial identity of the elite. Rather we are called to pursue a new vision of an equitable and just society living in relationship with a flourishing non-human creation. A new society bought about through the empowerment of the powerless. Such a society ought not to measure itself by the standards of material wealth but rather by a holistic conception of human well-being in community.

Shalom will only be fully established at the eschaton. Thus all attempts to establish penultimate manifestations will remain partial and incomplete. The establishment of such expressions will inevitably involve compromises. However these compromises must always be in favour of the poor and marginalised.[18] Yet the Christian

17 See Bruce Birch and Larry Rasmussen, *The Predicament of the Prosperous* (Philadelphia: Westminster, 1978)

18 See Charles Villa-Vicencio, *A Theology of Reconstruction: Nation Building and Human Rights.* (Cape Town: David Philip, 1992), p 31.

gospel proclaims that in Jesus Christ and through the work of the Spirit the *eschaton* has broken into human history. The establishment of penultimate expressions of *shalom* can thus be attempted in the hope of success. God is at work in the world and uses human efforts to give expression to God's goal for creation.

BIBLIOGRAPHY

Adams, WM. 1990. *Green Development: Environment and Sustainability in the Third World.* London: Routledge.

Cock, Jacklyn and Koch, Eddie. (Eds). 1991. *Going Green: People, Politics and the Environment in South Africa.* Cape Town: Oxford University Press.

Daly, Herman E. and Cobb, John B. 1989. *For the Common Good: Redirecting the Economy Toward Community, the Environment and a Sustainable Future.* Boston: Beacon Press.

Daly, Herman E. and Townsend, Kenneth N. (eds). 1993. *Valuing the Earth: Economics, Ecology and Ethics.* Cambridge: MIT Press.

Downing, Alan B. 1990. *Apartheid's Environmental Toll.* Worldwatch Paper 95, Washington: Worldwatch Institute.

Environmental Monitoring Group, 1992. *Towards Sustainable Development in South Africa: A Discussion Paper.* Cape Town, Environmental Monitoring Group.

Goudzwaard, Bob and De Lange, Harry. 1995. *Beyond Poverty and Affluence: Toward an Economy of Care*, trans. by Mark R. Vander Vennen, Grand Rapids: Eerdmans.

Hallman, David G. (ed). 1994. *Ecotheology: Voices from the South and the North.* Maryknoll: Orbis.

Nash, James A. 1991. *Loving Nature: Ecological Integrity and Christian Responsibility.* Nashville: Abingdon.

Ramphele, Mamphela. (ed). 1991. *Restoring the Land: Environment and Change in Post-Apartheid South Africa.* London: Panos.

Rasmussen, Larry L. 1996. *Earth Community, Earth Ethics.* Geneva: World Council of Churches.

Redcliff, Michael. 1987. *Sustainable Development: Exploring the Contradictions.* London: Routledge, 1987.

Samuel, Vinay and Sugden, Christopher. (eds). 1987. *The Church in Response to Human Need.* Grand Rapids: Eerdmans.

The Constitution of the Republic of South Africa, 1996. As adopted on 8 May and amended on 11 October 1996 by the Constitutional Assembly, chapter 12, section 24.

White, Anne V. (ed). 1995. *Environment, Reconstruction and Development: A Report from the International Mission on Environment Policy.* Building a New South Africa, vol. 4, Ottawa: International Development Research Centre.

Wilkinson, L. (ed). 1991. *Earthkeeping in the Nineties – Stewardship of Creation.* Grand Rapids: WB Eerdmans.

15 The ethics of reconstruction

Len Hulley and Louise Kretzschmar

The Reconstruction and Development Programme (RDP) of the government has been criticised by many people, but there seems to be general consensus on the need for something to be done about the social conditions of large sections of the population. The most visible aspects of the programme are the provision of water to areas where it has not been freely available before, building houses for the homeless and shack dwellers and the setting up of clinics to serve the health needs of the community. Critics are either of the opinion that the government is not delivering quickly enough in terms of its promises, as in the case of housing, or that we cannot afford to provide the services, as is said of the overall health programme, which includes the clinics. What is clear though, is that the government believes that the present state of affairs is not acceptable and that it is an unjust legacy of past government policies. These policies ignored the needs of the poor sections of the population. They were virtually all black. The government did not provide services to them nor did it empower the people to alleviate the inequalities of the past for themselves. Even a brief examination of South African society is sufficient to convince one that there are enormous disparities in income and living standards between the various social and race groups. The majority of those at the poorer end of the social and economic scale are black. This is not to deny that there are whites who are poor and unemployed, but the majority of those in these categories are black. It must also be acknowledged that there are blacks who are upwardly mobile, and some who are very wealthy, but these numbers are still small. In general there is still a strong correlation between race and class in this country. Indeed, black women make up the largest proportion of the most economically deprived group (see Haddad 1996:199–210).

Therefore, in his introduction to the White Paper on the RDP, President Mandela says that the government is committed to ameliorating "the problems of poverty and gross inequality in almost all aspects of South African society" (White Paper 1994:i). While it is clear that the RDP is aimed at improving the lot of the poorest sections of our society, it will prove beneficial for the whole country. Reconstruction and development cannot be achieved, he argues, unless the economy is in a healthy state. Unless the economy is growing, development cannot take place, in fact, there is a reciprocal relationship between growth and development (see White Paper 1994:i; also Todaro quoted in Swanepoel et al. 1993:44). As you improve the lot of people by development, you create a larger domestic market. This in turn means that manufacturers have a larger market for their products, which means that they need more labour and also generate more profits. Higher profits mean more tax revenue for the state. The RDP is a good example of a social policy, as distinct from social ethics, as discussed by Motlhabi elsewhere in this volume.

The government has closed down the RDP ministry, redeployed minister Jay Naidoo and transferred the responsibility of the programme to the various departments such as Housing, Health and Water Affairs. Overall responsibility for co-ordinating the programme was transferred to Vice-President Mbeki's office. While talk about the programme is not so common these days, its objectives remain part of what the government is trying to do. One vital problem with the RDP, however, is the problem of delivery. In a recent article in the magazine *Challenge*, Z Mokgoebo (June/July 1996:20f) asks whether the programme can still function effectively now that Mr Naidoo has been moved to another position in the cabinet.

Despite this, the government still seems to be pursuing the original aims of the RDP. We will now discuss these.

Guaranteeing human dignity

When President Mandela introduced the White Paper on the RDP to Parliament, he said that the aim of the programme was to fundamentally transform our society:

> My Government's commitment to create a people-centred society of liberty binds us to the pursuit of the goals of freedom from want, freedom from hunger, freedom from deprivation, freedom from ignorance, freedom from suppression and freedom from fear. These freedoms are fundamental to the guarantee of human dignity (White Paper 1994:1).

Some years ago Pope Paul VI issued a very important encyclical on human development. In that encyclical he expressed a very similar view. He held that development was a "transition from less human conditions to those that are more human" (Paul VI 1968:12). From the contexts of both these documents it is clear that human dignity is seen as something that is *extrinsic* to human beings. Indeed, in the White Paper development means "securing for each citizen liberty, prosperity and happiness" (White Paper 1994:4). In both of these documents it is held that if we create certain conditions for living we will guarantee self-respect among people. It is doubtful that an improvement in living conditions will guarantee that people have self-respect.

We believe that we should regard dignity as *inherent* (or intrinsic) in human beings because they have been created in the divine image (Gn 1:27). The conditions under which people live must therefore reflect a recognition of that fact. If a government, or a society, by its policies, or as a result of neglect, creates conditions which make it difficult for people to live dignified lives, then those conditions become an indictment against it. The kind of conditions we seek to create for living should be such that it is an appropriate environment in which people who possess an inherent dignity can live. In creating these conditions we ought to take people's own concerns into account, we must empower them to be the subjects of their own destiny. Many social upliftment programmes are imposed upon people, which is to completely disregard their dignity. The people themselves must be empowered to determine where it is they want to go: "Development is the process of people taking charge of their lives ... [T]o develop is to gain an increasing power to define, to analyse and to solve one's own problems" (Kent 1981:313).

Some years ago SL Parmar, a scholar from India who participated in WCC discussions, also related development to human dignity:

> If poverty and injustice are the main facts of economic life, the potentiality of the poor must be the main instrument for overcoming them. This would be possible if the people in the developing countries discover a sense of dignity and identity within their socio-economic limitations. To assume that only when we have more, when we are nearer the rich nations, we will have dignity and identity, is a new kind of enslavement to imitative values and structures, an enslavement that dehumanises (Parmar 1975:34).

The purpose in quoting Parmar is not to try and convince the poor in South Africa, or those who lead them, that they should settle for an inferior standard of living, a standard in which it is difficult for human dignity to flourish. We should rather aim at levels of development which are within the means of both the country and its peoples. Minister Kadar Asmal has often made the point that we are a water-poor country but that we should nevertheless aim at providing water to every person in the country. We do not have the water reserves for every person in the country to be able to use that commodity at the rate at which it is used in the wealthy suburbs of our country. What we will have to do is for all of us to use less water so that there is sufficient to go around. This whole approach to development is not an easy one to accept, especially in South Africa where both First and Third World living standards are to be seen. Many people aspire to the standard of living which they see in the wealthy suburbs, and also in wealthy countries. This is not merely a regional matter within countries or continents, but also an international problem: "The good life, or development as commonly understood in the west, cannot be sustained by the earth and cannot be extended to the five and a half billion people alive today, much less to the 10 billion who will inhabit the planet within four or five decades" (Visser 't Hoof Endowment Fund 1993:15; see also p 67).

The problem not only relates to the resources we may have available, in our case a limited water supply, but it also has to do with the health of the environment. We are polluting the environment, and here the First World is the greatest culprit (Visser 't Hoof Endowment Fund 1993:101). Something needs to be done: "The rich industrialised countries ... have a primary responsibility to take immediate steps to transform their economic systems so that they are globally sustainable in the sense that their patterns of resource-use could be followed by the whole world without causing ecological collapse" (Visser 't Hoof Endowment Fund 1993:21; see also Goudzwaard and De Lange 1995:18–31). We do not wish to discuss this matter any further as David Field examines the issue of sustainable development in this book. What it does suggest, however, is that we must all aim at a more modest life style, thereby ensuring that there will be sufficient resources for us all. It would then be possible for us all to live in a manner that befits persons who possess an intrinsic worth and dignity.

The basic principles on which the RDP is based

The programme envisages itself as being encompassed in five complementary programmes. These are: meeting basic community needs, developing human resources, building the economy, democratising the state and society and implementing the programme itself. The programme rests on six basic principles. These are briefly outlined below.

An integrated and sustainable programme

To integrate and sustain such a programme will require co-ordination of a high level. The White Paper (1994:6) sees this being done by the Government in co-operation with other organisations within society. However, because of the need for an overall plan, it seems obvious that the State will necessarily have to drive the programme. This is further borne out by the nature of the other principles underlying the programme.

Peace and security for all

To achieve this objective, the security forces will be integrated in terms of race and gender so that they represent the racial and gender make-up of the population at large. A similar process will be undertaken in respect of the judicial system to "provide fairness and equality for all before the law" (White Paper 1994:6). Of necessity, the steps to implement such a programme will have to be in the hands, or at least driven by, the central Government.

Nation-building

After peace and stability have been achieved, the White Paper (see 1994:6) sees the next step as embarking on nation-building. A point is made under this principle that the country has a single economy, apparently contributing to the idea that we are building a single nation. However, Nürnberger (1988:38–78) has shown that the South African economy exhibits the characteristics of a centre-periphery structure. In the centre there is economic development and power while the periphery is poor and powerless. The centre-periphery phenomenon in South Africa corresponds to the large cities and the rural areas respectively. This is further borne out by the need to provide water to the poorer rural areas. This would require a balancing act between urban investment and rural development. The new Director of the Land and Agricultural Bank, Dolney (1991:209), had this to say:

> In South Africa we need to balance resources required for the development of
> rural areas against investment in urban based manufacturing industries which
> are regarded as the driving force of a growing economy. ... There is general
> agreement among major political players that without growth there cannot be
> a redistribution of wealth.

We need to develop a national identity which is not completely based on the economy functioning as a single unit. There are, of course, implications for the whole
country which emanate from the state of the economy, for example, when unemployment is high everyone suffers, both in the urban and rural areas.

Democratisation

The White Paper sees the process of democratisation as an "active process enabling
everyone to contribute to reconstruction and development" (1994:7). The idea that
people must participate in the planning and implementation of the RDP is important, it guarantees better outcomes for the following reasons:

> First, planning is always contextual; ... Local people always know ... the local
> context better than any outsiders ...

> Secondly, broad participation in planning expedites the implementation of
> plans ... [because] ... the goals and motivation are wholly internalised ...

> Thirdly, there is the issue of justice. ... When people plan for themselves, they
> may make mistakes and they may harm themselves, but they will not nor-
> mally be unjust to themselves (Kent 1981:315).

Reading Kent's statement one gets the clear impression that the planning and projects refer to limited local objectives. In the White Paper, matters such as "job creation, land reform, housing, services, water and sanitation, energy, telecommunica-
tion, transport, the environment, nutrition, health care, social security and social
welfare" (White Paper 1994:8) are mentioned. These are beyond the capabilities of
local communities, they are part of a national policy that must be driven by central
or regional governments. To empower local communities, the projects must be more
modest and related to the local situation, the people can then participate in the planning and implementation, otherwise we have top-down development. When the
people do the planning, or at least participate in the setting of priorities and implementing the plans, the whole may not be as tidy, but they are then "sharing in the
adventure of seeing development take shape, invented step by step by the people
themselves" (Drabek 1987:xv).

Development and the Christian faith

People sometimes suggest that the Church has no business getting involved in economic issues. This view is sometimes put forward by people in the government service who suggest that the government is responsible for that aspect of the life of the
community. One also finds people in the Church expressing the view that it should

keep to its sphere of work, presumably working for the conversion of people and not getting involved in socio-economic affairs. For centuries, the concern of the Church for people has stretched beyond preaching to them. For example, from the 6th century onwards, the Benedictine monasteries were involved in health care, agriculture, writing and preserving manuscripts. They also served Europe by preserving learning when education was at a low ebb. The Church has also long been involved in welfare work and health care services. During the last two centuries, missionaries in many parts of the world have: established missions' reduced many languages to writing for the first time; founded printing presses which printed the first written literature in a language – usually parts or the whole of the Bible, as well as novels, grammars etc; founded hospitals and schools; taught people trades such as carpentry and also improved agricultural methods. Churches and missions were often the pioneers in these areas which were later taken over by governments or other institutions.

This raises the question of the relationship between the Christian faith on the one hand and the world in which we live, including social and economic development, on the other. Saying that Christians should not become involved in developmental matters suggests a very narrow understanding of the Christian faith. When you pray for God's "kingdom [to] come on earth as it is in heaven", surely one is praying, among other things, for peace and justice. In this regard, the Old Testament concept of *shalom* comes to mind. *Shalom* includes the welfare of the whole earth and its people. The same idea of comprehensive *shalom* is also expressed in passages like Romans 8:1–25 and Colossians 1:13–29. From the foregoing it is clear that as Christians it is part of our calling to become involved in that which contributes to the welfare of our neighbours as well as the rest of creation.

In the 1950s, a number of theologies of development emerged. These theologies largely reflected the views of development current at the time. These theories of development held that for the underdeveloped countries of the Third World to develop, they had to follow the same route as the developed countries in the northern hemisphere belonging to the so-called First World. The kind of development aid they offered was to supply the technologies current in their own countries. These often presupposed a highly developed infrastructure and suitably trained labour. These development programmes were generally inappropriate and ended in failure. The projects did not take sufficient account of the needs and desires of the people on the ground, nor could they sustain the projects in the longer term. They did not "own" the projects. One of the results of these failures was the growth of liberation theologies, which we will discuss in the next paragraph. The developmental ideas did, however, contain an important element of truth:

> The concept 'development' includes the elements of design, planning, and consciously thought out and deliberately effected change. The term is no less dynamic and no less political than the term 'revolution'. But it is more complex because the term 'development' also includes a reference to interdependence and to the participation of all productive powers (Sodepax nd:208).

All those for whom development is intended must therefore be involved not only as recipients of development, but also in the planning and execution of the programmes, as is envisaged in the White Paper. What is generally needed are roads, schools, educational programmes to train adults, clinics and other infrastructural elements, like means of communication and transport. These contribute to the sense of fulfilment in a community, they feel that they have arrived. Thus, even after political liberation one needs these to achieve economic liberation. This is reflected in the view expressed by President Nelson Mandela (1994:67): "The truth is we are not yet free; we have merely achieved the freedom to be free, the right not to be oppressed. We have not taken the final step on a longer journey, but the first step on a longer and more difficult road".

Concern for the welfare of people, as part of our Christian responsibility, was partly responsible for the development of liberation theology. In South America, where liberation theology originally developed, Christian theologians felt that we could not limit liberation to liberation from personal or private sin, but that it had to include all of life. Initially, some seemed to limit liberation to political and economic matters, the mirror image of the problem to which they originally reacted, the privatisation of religion. This vision is now broader, taking all aspects of personal and structural human sin into account, thus including both the spiritual and material spheres as matters which demand the attention of Christians. This new understanding of liberation is expressed clearly by two Brazilian theologians, Moser and Leers (1990:102): "liberation from sin no longer ends on the socio-political level, but takes on a soteriological and therefore trans-historical character. Henceforth, socio-political liberation draws its force from soteriological liberation". Among liberation theologians, those of an evangelical persuasion such as René Padilla and Orlando Costas strongly advocate the integration of the spiritual and material aspects of life. This integration of the various aspects of life is compatible with the African world-view which does not divide life into compartments, but sees it as all of a piece.

A theology of reconstruction

Over the past several years in South Africa, the church's energy was engaged in fighting a battle against the system of apartheid, which oppressed and dehumanised people. In the homeland system, it also provided a kind of "separate development" which would perpetuate the subservience of Blacks. The church must now contribute to "restoring the years the ... locust has eaten" (Jl 2:25). The church needs to develop a theology of reconstruction. Initially it must remind the people that they are a people who, as individuals, possess an inherent dignity because they have been created in the divine image (Gn 1:27). Nothing, and no one, should be able to disregard or remove this dignity. The people also have been entrusted with the task of being stewards of the earth (Gn 2:15). This means that human beings are entrusted by God with the creative task of making the place where they live an environment fit for them to live in. But, as Field clearly shows us, that means that we have a responsibility to care for the earth as well as to use its resources. In a sense, the earth is our home and we must keep it in good condition. Today we need to reconstruct South Africa into an environment which is fit for the peoples of this land.

The Bible also provides us with images that serve to motivate us to build a new communal future. In the post exilic literature – Haggai, Zechariah and Isaiah 56–66 – we find people rebuilding their country. The books of Nehemiah, Ezra and Joel are also important sources for a theology of reconstruction (Villa-Vicencio 1992:27–30). These books express the need for, and efforts at, the reconstruction of the people of Israel and their country after they returned from the Babylonian exile. They show that individuals who belong to the community and who have a vision can bring about significant change by motivating the community for the benefit of all. But visions of themselves are not enough, they need to be brought down to earth, as it were. The churches needed to become involved in the efforts to realise these visions, they should be involved in the programmes to reconstruct our society:

> The churches, based on their understanding of who God is and what God wants for humanity, need to be involved in the attempts to provide housing, education, and employment to a very needy population. They also need to constantly be on the watch for abuses of human rights and the misuse of political and economic power. The point becomes even clearer when one considers some of the possible obstacles that prevent reconstruction and development from taking place. These include selfishness and corruption on the part of the people who are supposed to be putting programmes into place. ... Political rivalry, at either local or national level, may prevent excellent schemes from bearing fruit (Kretzschmar 1996:59).

Although the church does not have endless resources at its disposal, it can maintain a credible prophetic witness in the situation where the government and other agencies are engaged in reconstruction. It can keep those involved to their promises. It can also help to motivate the people to participate in the programmes as agents of their own destiny and not merely as recipients of the largesse of others. This can be done by both teaching them of their own identity, in terms of their divine image, and giving them a vision for the future.

Reconstruction as building the future for people and communities

In the previous paragraph we mentioned the need to have a vision, that means that we are looking towards the future as something for which to strive. Together we must build our own future. In any such exercise, the people at grassroots are those who are likely to be both the most deprived, socially and economically, and the most powerless. Their experience of not being able to do much to change their situation is confirmation of their powerlessness in their own understanding:

> [U]nless ... [that group] is enabled to exercise its humanity by participating in its own development, the development programme is likely to fail or at least be retarded. Any growth that may take place but which bypasses these people

is defective because it does not meet the requirements of social justice. Conversely any growth which is imposed on them, to which they are not prepared to say 'Amen', is likewise defective. The ordinary people are both the object and the measure of development (Hulley 1980:192).

The RDP is necessary because of the lack of social justice in the country. Access to the resources of the country were made available in a very selective way to the inhabitants of South Africa. The RDP is justifiably seeking to correct that. The Bible teaches us that creation was part of the divine creation for humankind. Humankind was to use and care for the resources put at its disposal. It was, however, not intended to be the domain of a select few. Pope Paul VI (1968:13) expressed this very clearly:

If the world is made to furnish each individual with the means of livelihood and the instruments for his growth and progress, each man has the right to find in the world what is necessary for himself. ... God intended the earth and all it contains for the use of all men and all peoples.

Many people have been disempowered because they have not been able to participate in determining their own destiny. Over a period of time they develop a sense of inferiority, they have come to believe that they can do nothing to change the social conditions in which they live. Past attempts to do so which ended in failure, for whatever reason, only served to reinforce and confirm their lack of self confidence. In this situation they need to develop skills and acquire self confidence:

People need to learn to experience trust, autonomy, initiative, industry, ego identity, intimacy, concern for others and integrity. Because so many people in South Africa have experienced oppression and suffering, they have developed deep mistrust, self doubt, guilt, inferiority, identity confusion, despair, and an inability to relate meaningfully to others. Against this background the importance of human healing and development, not to mention empowerment, becomes patently obvious (Kretzschmar 1996:63).

This is nowhere more evident than among the Black women of our country. They are generally at the bottom of the socio-economic ladder. They are subject to their husbands, their in-laws and their employers. For them, survival is often the most important aspect of their daily struggle (see Haddad 1996:199).

People themselves need to be transformed. They need to be released from the shackles that have held them prisoners. Factors such as their own negative experiences during attempts at change and their own cultures can inhibit people from risking to create a new future for themselves: "[T]o be able to develop a people must be free from bondage to its past, this enables them freely to develop their potential but also freely to choose resources from their past which will make a positive contribution in the present" (Hulley 1980:190). In order for the people in the churches to do so, they themselves must be transformed so that they can exercise an appropriate ministry in the world (Rm 12:1–8). In the experience of Liz Carmichael (1996:185), who worked in Alexandra township for some years:

> Our own activity meets God's activity in both individual and social spheres. Just as in our individual spiritual life our own efforts to become new people meet the transforming power of God's grace, so in our efforts to create new societies we discover that we are co-workers with God in realising God's vision for the world.

But, in many cases, the church has not seen the world as the sphere of its service, except in a limited way. We need to catch the vision of the *shalom* of God as the purpose God has for the welfare of all people. According to Isaiah 65:17–25, this will include "housing and health, employment, good crops, reconciliation between former enemies, the ending of violence" (Carmichael 1996:184). Indeed, that vision from the prophet is not very far from the ideals set out in the RDP. As Christians we are called to participate in the realisation of that vision: "The church, if it is to follow the servant Lord, must consider itself the servant of the wider community" (Hulley 1980:191). It is significant that in the story of the judgement in Matthew 25:31–46, the people were judged not for the wrongs which they did, but for the good which they did not do. And there the failure was to respond to the physical and social needs of those around them, and not the failure to preach the gospel to them. Indeed, it calls to mind the old confession in which we confess before God our culpability for "the good we have not done".

In many attempts at reform, such as the RDP, the basic weakness in the whole exercise is that the decisions are not carried through, they are not implemented in a concrete way. There are a number of reasons for this, but an important factor is the matter of integrity. In South Africa we are increasingly suffering under burden of crimes which are committed at all levels of society. We also need a moral RDP if the development of our country is to succeed in the long run. Here the Church can make a great contribution – teaching and motivating people to live lives of integrity. We desperately need large numbers of people who combine integrity with ability:

> Administrative, financial, management and development skills are all vitally necessary, but need to be married to integrity. In short, the ability to get things done honestly and effectively is something without which reconstruction and development will remain a haunting mirage (Kretzschmar 1996:62).

Hope in the future

What people need to do is to turn their lives around. People who have been victims of their fate, whose circumstances have always militated against their being able to change their situation, lose hope. They come to accept that they will not be able to improve matters; they have no confidence in their own abilities. They must therefore be enabled to see themselves in a new light, as having dignity and worth, as being able to become agents in their own destiny, not victims of circumstance. This is possible with the help of the church, with the teaching that they have a dignity, worth and creative ability in the sight of God. Failures are then seen by the people as temporary set backs on the way to achieving their goals, not as further proof that they are unable to change their circumstances. By helping people to recover a belief in themselves the church can make a significant contribution to the future of the RDP:

> It is only as [people] ... recover a belief in themselves, as they see the possibility of changing their lot that they acquire hope and the courage to attempt to do so, for "hope looks to the future, not as the end, nor as a threat to what is, but as an open field of possibilities ..." (Hulley 1980:39).

BIBLIOGRAPHY

Carmichael, L. 1996. "Creating newness: The spirituality of reconstruction", in Hulley L, Kretzschmar L and Pato LL (eds). 1996. *Archbishop Tutu: Prophetic witness in South Africa.* Cape Town: Human and Rousseau.

Costas, O. 1994. *The Church and its mission: A shattering critique from the Third World.* Wheaton: Tyndale.

Dolney, H. 1991. "Economic growth, agricultural reform and the alleviation of poverty". In *South African Journal of Economics* 59:3.

Drabek. AG. 1987. "Development alternatives: The challenge for NGO's – An overview of the issues", in *World Development* Vol. 15. Supplement.

Goudzwaard, B. and De Lange, H. 1995. *Beyond poverty and affluence: Toward an economy of care.* Grand Rapids and Geneva: Eerdmans.

Haddad, B. 1996. "En-gendering a Theology of development: Raising some prelimnary issues", in Hulley L, Kretzschmar L and Pato LL (eds). 1996 *Archbishop Tutu: Prophetic witness in South Africa*, Cape Town: Human and Rousseau, pp 199–210.

Hulley, LD. 1980. *On being human: A consideration of human criteria for judging development and development aid.* Utrecht: Stigting Pressa Trajectina.

Kent, G. 1981. "Community-based development planning", in *Third World Planning Review* 3:3.

Kretzschmar, L. 1996. "Reading the bible in context: Reconstructing the lives of people and communities" in Kretzschmar L and Richards R (eds). *Reading the Bible in context: Reconstructing South Africa.* Johannesburg: Baptist Convention of South Africa.

Mandela, N. 1994. *Long walk to freedom.* Randburg: Macdonald Purnell.

Mokgoebo, Z. 1996. "Can a beheaded RDP still help the poor?", in *Challenge 36* June/July 1996 pp 20–21.

Moser, A. and Leers, B. 1990. Moral Theology: Dead ends and alternatives. Maryknoll: Orbis Books.

Nürnberger, K. 1988. *Power and beliefs in South Africa: economic potency structures in South Africa and their interactions wih patterns of conviction in the light of a Christain ethic.* Pretoria: Unisa.

Padilla, R. 1985. *Mission between the times.* Grand Rapids: Eerdmans.

Parmar, SL. 1975. Cyclostyled paper, being comments to section 4 of the WCC Conference, Nairobi.

Pope Paul VI. 1968. *Populorum Progressio*. London: Catholic Truth Society.

Sodepax nd. *In Search of a theology of development*. Geneva: Sodepax.

Swanepoel, HJ., Kotze, DA., Pretorius, A. and De Beer, FC. 1993. *Development Administration OAD303–4*. Pretoria: Unisa.

Villa-Vicencio, CA. 1992. *Theology of reconstruction: Nation building and human rights*. Cape Town: David Philip.

Visser 't Hoof Endowment Fund 1993. *Sustainable growth – A contradiction in terms?* The Visser 't Hoof Endowment Fund for Leadership Development, Geneva.

White Paper 1994. *White paper on reconstruction and development: Government's strategy for fundamental transformation*. Cape Town: South African Government.

16 Business ethics

Len Hulley

When one engages in conversation about government or business today, it does not take very long before the matter of honesty and integrity in the workplace is raised. Paradoxically, it seems that many people seem to be oblivious of the ethical implications of their actions or, if they are aware of them, seem to be quite happy to ignore them so long as they benefit from their actions. The paradox arises because although the perpetrators feel that their actions are acceptable, other people are concerned about the morality of their actions. What are the kinds of actions that I have in mind? Let me spell some of them out so that the matter may become a little clearer.

In our newspapers we read about the phenomenon of the awarding of business contracts to relatives and friends by people who are in a position to make decisions on these matters. When confronted with such cases, those who award the contracts usually argue that there is nothing dishonest about the matter and that no loss was incurred as result of awarding the contract to such people. They sometimes add that they themselves were not enriched by such actions, as though that justified their actions. We nevertheless feel uneasy about such conduct, we intuitively feel that there is something wrong with doing things in this way. This is why such stories make front page headlines in the newspapers.

Many people do not seem to think that "helping yourself" from your employer is in any way problematic. This may be done in various ways, from taking things that belong to the company (even computers have disappeared out of offices) to claiming for overtime that was not worked or presenting fictitious invoices for payment. In the past, some people argued that the poor, generally Black, employees were justified in "remunerating" themselves with goods and services taken from their employers because they were badly paid and they were merely righting a wrong. This argument is not so prevalent today, but it has helped to create the culture of entitlement. Do the poor have to pay for services such as lights and water and the removal of refuse? Do the arguments that prompted them to refuse to pay for these services as part of the "struggle" still apply today? Is it dishonest to use services and refuse to pay for them?

Where do we draw the line?

Today it is such common practice to take prospective customers out to lunch that it has in fact become part of our corporate culture. But where does one draw the line?

Years ago when I was a city council employee, I had to make sure that people paid their accounts promptly. Failure to do so could mean that I would instruct the council's lawyers to take legal steps to recover the money. One day a businessman against whom I had taken such steps turned up at my home with a dinner service as a gift. I refused the gift because I felt that I would be compromised by accepting it. Recently the University of South Africa (Unisa) thought it necessary to issue a set of guidelines for persons who had to make decisions which affected the awarding of contracts. From the circular it became clear that there was concern that people were being offered gifts to make decisions in favour of the donors. These gifts were seen as significant enough that they could influence the awarding of contracts to persons or companies who had tendered to supply goods and services. The situation had reached the stage where it was no longer considered acceptable to the management of Unisa. Here again it is difficult to know where to draw the line between "entertaining" clients and bribery.

Moral questions on a larger screen

But are these problems always of the kind in which one person is responsible for making the morally correct choice? There certainly are cases where the problem is much more complex and numbers of people are involved. I just want to cite two examples. The first is an example which relates to South Africa. At present, our country is faced with the dilemma of the relationship between labour and business on the question of working hours and wages. Here we are faced with the questions: What is a fair wage? How much work should be done to justify earning that wage? How many hours should one work in a week? These are ethical questions, and they affect us as persons. But the matter is even more complex because the government is also involved. The labour movement is largely supportive of the government. Many former labour leaders are members of parliament for the ANC. Since coming to power, the government has become aware that some of the demands from labour could be to the long-term detriment of the economy of the country and, what is more, there is a large group of unemployed people out there whose future job prospects depend on an improvement in the economy. When actions are taken on the labour front by both organised labour and organised business, much of the rhetoric in negotiations has to do with the impact such actions will have on foreign investment in South Africa. Foreign investment and foreign tourism are seen as important factors in the creation of jobs in the country. As you can see, those in government have to consider the consequences of their decisions for the welfare of all the people in the country. This implies moral responsibility for the good of all our citizens. Here we see that business, economic and political ethics sometimes intertwine. We usually separate them, but life does not always fit neatly into our theoretical categories.

The second example is taken from the international business world. In 1970 the United Nations sponsored a meeting in Bogota, Colombia, at which they discussed infant feeding. In subsequent discussions it became clear that many babies in the Third World died because instead of being breast-fed they were being given infant feeding formulas which were not prepared in sterile conditions and/or not mixed in the correct proportions. The media began to unearth some of the practices of the manufacturers of infant feeding formulas:

1. Sales representatives dressed up as health care professionals to market the products in villages.
2. New mothers were given free samples of infant formula in maternity clinics.
3. Hospitals and clinics were given free or cheap supplies of the infant formula for use by mothers, thus making its use part of their routine, as an alternative to breast-feeding.
4. Labels on the containers failed to warn mothers of the serious consequences of incorrect usage.

This gave rise to several years of wrangling which led to the eventual boycott of the world's largest infant formula manufacturer, Nestlé. The outcome of this was that the boycott was called off when Nestlé developed procedures which took account of the concerns raised. The procedures were:

1. Embarking on an educational programme promoting breast-feeding as superior and having other advantages over bottle-feeding. This information would be included in all material dealing with the feeding of infants.
2. They would ensure that those who used their products were fully informed of the dangers of incorrect use, such as unclean water or utensils and incorrect storage.
3. Health care professionals would not be given gifts. Nestlé would also "avoid product-brand advertising in the distribution of technical and scientific publications" (Barry 1986:97).
4. They would refrain from supplying low-cost infant formula to health institutions where it would inadvertently discourage breast feeding. It would only provide such supplies where the use of breastmilk substitutes was warranted.

Such are some of the problems that face us when we consider the matter of business ethics. From the larger screen, we return to issues in which we as individuals have to make a contribution to ethical decision-making.

A framework for making decisions

The question then arises how we are able to cope with decision-making when we face moral issues in the world of business as Christians. To solve problems such as these is not always straightforward:

> A business person who may be sensitive to ethical issues and able to recognize those critical situations where an ethical issue may indeed be the determinative factor, may not be able to figure out how to take ethical decisions into ac-

count in the normal day-to-day decisions for which ethical issues may be relevant but not determinative (Forell and Lazareth 1980:24).

What the authors are alluding to here is that in many cases the issues are not always clear-cut. Where, for instance, does one draw the line when you are offered a gift by a seller of a product? As I mentioned earlier, this is recognised as a problem by Unisa. Is accepting a good ballpoint pen with the vendor's name on it acceptable? Can you accept an invitation to an international rugby or soccer match? There is of course the other side of the coin. To what extent can a company engage in such practices without transgressing acceptable ethical boundaries? Many people who are engaged in selling are faced with this question. Does it change matters when a person who represents a potential buyer lets it be known that a "gift" would ensure that you are awarded the contract? In some countries, government contracts are often apparently dependent on such payments to civil servants in charge of contracts, usually referred to as bribes.

What resources are available to us in such matters? I propose to set out some guidelines which I believe are defendable on Christian grounds as well as being acceptable to people who do not necessarily explicitly subscribe to Christian values. We have to do here with two levels of ethical decision-making. On the first level, we are faced with the behaviour of individuals. How do we as individuals decide what is the correct course of action when we are faced with a decision which includes ethical dimensions? The second level is where we act in an official capacity as officers of a corporate body. Our decisions are not seen as those of an individual, but of the whole undertaking; in a sense they represent the policy of the whole institution. The discussion which follows will, I trust, provide useful resources for making ethical decisions on both individual and corporate levels.

The most effective way to address the matter of making ethical decisions is to provide a number of "tools" that can be used when faced with moral issues. What we do at this level is to distinguish between moral decision-making and ethical analysis. Analysis helps us to identify, among other things, the types of arguments people use to defend or justify their actions and to try and forecast the consequences of actions based on their arguments. What we seek to identify here are the systems of values or beliefs that underlie people's moral values. To be able to do this we need to know something about ethical theories. If we are interested in the actions themselves, we are moving towards applied ethics. If we engage in ethics with a knowledge of the theories and how they are applied we are on the way to making intelligent ethical decisions.

Ethical theories can roughly be divided into three types of arguments. These are the deontological, the consequentialist and the personalist. Before we discuss these theories, we will consider the case for ethical relativism, another widely held theory.

Ethical relativism

One hears people say that you cannot prescribe for other people, they themselves must decide what is right for them. They are, in fact, saying that there are no commonly held values and individuals decide to what values they will adhere. It reminds one of the concern expressed in Judges 18:6: "In those days there was no king in Israel; all the people did what was right in their own eyes". The argument becomes even stronger when we are faced with people of different cultures, as we are in South Africa. Proponents of relativism then argue that what is wrong in one culture may well be right in another. The implication of these arguments is that there are no generally accepted standards by which we can judge the moral behaviour of other people.

Sometimes proponents of ethical relativism claim that the values which an individual or society holds to be morally correct are *correct for them*. If this were true, it would mean that we cannot really have disagreements on moral questions because every person's opinions would carry the same weight and have an equal claim to be right. In the history of human kind there have been some issues about which people are in general agreement. One such issue is slavery. At one time many people, among them Christians, practised and accepted slavery without question. Many of them even defended it. Yet today we would argue that slavery was as wrong then as it is wrong today. This is related to the question of human rights – slavery is a denial of a person's human rights as it involves taking away their freedom. Even countries who deny people their human rights do not argue that human rights do not exist; they try to justify their behaviour on other grounds. In South Africa, apartheid was official policy until the fairly recent past. Many of our fellow citizens believed implicitly in the theory and practice of apartheid, even justifying it theologically. In terms of the relativist argument, the world should have allowed South Africa to hold to its beliefs and practices. The argument being that it was right for the "peculiar situation" we have in South Africa. The latter point of view was often put forward by politicians at the time. Thankfully, their argument was not accepted by the outside world which joined with the victims of apartheid, and many other South Africans, in condemning it.

From the example of apartheid it is quite clear that people from various cultures and countries can strongly disagree on the rightness and wrongness of moral issues. In the case of apartheid, the disagreement was strong enough to affect the course of history.

A last comment on the matter of relativitism. One of the important aspects of human society, or societies, is that its continued functioning is dependent on a commonly held set of values which are transmitted from generation to generation. There has to be a means of recruiting people to adhere to a set of values and a means of enforcing those values (see De George 1982:37; Mitchell 1977:195). The business community is a social structure, within the larger societal structure, which is heavily dependent on commonly held values. Without commonly held views on how to negotiate and come to agreements, and how to keep those agreements, it would create a climate in which it would be difficult for business transactions to take place and chaos would result. Should parties to contracts not see the necessity of adhering to their terms and conditions, business transactions would grind to a halt. The continued functioning of the system depends, at the very least, on the participants holding these values in common. Disregarding the provisions of agreements in this sphere often leads to litigation in the courts which then enforce the terms agreed to by the relevant parties. Relativism is not much help in the sphere of business ethics and is problematic in other spheres as well. Van Niekerk discusses the failure of relativism in the last chapter of this book.

Consequentialism

One can easily recognise consequential arguments because they do not see morality as an end in itself, but rather as a means to an end. We find this kind of reasoning in the commandment to honour your parents "so that your days may be long in the land that the Lord your God is giving you" (Ex 20:12). Earlier it was argued that one could not conduct business on the basis of relativist ethical principals. The reason for the rejection of that approach was that it would result in chaos in the business world. This would obviously be a state of affairs which would be to the detriment of society as a whole. This constitutes an argument which holds that we cannot accept a certain set of values, and a way of doing things that arise from those values, because the social consequences would be negative. Gill (1985:6) has this to say of consequential arguments:

> At its simplest, one is enjoined to be good so that one may receive some reward – either in the form of some present or near future state, such as 'pleasure' or 'happiness', or in the more distant form of an earthly utopia or of a transcendent eternal life.

In this quotation we have what is clearly a consequentialist argument about receiving a reward in the future. Where there is talk of doing something to achieve a goal or objective, one can speak of consequential, or teleological, reasons for doing something. The word is derived from the Greek word *telos*, meaning end or objective. If, for example, you argue that you have a vision of seeking to bring the values of the kingdom of God into everyday affairs, that becomes your objective or aim. Similarly, if you are in the business world and you argue that in that environment there must be a commonly held set of values so that there can be an orderly business climate to facilitate trade, then you are thinking in terms of a goal and therefore using teleological or consequential reasoning.

There are a number of other consequential theories in ethics. Utilitarianism, seeking the greatest balance of good over evil (good often being defined as happiness); hedonism, arguing that pleasure is the greatest good; and ethical egoism, which says that each person should act so as to produce the greatest balance of good over evil for him or herself. Some people in the business world, particularly those who hold to capitalist and free trade convictions, use egoist arguments. So, for example, one hears it said that the country would be best served if each business person sought their own best interests. These best interests are sometimes qualified as long-term rather than short-term. The argument goes that if you establish a profitable business it benefits not only yourself, but also your employees and the country as a whole, but your first concern is your own self interest. These arguments echo the sentiments of Adam Smith, perhaps one of the most influential figures in the history of economics, whose book *Wealth of Nations*, published in 1776, is still quoted. Smith argued that if business people acted in their own self interest, this would lead to positive results. He wrote:

> ... [h]e intends only his own gain, and he is in this, as in many other cases, led by an invisible hand to promote an end which was no part of his own invention. Nor is it always the worse for the society that it was no part of it. By pursuing his own interest he frequently promotes that of the society more effectually than when he really intends to promote it (Newman 1962:52ff).

This statement from Smith has got some validity. Often dynamic entrepreneurs get a business undertaking off the ground because of their drive and innovative thinking. They are, in fact, seeking only their own advantage, but it has positive spin-offs. Because they are not hidebound by rules, they often manage to get things done where others would have failed. But, this way of doing things by their own rules can also create problems. Because they judge the moral goodness of an act or a course of action purely on the basis of consequences produced, they could quite easily ignore the rights of people, disregard the claims of justice, and even discount the intrinsic worth of human beings.

Deontology

"It is a feature of deontological arguments – derived from the Greek for 'necessary' or 'imperative' – that by nature they are absolutist. One cannot argue beyond them" (Gill 1985:5). People who use these arguments do not discuss the reasons behind their position, they merely reiterate their conviction or quote the rule which they apply. If you were to ask someone why they held murder to be wrong they would, for example, merely say "Because it breaks the commandment which prohibits murder", or "It is against the will of God". The appeal is to some absolute norm about which there is no debate.

There is one such norm which is widely accepted by people from both the religious as well as the secular perspective. That is the so-called Golden Rule, "Do unto others as you would have them do to you". This is also found in Kant's principle of universalisability, about which more is said in the next paragraph. Even people who have no intention of obeying the rule accept its validity.

Among philosophical ethicists, Immanuel Kant is the one who comes to mind when one speaks of unbreakable rules, what he called "categorical imperatives". He argued that we should not perform right actions because they would give rise to good results, but that it was our duty to perform them. We shall not go into the details of his argument, but merely note that he stated that there are two basic imperatives. First, you should only take an action if you thought it acceptable that everybody did the same thing. If you were not happy that it become a general rule, that it should be universally applicable, you should desist. This is known as his principle of universalisability. Second, he held that human beings should never be merely treated as means to ends, but always as ends in themselves. When someone repairs your car or builds a house for you, that person is a means to an end, but you do not act towards them as though they were merely objects that satisfy your needs, you still treat them as human beings or, to use Kant's terminology, as ends in themselves. This view is compatible with Christian convictions as is demonstrated in the following quotation from a theological ethicist:

> Christian faith offers no unique technical solutions to labour issues, but it does hold up a vision of work and humanity that keeps workers from being regarded as mere resources of production (Owensby 1988:54).

The advantage of deontological theories is that they take rules and rights seriously. You cannot merely disregard them for reasons of expedience. Taking Kant's view of human beings into account means that you cannot ignore the intrinsic worth of humans for the sake of expediency or other supposed advantages. These theories, however, do not provide much help when it comes to clashes between rights and duties. Because you cannot question the rules there is no way of resolving such dilemmas.

This discussion of Kant's view of human beings takes us into the next set of theories, those of personalism.

Personalism

In personalism, one views the ethical enterprise from the point of view of the person making the ethical decisions:

> It is a feature of personalist arguments that they view morality, not as obedience to autonomous, absolute principles or as a means to something else, but as an expression of individual feeling, conscience or love (Gill 1985:8).

To the list of feelings, conscience and love one can add respect for persons as normative criteria in personalism. It is a very personal, individualistic way of doing ethics in which the situation or context also plays an important role. When a person using this approach to ethics is asked why a certain course of action was chosen, for example, refusing to pay a bribe to clinch a business deal, one could receive answers like: "I just felt that it was wrong" or "Because I could not reconcile it with my conscience". Other circumstances could arise that one's view of a person would be the decisive factor in the decision. Some firms expect you virtually to sacrifice your family life to do the work they require of you. A personalist would see that expectation as a negation of an aspect of his/her humanity. Some theological ethicists find personalism attractive because they feel that it reflects the anti-legalistic attitude they see in Paul or that it allows for Jesus' command to love.

When one examines personalism, you notice that the system is extremely individualistic. In fact, it could be seen as contributing to a relativistic attitude because moral decisions are made by each individual according to their feelings or convictions. Although the individuals may use either consequential or even deontological reasoning to arrive at their decisions, they are still personal and private judgements. One cannot have a moral system in the world of business where common values according to which business is pursued are purely coincidental. There is, however, a positive aspect to this approach which is that people take responsibility for their own decisions.

Bringing ethics and business together

It may seem strange that I have spent so much time discussing ethical theories when what this article is concerned about is ethics in business. My reason for doing this is that one needs a thorough understanding of how ethics works in order to be able to apply it in business, or any other, sphere. The following quotation is apposite in this regard:

> A manager who would be appalled if someone suggested that any reasonable person of goodwill could do an adequate analysis of the financial aspects of a corporate decision is likely to be surprised and sceptical at the suggestion that these qualifications may not be sufficient for an adequate analysis of the ethical aspects of that decision (Forrel and Lazareth 1980:21).

In other words, just as one needs accounting expertise to analyse the financial implications of a business decision, one needs some ethical expertise to make ethical decisions.

Attempting a synthesis

You will have noticed that there are advantages and disadvantages in the two main sets of ethical theories, namely, deontology and consequentialism. At first glance, these two sets of theories are incompatible but, a philosopher, Vincent Ryan Ruggiero, suggests that there is common ground between them. He identifies obligations, ideals and effects as that common ground. We shall consider them in turn.

Obligations

Ruggiero argues that every significant human action takes place in the context of human relationships. Within these relationships obligations arise. Because of these obligations, we cannot merely act as we wish. Our behaviour is restricted in terms of these obligations. Kant has argued that we are then duty bound to do certain things and to refrain from doing others. This is a softer version of the deontological argument. Other people who use deontological type arguments have proposed that there are several such duties. They are the following: "fidelity, gratitude, beneficence, self-improvement, noninjury and justice" (Barry 1986:64).

Ideals

From the teleologist's unbreakable rules we also derive the concept of ideals, which is likewise a more flexible way of expressing rules. An ideal represents a common goal towards which we can all strive. Earlier I already mentioned the Golden Rule which is almost universally accepted, though often more honoured in the breach than in the keeping of it. Even those who do not keep it acknowledge that it is an ideal for which to strive. In Southern Africa we have the commonly mentioned ideal of *ubuntu*. This is an expression of the common humanity we experience and give expression to in community, and it is only as we are in community that it is possible. As individuals we live out our full humanity in community. *Ubuntu* would include such ideals as acceptance, caring, justice, fairness and respect for each other as persons. These form the moral basis of society. In the business world there are also several objectives or ideals of which we must take note. They are: "profit, efficiency, productivity, quality, stability" (Barry 1986:65). In the long run, no business undertaking can survive without some or all of these, the ideal of profit being dependent on the others and without making a profit in the long run any undertaking is doomed.

Effects

This is a compromise which the deontologists have to accept. One cannot merely ignore the effects of what one does, even when you think that you are right. If the rule you adhere to consistently causes negative effects, something must be wrong and you need to think again. If a business decision has disastrous consequences for the undertaking, or for the community, you certainly need to reconsider what you are doing.

Ruggiero has identified obligations, ideals and effects as three concerns common to both deontologists and consequentialists:

> A useful definition of "right" and "wrong" in an organisational context will reflect these considerations: the obligations that derive from organizational relationships, the ideals involved, and the effects or consequences of the action in question (Barry 1986:65).

Getting down to business

It should be obvious that one has to have a thorough understanding of the business issues involved if you want to make an adequate ethical judgement on issues that affect the undertaking. Christians are sometimes charged with making ethical pronouncements on business and economic issues without fully understanding the implications of the situation. Often, however, the ethical issues are clear. For example, dumping toxic waste into river systems is sometimes practised by undertakings because it is cheaper than treating it. That practice cannot be justified, however strong the economic argument, because the social and environmental effects are too severe. From this example it is also clear that keeping to high moral standards is not always the cheapest or most profitable way of doing business. It is strange, however, that in a society that often advocates ethical relativism that we are insistent that large corporations act in a morally responsible way. In any case, the first thing that one has to do is to gather all the facts, accurately identify and define the problem. The way to do this is to look at it from the point of view both of the undertaking and of someone who has no monetary interest in the matter, that is, from someone who would not benefit from the action (see Andrews 1989:246), and even from the angle of people who may experience the project negatively. In the case of dumping toxic waste, the community and environmentalists would have to be consulted. It is important that this kind of dialogue be kept going throughout the ethical evaluation.

To show how these three criteria work, we will consider a case study quoted by Barry (1986:65), but include some other thoughts gleaned from other sources.

The executives of a large company are planning an advertising campaign for the coming season. They would prefer to put it strictly on an informational level and avoid the standard overstatement and "puffery" that goes on in marketing. But their competition relies on exaggeration, distortion, psychological manipulation, and all manner of technically legal but unseemly devices to sell its product. The executives fear that if they don't "fight fire with fire" they will not be competitive. Should they use the same tactics as the competition?

The first thing to do is to consider the *obligations*. They have obligations to their customers to provide good reliable information on their product. They also have to consider their shareholders who expect them to make decisions that will provide a profit in the long run, so that they will be paid healthy dividends.

Second, they must consider the *ideals* involved. It is clear from their reasoning that they are turning the Golden Rule on its head by considering to retaliate in kind, that is, they are returning evil for evil rather than good for evil. By being dishonest in their advertising they would be misleading their customers, it would also be unfair to them. People buying their product on misleading information would be financially injured. Deceiving people, as Kant points out, shows a lack of respect for them as people. In terms of ubuntu, this would be a serious disregard of their humanity.

Turning to the *effects* of such an advertising campaign, the intention may be that there should be higher profits. Although there may be short-term gain in higher profits, there is no guarantee that misleading advertising would provide them with a competitive edge and higher profits in the long run, it may possibly even lead to the reverse as people begin to mistrust their product information and stop buying their products. In the spirit of ubuntu, in which you do not engage in activities which injure people and the community, causing mistrust in the community is counterproductive. In fact, this mistrust could boomerang on the company. People would no longer have confidence in their advertising and disregard claims made for their other products. This could have negative long-term implications for the company. Their profits could suffer. If the company has confidence in the quality of their product, they should concentrate on this in their advertising.

As you can see the whole exercise is one of drawing up a lists of pros and cons in terms of the three criteria. In this case it seems that considering all three of them suggests that on balance one should decide against the action on moral grounds. It also seems to make better long-term business sense.

Conclusion

We have noted that without a set of commonly accepted values, business cannot function. These values form the foundation on which business transactions take place and are a precondition for continuing to engage in business deals. This is a very significant point. What it is conceding is that a moral environment is essential for business. The question is merely which values we live by in that context.

Although we accept the necessity of that common morality, we are nevertheless faced with difficult moral decisions from time to time. Those are the product of the values we live by. Having a knowledge of ethical theories, in the way we have discussed them here, clearly enables us to analyse the situation, to identify and evaluate the moral arguments for and against a course of action. We are therefore in a better position to reach a morally justifiable course of action when a difficult situation arises in the field of business.

BIBLIOGRAPHY

Andrews, KR. 1989. *Ethics in practice: managing the moral corporation*. Boston: Harvard Business School Press.

Barry, V. 1986. *Moral issues in business* (3 ed). Belmont: Wadsworth Publishing Company.

De George, RT. 1982. *Business Ethics*. New York: Macmillan.

Forell, GW. and Lazareth, WH. 1980. *Corporation ethics: the quest for moral authority*. Philadelphia: Fortress Press.

Gill, R. 1985. *A textbook of Christian ethics*. Edinburgh: T and T Clark.

Hoffman, MW. and Moore, JM. 1984. *Business Ethics: Readings and cases in corporate morality*. New York: McGraw Hill Book Company.

MacQuarrie, J. and Childress, J. 1986. *A new dictionary of Christian Ethics*. London: SCM Press.

Mitchell, GD. (ed). 1977. *A dictionary of sociology*. London: Routledge and Kegan Paul.

Newman, PC. 1962. *The development of economic thought*. Engelwood Cliffs: Prentice-Hall.

PART 5

Where do we go from here?

17 Challenges for moral systems

André van Niekerk

The criticism of morality is an important ethical task in itself. In criticising narrow minded, conventional, and power-abusing forms of morality, the critic reveals his or her commitment to genuine morality. The achievement of a healthy and empowering form of morality is an ongoing process. In a closed moral system which allows no criticism, such as is found in many forms of religious fundamentalism, morality becomes fixed and inflexible.

Requirements for moral systems in the future

Due to the limitations of space, in this last chapter I would like to mention four ethical requirements which I believe are crucial for our planet's well-being in future.

A holistic approach

If a moral system emphasises only one aspect of life, it generates more problems than it can solve. For example, some systems emphasise only the personal life of the individual and the family, but leave the political and societal spheres without norms. This ethical vacuum is then inevitably filled with norms which promote the interests of the ruling power elite. The decisions that the powerful take may be decisions based on a value system that is diametrically opposed to the system that ordinary citizens nurture at home. Thus, the migrant labour system was put into practice in Apartheid South Africa even though it conflicted with what individual believers regarded as necessary for proper family life. Other moral systems concentrate only on the societal level, for example, they stress justice in the work place, but they give no guidance to the individual's personal conduct or family life.

A very good example of the lack of holistic vision is seen in some ethical approaches' view regarding nature. Although the first chapter of this volume stresses humanity's role as guardian of creation, the ethical systems of Christians became so human-centred that the dignity of fauna and flora were ignored. The moral right of humankind to "develop" nature was over-stressed and, without ethical norms to control it, the technological revolution has created a world view and an economy which now threaten all forms of life – including the future existence of the human species. We are in the worst mass extinction period in the life of the earth: 300 species of life are killed daily!

A system of morals should not tolerate dualism. All things belong to one created system. All things are interrelated. Therefore, we must have a holistic (one whole world) approach. Economic growth should not endanger the prospects of future generations through the consumption of the earth's resources. Moral values must be all inclusive – they must include economic and ecological facets, the Northern and the Southern hemispheres' interests, the value of trees and of humans, personal and the societal dimensions, the physical and psychological, both masculine and feminine, the present and the future. Ethical reasoning should strike a balance between various interests; it should critique the emphasis on personal and short-term interests at the expense of the social and future interests of our planet.

The fostering of responsibility

Unfortunately, present moral systems do not foster responsibility on a large scale. People who profess moral connections may, in principle, support a moral lifestyle, but they often do not apply these moral principles to all levels of their daily lives. Large numbers of people within our societies actually have no interest in morality, but only in the promotion of what they perceive to be their best interests. The notion of being a morally responsible person, let alone taking a measure of responsibility for others and our planet, is often ignored, if not despised.

Responsibility is the ability to respond to reality with integrity. It is based on an affirmation of the interdependence of all things in the system of life, as was discussed above. It is to make other people's problems your problems, whether they are in the past, present or future. The challenge facing moral systems is to enable people to take responsibility both for immediate dangers (eg a hurricane) and for possible future disasters (eg the negative weather changes which could result from global warming) (cf Hüber 1993:576). An ethics of responsibility should therefore be at least pro-active, future orientated, and altruistic.

A character of tolerance

Differences can divide, but absolute differences can divide absolutely. Power elites have, in the past, used moral systems to manipulate people to uncritical loyalty by using religion, tradition and group interests to legitimise these systems. Differences between what is morally desirable and what is legally permissible are minimised by totalitarian regimes. Whether the legitimisation is effected through the use of ideology, state laws or both, the result remains moral inertia and conformity. Even today, people are "told" what to do by political and religious leaders or by merchants and media bureaucrats. Individual resistance can lead to social rejection. In the case of collective resistance, the conflict of interests can result in "holy" wars. To stop them is very difficult, as the Palestinian leader Yasser Arafat and the murdered Jewish leader, Yitzhak Rabin, had come to realise in relation to the conflict on the West Bank in Israel. If a morality of intolerance prevails, peace seekers have tremendous, if not insuperable, barriers, to overcome.

As the world population grows and living space becomes more limited, people who hold differing values and differing concepts of the nature of responsibility will have to live and work towards a common future. If their ethical tools preclude toleration of other people's views, these tools are turned into swords – instead of being used as ploughs.

The articulate German ethicist, Wolfgang Hüber (1993:589), applied the following "golden rule" to the problem of differences in principles:

> Respect the principles of others as much as you want others to respect your own ... respect other people in their dignity, independent of your judgement about their principles ... exclude all kinds of violence from the controversies about principles or truth questions ... convictions can be fostered only by communication, not by coercion, by word and not by violence.

Hans Küng (1990) goes even further. He pleads for a world ethic (Projekt Weltethos). In an atmosphere of tolerance, world religions should talk for the sake of peace among the religions. Peace among the religions could lead to a world ethic. A world ethic could lead to survival of life on earth.

The ability to empower the downtrodden

The world has always had some or other form of moral values and norms. The problem with this morality, however, has been that these laws or the principles based on these moral values were usually not to the benefit of women, ethnic minorities, and the powerless. Either the system did not treat people equally, or the norms were not relevant or did not ameliorate the condition of the downtrodden. Traditional customs which were unjust were legitimised through silence. A clear example is the way in which the Hindu upper classes developed a system in which 80 % of the lower classes in India were kept in an inferior position and impoverished by means of the caste system. In the eyes of the oppressed, morality is often perceived to be a servant of the culture which is oppressing them. The tendency is, thus, to throw the baby out with the bathwater, that is, to discard morality as such rather than those aspects of moral systems that are unjust or oppressive.

One important way of testing moral systems is to ask whether these systems really improve the humanity of the downtrodden people like the poor, minority ethnic groups, women, children, the disabled, and the poorly educated. It should be clear that this means that moral systems should be contextual and have a concrete influence on the welfare of people.

Furthermore, it should be clear that the requirement of justice for the marginalised means that moral systems should be sufficiently adaptable so that they can be applied contextually and achieve concrete results. For example, the principle of justice should be contextualised in regulations that make democratic accountability obligatory in a particular region. It would be unjust if democratic measures were manipulated by powerful groups and only an illusion of accountability remained. The present democratic system of the USA with its lobbies, financial power blocs, and extensive use of the media by the powerful elite, makes the political processes within that country look somewhat "undemocratic" in the real sense of the word.

The argument so far

For morality to be an orientation to life, to constitute the social fabric of a humane society, and to guide us into the future, four requirements are proposed. An ethical system should first be holistic in its approach, because of the interdependence of all of life. It should also be self-critical and avoid dualistic tendencies. Secondly, ethical systems should foster an ethic of responsibility so that people become proactive, future orientated and altruistic. The third requirement constitutes a warning against fanaticism and pleads for a character of tolerance. The fourth requirement provides a vital testing ground: does a particular moral system really serve the concrete needs of downtrodden people?

If these are some of the requirements for ethical systems in general, what is the challenge for Christian ethics in particular?

The challenge to Christian ethics

Ethics is a necessity to sustain life. The new historical possibility that human technology can provide the means to annihilate all forms of life makes the task of ethics even more urgent. The ethical direction which our ecological and economic, our sexual and political activities take is therefore crucial. We can no longer separate life into different compartments. Each aspect – whether economics, politics, or any other facet of human activity – should be seen as having moral implications. We need morality for life itself. But, what about religion? Does morality need religion, and Christianity in particular? It is with this issue that we will be concerned in this last section.

In modern times, the pre-modern perspective which wedded morality and religion together was criticised as authoritarian. In its place, the modernists proposed autonomy. Morality, in their view, could and should operate successfully without religion. Today, this view is being criticised by many. As we move into what is vaguely called the "post-modern era", with its openness towards what it terms "transcendence", the viability of Christianity is at stake. Can Christianity provide a credible ethical system for the future?

It is argued below that neither an absolutist nor a relativist approach can provide a plausible foundation for Christian ethics. Instead, a third approach is proposed.

The danger of absolutism

In the search for an infallible foundation for ethics, the Bible, as a sacred revelation from God, was and still is regarded by many Christians as the obvious solution. This quest for an infallible foundation, typical of all legalistic religions, is called fundamentalism and, when it refers to the Bible, biblicism (Nürnberger 1988:211). Although evangelical Christians are conservative in their theological position, not all of them treat the Bible in a fundamentalistic way.

A fundamentalist approach to ethics is not without advantages. When people can determine what is right and good just through what God has revealed, it gives people a sense of certainty and stability. However, the problems of fundamentalism significantly exceed its advantages.

In the first instance, the nature and literary style of the various parts of the Bible are not taken into account. Because the historical and human character of the Bible are not respected, it becomes something of an idol. The testimonies of faithful people living under specific historical conditions are ignored. Poetic verses, historical narratives, fables, law codes, songs of praise and causal explanations, through which the Spirit of God could guide us today, are changed into a dogmatic system of revealed truths. In my view, this is an overly rationalistic and simplistic approach to the Bible which does not take the Bible's actual character into account and misunderstands the nature of God's revelation in the Bible.

The second problem with fundamentalism is the historical distance between the biblical cultures and our personal and societal problems today. Instead of exhibiting a humble attitude about our knowledge of the ancient world, enthusiastic believers sometimes force analogies and exegete the Bible so subjectively that they actually end up misusing it.[1]

The third major problem with fundamentalism is its track record. Like all literature that is regarded as sacred, the Bible has been manipulated in dangerous and oppressive ways. The religious wars of the 17th century in Europe revealed this abuse of the Bible by various groups. Nevertheless, during the 20th century, German Christians used the Bible to legitimate Hitler's Nazism and in our own country Afrikaner Christians similarly legitimated apartheid. Numerous examples can also be cited where individuals use the Bible selectively to further their own selfish interests at the cost of nature and other human beings. We all know persons who, although they may be sincere, interpret "God's will" so subjectively that the credibility of Christians, the church and the Bible are called into question. Ironically, non-Christians are sometimes more aware of this than Christians themselves. We often fail to hear their critique, instead we counter it by attacking their "non-spirituality" or "lack of faith".

A fourth problem is the tendency of some fundamentalists to become uncritical and "sectarian". Church and world are separated into different "sectors". The "true believers" or the "born again" are right and the "unbelieving" and "lost" are wrong. Salvation is restricted to activities within the church. Problems of an ecological and socio-political nature are regarded as "worldly". Christians should, it is argued, not become involved with them.

The misinterpretation of sacred literature may have a less decisive influence in

---

1 See chapter 2 of this volume.

the secularised Western world today, but it is still an immense danger. This danger is demonstrated in the rise of obscure cults with the approach of the mystic year 2000. People are deceived into following a manipulative charismatic leader. One of the largest mass suicides in the USA occurred under the leadership of 65-year-old Marshall Herff Applewhite in March 1997. His "Heavens Gate" philosophy consists of a mixture of Christian fundamentalism, the gnostic heresy that regarded the body as a burden from which the soul longs to be freed, and astronomical interests in the "other world". His 38 followers saw the arrival of the comet Hale-Bopp as a signal from God to kill themselves in order to link their souls up with an expected UFO (cf Gleick 1997).

In the Islamic world, to give another example, proponents of freedom and critics of fundamentalism like Salmon Rushdie are officially condemned. The Bangladeshi feminist author, Taslima Nasrin, has to live with death threats made by Muslim extremists because she is a proponent of women's rights.

Africa is an extremely religious continent. The Rwanda catastrophe is an example of conflict that will haunt the world for decades to come. These "tribal skirmishes recall the wars of the middle ages, when religion and politics and economics and social conflicts were all messily intertwined" (Gibbs 1994:28).

It is clear that religion is extremely dangerous when it is treated in an absolute manner. In this sense, we must agree with the critics that morality is better off without religious absolutism. When any humanly formulated creed, principle or ethical system makes use of ultimates in an absolute manner, an extremely dangerous situation is created. People desperately looking for change and meaning in life often cannot see the difference between God's will and the human formulation of God's will. They would risk their lives and those of other people "to do God's will".

The failure of relativism

It is not only fundamentalism that needs to be questioned, relativism is also open to critique. The liberal ethics of the Enlightment led to an autonomous morality with freedom as its highest value. Due to the development of modern communication, people of widely differing beliefs and values began to interact on a scale far greater than ever before in history. The interaction between liberal ethics and many other cultures led to moral pluralism. Pluralism in morality means that there are no longer pre-eminent ethical systems which the majority in a society accept. A plurality of moral views, opinions, alternatives and lifestyles exist from which each person is free to choose or create his/her own lifestyle. This is true of all Western countries and also of some developing countries. Traditional Muslim countries still hold to a mono-culture with one generally accepted moral system. It is religiously legitimated and defends itself, sometimes fanatically, against the moral (or immoral) systems of other cultures.

Pluralism leads to relativism, while relativism promotes plurality. They reinforce one another. Relativism in morality means that all notions of absolute truth are rejected and each generation, group or individual must develop its own system of meaning and morality.

In recent years, criticisms of liberal ethics have grown apace. These criticisms are voiced both by fundamentalists and non-fundamentalists. The criticisms are basically of two kinds, first, liberal morality has not lived up to its expectations, and second, the freedom of a liberal moral system is a negative freedom.

The disappointment that has resulted from liberal morality

Our socio-technological and bureaucratic society, which is based on a materialistic world view, tends to regard social issues as technical problems. From a conservative view, Colson (1993) refers to crime statistics in the USA to prove his point. According to the liberal view, crime is caused by environmental factors like poverty, racism, oppression and lack of opportunity. But in the Great Depression of the late 1920s and early 1930s, when 34 million people were unemployed in the USA, the crime rate dropped. The crime rate also decreased during the period of rapid urbanisation. Conversely, during the good economic years of the 1920s, crime rose. By means of these statistics, Colson wants to substantiate the views of the Harvard professors, J O Wilson and R J Herrnstein, who argue that the cause of crime is a lack of proper moral training among young people during the morally formative years, particularly ages one to six.

In the Netherlands, the "Social and Cultural report" of 1992 affirmed the disappointment of many with regard to liberal morality. The report compared the morality of the 1980s with reports from 1958 and identified certain tendencies. From the late 1950s, morality broke away from authoritarian systems legitimated by the Christian religion and became egalitarian. Freedom and equality became the main pillars of this individualistic approach to morality. The shocking information is, however, that criminality rose by 1000 % from 1958 to 1993 (Kapteyn 1993).

Before we draw hasty conclusions from these studies, let us refer to the work of Loek Halman (1993). According to Halman, moral permissiveness does not increase in direct proportion to secularisation. Scandinavian countries, for instance, are very highly secularised with very low church attendance, yet they have a strong civic morality, *burgerschaps moraliteit*. They also are less permissive than the Netherlands, which has much stronger church affiliation and attendance. This indicates that many factors are involved but that, at the very least, we can only say that liberal morality doesn't live up to what it promised.

Liberal morality's freedom is a negative freedom

The Canadian philosopher, Charles Taylor (1989), has written convincingly about the impoverishment of liberal ethics' individualistic approach. Morality is minimised to judicial procedures so that each person decides for him/herself what is good. The freedom it proposes is negative. It has no content. The ethical good is regarded, in principle, as pluralistic and therefore subjective. Each person decides what is good and right. There are no limits. This makes it dangerous. Ethicists from a more conservative stance than Taylor, such as Hauerwas and McGrath, agree that without a stress on the public good, individual selfishness will prevail.

Eibach (1994) illustrates the concrete results of the change of values from an authoritarian to autonomous source. If a person's value system is concerned only with self-fulfilment, loyalty towards a life partner and children, for example, will diminish. The high rate of broken relationships can be traced to this egoistic attitude, fostered by liberalism's stress on individual freedom.

From an environmental point of view, C de Witt (1993) argues that neither political and technical responses, nor a secular environmental ethic will provide a concrete solution to the crisis our planet faces because secular ethics has no place for the "intrinsic worth" of nature. The challenge, according to him, is up to Christian ethics.

The challenge to renew Christian morality

Can Christian ethics avoid both the dangers of absolutism and the failures of relativism and foster credible moral systems which would be holistic, responsible, tolerant and empowering? It is my view that this challenge can be met if Christians pray for and work at being co-creators of a new public morality. In order to achieve this, the following methodological parameters should be followed. Morality should firstly develop a two-fold thinking process, that is, listening to God as well as being aware of what is going on in the world. Secondly, it should relate freedom to responsibility. Thirdly, it should give stability, show flexibility, and be anchored to the person's deepest transpersonal convictions.

A two-fold way of thinking

The Christian sociologist, Peter Berger (1992), has criticised both the fundamentalists and the relativists. On the one hand, fundamentalists seek to retrieve religious security – but this is no longer available without self deception and the sacrifice of the intellect. On the other hand, relativists and "liberal Christians", in particular, have tended to abandon the distinctiveness of Christianity in their zeal to accommodate contemporary culture. Berger tries to avoid both the fundamentalist and relativist options. While there is, in my opinion, no easy "middle of the road" alternative, we need to look for a model of Christian ethics which will be able to grow in terms of both content and credibility.

Berger's notion of an ambiguous experience of transcendent reality can be misunderstood; divine reality is not alien, it is part of ordinary human reality. Karl Barth's approach, which stresses the transcendent aspect of God's revelation, can also be over-emphasised. The challenge of Christian ethics should rather be to develop an "incarnational" morality in line with Bonhoeffer's ethics. The belief of the Church that God incarnate in Jesus Christ reveals a God who can be manifested in us and our world. A morality based on the incarnation prevents us from a dualism between profane history and salvation history (cf Pannenberg). Furthermore, the incarnation of God in our world gives us a theological explanation for taking both revelation from above and circumstances from below seriously.

In ethical thinking there is fortunately a growing consensus that thought and experience from both "above" and "below" are important. Fundamentalists claimed that they work from above (revelation) to below (the situation). The sociology of knowledge and liberation theologians have shown that this deductive approach is false. All thinking is inevitably closely related to our context although people often try to hide their personal and interests behind a legitimation from "above".

An evangelical of the stature of John Stott (1992) therefore pleads for "double listening". Christians should work hard both at hearing the Word of God and listening to the ideas, questions and aspirations of the world of God. We must seek to relate the two, not isolate them from each other, as also discussed by Hulley in the chapter on biblical ethos.

The mature modern ethicist, Trutz Rentdorff (1986), operates openly with an inductive (from below to above) approach. The starting point of his ethicising is the present ethical realities of life. He therefore calls his approach "ethical theology" rather than the more deductive name "theological ethics". For Rentdorff, the three basic elements of life are the givenness of life, the giving of life and reflection on life. In his ethics, he avoids a compendium of prescriptions (from above) but offers a guide for discernment. Discernment brings us to our second parameter.

A morality of freedom and responsibility

If the inductive way of doing ethics is growing, we can expect a closer relationship between theology and cultural modes of thinking. Few modern ethicists want to discard modern society's high regard for freedom. However, many ethicists want to move away from the "negative" freedom of pluralistic culture. They stress that freedom must be linked to responsibility. The value of this emphasis can be illustrated by means of two examples.

The first example is from the 1993 Papal encyclical on morality entitled *Veritatis Splendor* (The Splendour of the Truth). An encyclical is a letter from the Pope to the Roman Catholic Church. John Paul II argues that the modern world's emphasis on freedom is good, but that it must be grounded in truth. Freedom without truth is a delusion. It degenerates into license which is the enemy of real freedom. Without absolute truth all arguments, and relationships, become nothing more than the "will to power" (as Nietzsche argued). John Paul's central text for his argument is John 8:32: "You will know the truth and the truth will make you free". The Pope's use of biblical quotations and his sharp reaction to the relativistic wilderness are valuable, but are not completely convincing. In particular, the Pope's use of a natural law ethic and his continued unwillingness to allow Catholics to make use of artificial means of contraception make for serious shortcomings in his approach to ethics. In my view, one of the most serious problems in our modern world, the high birth rate amongst the poor, is treated in an irresponsible manner by the Pope.

The second example is the moral-theologian from Tilburgh (Netherlands), Karl-Wilhelm Merks (1994). Merks is also a Roman Catholic, but his views differ from those of John Paul II. Merks uses freedom as a central concept to develop an ethics of responsibility, while John Paul II clings to an ethics of obedience. In order to adapt to our modern pluralistic culture, Merks is of the opinion that the language and thought systems of traditional morality should change. If this is not done, the churches will lose their influence. Moral norms should be seen as the product of the use of our God-given freedom to choose what is good and right. The benefit of this approach is clear. The individual conscience has the responsibility before God for what is right and we cannot blame some source outside themselves – whether it is the Bible, the state, the church or nature – for not knowing what a person's moral plight is in a specific situation. The identity of a modern "morality of faith", *Glaubensethik*, is fundamentally the same as previous Christian models of morality. Faith should be a synthesis of the experience, *Erfahrung*, of God, the world and the self. Merks is very clear that the freedom of individual persons is not the same as egoistic individualism. The respect for the worth of other human beings is inseparable from this freedom. It is unfortunate that Merks does not explicitly speak of the worth of all creation as well.

The integration of flexibility, stability and conviction

If Christianity wants to create credible moral systems which will be relevant to our present and future problems, it should use an inclusive approach. Three elements derived from different moral approaches should be integrated, namely, flexibility, stability and inner conviction. Each element in itself is insufficient, but together they will enable Christians to contribute to world cultures in which God-given life can be fully lived.

Flexibility

Flexibility is necessary for morality because life is not static, but dynamic. A Christian moral system must be versatile enough to cater for life's endless possibilities. In these situations, people should be able to discern between different options, long and short term consequences, different relationships, clashing interests, opposing values, and even between different lives. A rigid legalistic approach is clearly insufficient for the nuances of such complexities. When it is rigidly applied, it only gives the semblance of morality, while it actually acts from immoral motives. It is like the loud, but hollow, arguments of the preacher who writes a note in his sermon: "Weak argument – shout like hell!"

Flexibility is prominent in ethical approaches such as utilitarianism and situation ethics. An ethic which concentrates on goals and motives is reconcilable with traditional Christian morals as is reflected in my favourite biblical text: "I pray that your love will keep on growing more and more, together with true knowledge and perfect judgement, so that you will be able to choose what is best ..." (Phil 1:9–10; Good News).

When the historical character of the Bible and tradition is respected, the fundamentalistic tendencies to harmonise the different moral insights is avoided. The differences could then be seen as creative tensions which encourage our God-given responsibility to cultivate a credible morality. The new and even unknown challenges before us, and the various levels of application, underline the fact that flexibility should be an indispensable element in Christian morality.

Stability

This criterion reveals the weakness of situation ethics. In order to cultivate responsible moral deeds, arbitrariness should be prevented. Merks' (1994) observations of the processes in modern culture are significant. Together with the development of pluralism, an opposite process is emerging, that is, the development of a communal moral system. The development of universal human rights is balancing the individualisation of morality and preventing it from sliding into egoism. To live our lives responsibly, we need an overarching system of meaning and of morality which can provide stability.

The advantage of ethical approaches like legalism is the stability they provide. Roman Catholicism's natural law, Immanuel Kant's categorical imperative and the "ethics of principles", which deduces ethical principles from the Bible, are examples of this approach. We must differentiate between the positive and negative results of these "ethics of norms, laws and rules". We should not throw out the baby with the bathwater. We need norms to help us to discern whether a decision enhances or obstructs life.

The development of the concept of human rights is reconcilable with the basic intention of the Bible and the Christian tradition. In his quest for a set of ecumenical criteria to discern true religion, Küng (1986) convincingly argues that the ethical categories of good and evil, true and false can be distinguished according to the fundamental ethical norm of authentic humanness: "That is morally good, then, which allows human life in its individual and social dimensions to succeed and prosper in the long run, which enables us an optimal development of human beings in all their levels and dimensions" (Küng 1986:15). This means that religions must firstly be measured against their own authoritative teaching (the Bible for Christians) and authoritative figure (Christ for Christians). Secondly, they should be measured with the ethical criterion of the *humanum*. In the case of Christianity, the proclamation of the reign and the will of God in the words and behaviour of Jesus aims at nothing more and nothing less than a new, true humanity which manifests itself in solidarity, even with the enemy. Thus the biblical and Christological ethical content could fulfil the requirements of tolerance and empowerment as argued above.

Inner conviction

It would help very little if people know what is good and right, but are not motivated by a profound conviction to participate in concreticising what is good and right in their individual and communal lives.

Moral approaches as different as the Marxist reconstruction of reality through revolution, the morality of discipleship of Jesus, and the "community of virtue" approach by ethicists like Stanley Hauerwas, John Yoder and Ron Sider provide for the necessary inner conviction, which is a distinct advantage.

Inner conviction must be based on something or someone that transcends our human life. For ethicists like Fuchs, Janssens, Schüller, and Biestinger (De Tavernier 1994:37), the distinctiveness of Christian ethics is not the content, but the intention. The content is more or less in line with the *humanum*, but the intentional power comes from faith in God. When someone accepts God's love in Jesus Christ, that person takes responsibility for life in this world by following Jesus. Christian morality is not reflexive ethics in which rational arguments are developed to seek to discern moral truth. Christian morality is parenetic – it focuses on a person and the will – and not primarily on reason. The French philosopher, Paul Ricoeur, is of the opinion that the strategic level on which evangelical morality functions is ethical intention (De Tavernier 1994:41–42). Evangelical morality frees us to be responsible; it then challenges us to recognise the freedom of others which in turn frees me; the kingdom of God is the symbol which invites us to be a community of truly liberated people. Ricoeur's research of the New Testament's literary genres convinced him that the New Testament's imperatives orientate us through the disorientation of the traditional ethical order and by means of imagination.

Although restricting the relevance of Christian morality to intentions, as Ricoeur does, is not necessarily valid, the intentional aspect is reconcilable with our understanding of how faith works in our lives. But, it is not only the New Testament's eschatological structure (the emphasis on the Kingdom which is already present, but not yet fully consummated) which motivates us. According to Birch (1988), the moral power of the Old Testament narratives expose reality, shatter or transform world views, and challenge the reader to embark upon a practical response.

Hüber (1993) and Smit (1994) criticise recent theories of responsibility because they lack the notion that there is someone to whom we as human beings are responsible. With reference to Matthew 25, they conclude that the criteria on which the judgement of God is based is whether our actions express concern for those who are weaker than we are.

In my opinion, the relation between faith and morality is worked out more logically and convincingly by the South African theologian Klaus Nürnberger (1988:9, 10; 1987) than by anyone else. This is already clear in Nürnberger's definition of ethics as "a reflection on what ought to be and on how we can be liberated and motivated to bring it about". The soteriological problem of redemption is put on the same level as the problem of finding norms. Nürnberger maintains that Christian ethics is part of God's mission to redeem this world. Through grace we share the new life of Christ in the power of the Spirit and are invited to participate in God's own creative authority, redemptive love and comprehensive vision for the world.

From this it should be obvious that Christian morality can fulfil the requirements both for a holistic approach to creation and the need to foster responsibility.

Conclusion

Morality should at least promote a holistic vision, foster responsibility, have a character of tolerance and be able to reach out to and empower the downtrodden.

The challenge to Christian morality, in particular, is to avoid both the danger of absolutism and the failure of relativism. Christian morality should be renewed through the use of both deductive and inductive reasoning. It should integrate modern society's stress on freedom with the responsibilities and moral duty stressed in the Christian tradition. Thirdly, in order to constitute a credible morality, it should integrate flexibility, stability and inner conviction. If this is achieved, we will be both true to God and true to life.

BIBLIOGRAPHY

Please note: The abbreviation JTSA refers to the Journal of Theology for Southern Africa.

Berger, Peter. 1992. *A Far Glory, The Quest for Faith in an Age of Credulity*. Free Press.

Berger, PL. 1993. "Wenn die Welt wankt. Pluralismus ist eine Chance für Christen", in *Lutherische Monatshefte* 12/93.

Birch, B. 1988. "Old Testament Narrative and Moral Address" in GM Tucker, DL Petersen and RR Wilson (eds). *Canon, Theology and Old Testament Interpretation: Essays in Honour of Brevard S Childs*. Minneapolis: Fortress: 62–74.

Bordewich, F. 1995. "The country that works perfectly, in *Reader's Digest* 146:41–46.

Caroll, RP. 1991. *The Bible as a problem for Christianity*. Philadelphia: Trinity.

Colson, C. 1993. "Crime, Morality and the Media", in *Christianity Today*, 16 August: 29–32.

Cronk, L. 1994. "Evolutionary Theories of Morality and the Manipulative use of signals", in *Zygon* 29(1):81–101.

De Tavernier, J. 1994. "Vraagt etiek om geloof? Ethische verkenningen in het spoor van E. Schillebeeckx", in *Tijdschrift voor Theologie* 34:24–48.

De Witt, C. 1993. "A Scientist's Theological Reflection on Creation", in *Transformation* 10(2): 12–16.

Eibach, U. 1994. "Der Wandel moralischer Werte – Eine Herausforderung für die Kirchen", in *Kerygma und Dogma* 40:80–100.

Gibbs, N. 1994. "Why? The Killing Fields of Rwanda", in *Time International* 16 May: 22–29.

Gleick, Elizabeth. 1997. "The Marker we've been waiting for", in *Time International* April 7, 22–30.

Halman, L. 1993. "Permissiviteit sterk toegenomen", in *Een-Twee-Een* 21(13):11–14.

Hüber, W. 1993. "Towards an Ethics of Responsibility", in *The Journal of Religion*. 73(4):573–591.

Kapteyn, P. 1993. "Verontrusting over de vaderlandse moraal: Sociaal en Cultureel Rapport 1992", in *Socialisme and Democratie* 50(3):113–117.

Küng, H. 1980. *24 Stellingen over de vraag naar God in deze tijd.* Hilversum: Gooi en Sticht.

Küng, H. 1986. "What is true religion? Toward an Ecumenical Criteriology", in *JTSA* 56:4–23.

Küng, H. 1987. *Why I am still a Christian.* Edinburgh: T and T Clark.

Küng, H. 1990. *Projekt Weltethos.* München: Piper.

McGrath, AE. 1991. "In what way can Jesus be a moral example for Christians?" in *Journal of Evangelical Theological Society* 34(3).

Merks, KW. 1994. "Das Recht anders zu sein: Eine Chance für die Moral. Pluralismus zwischen Freiheit und Verantwortlichkeit", in *Bijdragen – Tijdschrift voor Filosofie en Theologie.*

Moltman, J. 1989. *Creating a Just Future.* London: SCM.

Nürnberger, K. 1987. "Ethik" in K Müller and T Sundermeier. *Lexikon Missions – Theologischer Grund begriffe.* Berlin: Reimer.

Nürnberger, K. 1988. *Theological Ethics: Only study guide for TEA100–4*, Pretoria: UNISA.

Pope John Paul II. 1993. *Veritatis Splendor.* Vatican.

Rentdorff, T. 1986. *Ethics volume one: Basic Elements and methodology in an Ethical Theology.* Philadelphia: Fortress.

Schönfeld, M. 1992. Who or what has moral standing? in *American Philosophical Quarterly* 29(4):353–362.

Smit, DJ. 1994. "Morality and Individual Responsibility", in *JTSA* 89:19–30.

Steen, W. 1994. "Herausgefordert zu Frieden und Gerechtigkeit in der Welt", in *Materialdienst des Konfessionskundlichen Institut Bensheim* 45(5):87–92.

Stott, J. 1992. *The Contemporary Christian.* Leicester: Inter-Varsity.

Swanson, G. 1960. *The Birth of the Gods.* Ann Arbor: Univ of Michigan Press.

Taylor, C. 1989. *Sources of the Self: The Making of the Modern Identity.* Cambridge (Mass): Harvard.

Toffler, A. 1970. *Future Shock.* New York: Random House.